AN
INNER VOICE
FOR
PUBLIC
ADMINISTRATION

Nancy Murray
Foreword by Charles T. Goodsell

PRAEGER

Westport, Connecticut
London

Library of Congress Cataloging-in-Publication Data

Murray, Nancy (Nancy Bott)
    An inner voice for public administration / Nancy Murray ;
foreword by Charles T. Goodsell.
        p.   cm.
    Includes bibliographical references and index.
    ISBN 0–275–95250–9 (alk. paper)
    1. Public administration. 2. East and West. I. Title.
JF1351.M85 1997
351—dc21   97–5590

British Library Cataloguing in Publication Data is available.

Library of Congress Catalog Card Number: 97–5590
ISBN: 0–275–95250–9
First published in 1997

Praeger Publishers, 88 Post Road West, Westport, CT 06881
An imprint of Greenwood Publishing Group, Inc.

Printed in the United States of America

The paper used in this book complies with the
Permanent Paper Standard issued by the National
Information Standards Organization (Z39.48–1984).

10 9 8 7 6 5 4 3 2 1

In memory of my parents
Philip J. Murray
Eugenie Siddle Murray

Contents

Foreword *by Charles T. Goodsell*   ix

Preface   xiii

Acknowledgments   xv

PART 1
Commentary on Public Administration Today

Chapter 1. The Need to Rethink Public Administration   3

PART 2
The Influence of Modernism on Public Administration

Chapter 2. Logical Positivism and Twentieth-Century
            Government   27

Chapter 3. Insights into New Theories for the Twenty-First
            Century   51

PART 3
Ideas for Administrative Theory from the East

Chapter 4. Lessons on the Self: Lao-tze to Jung   77

Chapter 5.   The Legacy of India: Beyond Thought Toward
             Silence   95

Chapter 6.   The Legacy of China: Perspectives on Taoism   117

Chapter 7.   A Meeting of the Minds: Beyond Isolation Toward
             Unity   145

PART 4
Commentary on Public Administration Tomorrow

Chapter 8.   Journey's End   167

Selected Bibliography   179

Index   185

Foreword

Public administration is a field in which many books are written that add only marginally to our insights and are soon forgotten. This book is an exception. It is stunningly original and will be remembered for a long time.

Dr. Murray stretches our minds and our field in new directions. She attempts nothing less bold than to introduce an entirely new perspective to the field. At the same time, she adds more than she subtracts; unlike most "radical" treatments of public administration, such as the typical postmodernist manifesto, she is not so much preoccupied with destroying the old order as adding to the richness of our current attempts to make the world better through collective public action.

The core thesis of this book is that public administration's philosophical roots of rationalism, positivism, scientism, and progressivism have contributed to making the personal life of the public servant a hollow shell. The field's preoccupation with the external world, and its confidence that this external world can be consciously and deliberately manipulated, have smothered the inner world of self-reflection occupied by the individual public administrator. Dr. Murray's intention is to give us the ideas and license through which we can open up our inner personal worlds to greater heights and awareness; not just to make us healthier human beings, but also more helpful and devoted contributors to the public weal.

The book asserts that an *inner voice* can be developed for public administration. This voice is individual, and hence its development cannot become a standard organizational or disciplinary practice. A new element for the standard MPA curriculum is not proposed here. Rather, each of us is called upon to develop his or her own inner voice. By means of it, we articulate to ourselves our ongoing, tentatively-held moral and psychological self-understandings and, in some crude sense, a personal metaphysical interpretation of life. But also, by means of this liberated and awakened inner voice, we are called upon to provide more complete service to others. For it is the more reflective, self-aware individual that is able to give the special energy, sensitivity, and caring that produces an enhanced contribution to others.

Dr. Murray's position is not emergent from the latest chic intellectualism of the field. Nor is it a rearrangement of old intellectual furniture. Rather, she builds a new house for public administration, on her own, guided by a unique vision that seems to have sprung from the cries of her own inner voice.

Her position can be thought of as insisting that we connect salient points of eastern philosophy to western thinking. From Confucianism, Buddhism, Hinduism, and Taoism, Dr. Murray derives a series of ideas that pertain directly to the experience of the thoughtful administrator. These are practical ideas, not "new-age" romanticisms or an attempt to indoctrinate us in some other culture's religious practices. The ideas are given serious scholarly attention, even though the author does not claim original scholarship in eastern philosophy. Moreover, they are not presented in isolation, but in the context of the broader philosophical systems involved, as well as the lives and writings of their originators and disciples.

These insights are then held up against assumptions of the familiar thinkers whose ideas forged the basis of western rationalism, namely Descartes, Hume, Kant, and Newton. Their philosophical tenets underlie modern public science, policy, and hence administration. The author's view is that, because of the influence of these tenets, public administration's world view gives almost exclusive attention to the external, objectified world over and against the internal, interpreted world. The consequence is organizationally complete administration run by individually incomplete administrators. Public servants are imagined by their superiors and themselves as adjustable machines capable of controlling events, not frail human beings trying to cope responsibly with an unpredictable world on a day-by-day basis.

The ways by which the author builds bridges between the ideas of east and west are ingenious and a pleasure to discover as one reads through the chapters. A connecting link is the analytical psychology of Carl Jung. This seminal Swiss thinker was a close student of eastern philosophy and incorporated much of it into his own work. Another bridge is quantum physics. Its revolutionary departure from Newton's understanding of the natural world is seen by Dr. Murray as analogous to holistic precepts of eastern metaphysics. The author also establishes connections with the help of several western interpreters of the eastern ideas, such as Joseph Campbell, Will Durant, Aldous Huxley, Thomas Merton, and Raymond Van Over. While these figures are well known generally in the world of letters, their insights are seldom explored by students of our splendidly philistine field of public administration. We can be grateful for Dr. Murray's wide-ranging exploration of the shelves in her university library.

The most striking means used by Dr. Murray to engage us in eastern thinking is the parable. The concepts she finds so promising for enriching the inner life of the administrator are difficult to present in the normal western mode of direct descriptive exposition. Hence she supplements straight narrative with this creatively indirect means of presentation.

The principal parable of the book is about Emily, a retired public administrator living in Chicago. You will meet Emily, learn about her life, and peer within her soul. Emily's remembrances of childhood winters and adult crises at the office are profoundly human and quite unforgettable. Contemplations on what they mean, and how they relate to eastern ideas, surface again and again as we turn the pages. Even Jung himself is called in to respond hypothetically to some of Emily's dreamings.

The book's pages therefore open before us as a creative and unusual tapestry of thoughts, fiction, ideas, and comments on things big and small. And the whole piece of art hangs together, with scarcely a wasted word. The author not only expresses new insights for our field, she offers new insights into how to express ourselves about it. Let us hope others in the field follow in her footsteps.

What are some of the ideas about eastern philosophy to which you will shortly be introduced? Their utter simplicity will take you by surprise. No Germanic philosophical abstractions here, nor unintelligible doctrines of French deconstruction. The challenge of this book is not to cognitively understand what is being said, but to personally respond to it.

One idea is silence, the need to stop incessantly running at the mouth to each other throughout the working day. We should rethink the textbook admonition to "communicate" clearly and persuasively with all comers. Instead, we are invited to learn from each other by quiet observation. Then too, we must be still at those moments when our inner voice is saying something to us, usually at low volume.

Another concept is wu-wei, roughly translated as "nonaction." This is the notion that rather than being primed as macho bureaucrats to intervene "proactively" in all situations at all times, we should learn to allow events to unfold when we sense they are doing so. In Dr. Murray's eloquent words, good administrators know the rhythm of the seasons and understand that an ear of corn does not grow in winter.

A third principle is unity, or the essential oneness of life. It warns against the tendency to disaggregate all complex situations in order to analyze their separate parts and causal interrelationships. We may wrongly assume that A causes B or that causation even exists in the first place. An indispensable start to a wise analysis of the human condition is the realization that each human being is an indivisible whole.

I should apologize for listing these ideas in this seriatim manner. This sequential form itself, with its neat order, runs counter to the very substance and spirit of the items listed. Dr. Murray's own writing style is much more in accord with the ethos of her message, as it should be.

The author's manner of exposition brings into play a variety of evocative literary devices, each of which has its special advantages. These include: (1) the introduction and reintroduction of material, at varied points and for different purposes; (2) calling upon the emotive power of poetry, from the pens of the ancients as well as moderns like Robert Frost; (3) taking us before Aldous Huxley's hierarchical gate to self-knowledge, first at the beginning of the book and then at its end; (4) introducing us to Emily and a gang of other interesting characters from eastern writing; (5) offering small remembrances of the author's own early life as a New Englander, such as studying book titles and trying to decode their index entries; and (6) even observations that draw on the mundane details of everyday living, e.g., fending with traffic, answering the doorbell, brewing good coffee.

Clearly, this book is an expression of its author's own inner voice, given with feeling and authenticity. In this sense, the volume possesses its own internal integrity. Perhaps we readers can each try to be, in our more passive role, just as honest—and listen for our own inner voice.

Charles T. Goodsell

Preface

The time has arrived for the field of American public administration to engage in self-evaluation as it approaches the twenty-first century. The interest of the public in the role of government has reached major proportions in recent years. There are those who argue that the problems government is expected to solve are beyond its scope. The opposite view posits that the role of government should embrace all aspects of society. Those who are caught in the trenches of the controversy are the professional men and women who have chosen to work for government.

These public administrators have been the target of criticism by both elected officials and the public. The charges against them have ranged from accusations of incompetence to the use of excessive power. While I believe that the criticism is largely undeserved, I also believe that it provides us with an opportunity for reflection. The practice of public administration has benefitted from attention to its more practical needs. The public sector work force has been educated and trained in the skills necessary to conduct the public's business in an efficient and effective manner, criticism notwithstanding.

It is time for those of us who practice public administration and those of us who teach to attend to aspects of the field that we have been too preoccupied to consider; it is in great need of philosophical definition. This book was written to initiate a dialogue that will result in a philosophy of administration that can be applied to individual public administrators. The ideas presented here are founded upon the teachings of eastern metaphysics and the insights of the Swiss psychoanalyst Carl Gustav Jung. Ideas and perceptions of western philosophers, poets, and scientists are also included.

Stories modeled on ancient parables are designed to engage the reader's imagination. The characters in the stories serve as metaphors and are, therefore, not fully developed. The leading protagonist is an American public administrator whose background and experience reflect our western culture. There is a lyrical quality to much of the writing that is in keeping with the nature of the material being presented. The following format is used for in-text citations of multivolumed works.

- *Bhagavad Gita*—translator's name and year of publication, followed by poem number, followed by verse number—example; Mascaro 1980, 2.31

- Descartes' *A Discourse on Method*—paragraph number, followed by page cited—example; 60:189

- Jung's *Collected Works*—volume number, followed by paragraph number—example; 10:154

- Kant's *Critique of Pure Reason*—translator's name and year of publication, followed by designations for the 1781 and 1787 translations, followed by page number—example; Politis 1993, A91/B124, 95

- Lao-tze's *The Canon of Reason and Virtue*—chapter number, followed by section number—example; 39:1, 2

Lao-tze's *Tao Teh King* has been translated into the English language by a number of sinologists who employ a variety of ways to spell both his name and his work. R. B. Blakney, Arthur Waley, Holmes Welch, and Richard Wilhelm, well known translators, spell his name Lao-tzu and his book *Tao-Te-Ching*. Differences in spelling can be confusing for readers. In the interest of consistency, I have adopted the spelling used by Carus and Suzuki throughout this book.

Acknowledgments

I am indebted to some wonderful people whose support made this undertaking possible. Charles Goodsell's encouragement gave me the confidence
I needed to develop ideas that I thought might be too "far out." Charles'
insights and probing questions added richness and depth to my own search.
He has been an invaluable colleague and friend. The guidance I received
from Budd Kass early on was inestimable. As I reviewed my notes from our
many telephone conversations, I realized how crucial his influence was.
Budd helped me focus my thoughts and clarify my intent. My colleagues
at the Public Administration Theory Network taught me how good scholarship can lead to stimulating dialogue. I have been significantly influenced
by them and inspired by the scope of their intellectual achievement.

Pace University deserves recognition for its continued support of my
scholarly interests. Charles Masiello, Dean of the Dyson College of Arts and
Sciences, approved my sabbatical during the spring 1995 semester. This
uninterrupted time allowed me to continue my research and write the first
draft of this book. Thanks are also due Joseph Morreale, past chair of the
Department of Public Administration, and Joseph Ryan, current chair. My
colleagues in the department, Tony Cupaiuolo and Modestine Rogers, are
always ready to listen and help when needed. Susan O'Hara, program manager, and Isabel McHugh, program secretary, are the best support staff an
MPA program could have. They can always be relied upon. I am grateful
to my research assistant, Dina Dos Santos, for the many hours she spent
editing and commenting on the final manuscript.

Finally, my friends and family have earned special thanks. When the book took precedence over their company, they assured me they'd be there at a more propitious time. I have been blessed with an unusually supportive family. To Bob Bott, Roberta Bott, Jonathan Bott, and Lorri Macleod Bott— a very big thank you!

PART 1

Commentary on Public Administration Today

CHAPTER 1

The Need to Rethink Public Administration

A CERTAIN PERSPECTIVE

I was always intrigued by the titles of books I read when I was a child. Somehow, I felt they were a code to the mysteries that lay within and if I gave enough attention to the title, I would be able to crack the code. I became so engrossed in this practice, it took on the dimensions of a game. Besides, it gave me an opportunity to interject some of myself into the book. After all, if I could figure out why a book was called *The Arabian Nights*, I could decide whether I wanted to delve into the secrets it contained. My game was sort of an immature prelude to looking at the index of a book, a practice I developed much later when I read for knowledge as well as pleasure. It is interesting how the habits of childhood stay with us, especially when we choose to remember them and make them a part of our adult lives.

I am far beyond childhood now, and still believe that all books unlock mysteries. However, I can no longer distinguish between what I read for pleasure and what I read for knowledge. These days, the index of a book is as intriguing to me as its title. *An Inner Voice for Public Administration* may seem to be an unusual title for a book in this field, and I admit that it is. For those who are put off by it, may I suggest a trip to the index? If you find no redeeming value there, this book is not for you, and I regret the loss of a reader with whom I might have had discourse. Those of you who are intrigued with the title have already entered into a dialogue with me and are entitled to a preview of the mysteries contained within this book.

I will attempt to describe the professional journey which led to its writing and to its unconventional title.

Like many others in the field of public administration, I have been disappointed in certain trends that have occurred over the last twenty years. Scholarship has focused on technological development and to a considerable extent excluded psychological and philosophical dimensions of the field. Curtis Ventriss (1991, 4–13) reminds us that public administration was conceived as an antidote to political corruption. Raised in the orthodoxy of the reform movement, its educational emphasis has been on preparing students for performing the functional tasks that assure economy and efficiency. It is generally believed that through rational means, corrupting influences can be curbed and the legitimate ends of government fulfilled. Schools of public administration concentrate on preparing students in the technical aspects of the profession. They do a good job educating students on how " 'to do public service,' " but not on how " 'to be public servants.' "

All professions seem to pass through a natural progression not unlike the passage of human beings from childhood to adulthood. Childhood is the time during which children master the material and physical environment so they will be equipped to meet the demands of the world. Public administration has mastered sufficient technological knowledge and provided its practitioners with the means necessary to meet the requirements demanded of the profession. This knowledge enables them to amass data, extract pertinent information, and finally reach workable solutions to complex situations. They are educated, trained, and in the world "doing" the business of public administration. The discipline has equipped them with whatever tools the external world can provide.

The Need for a Philosophy of Public Administration

What then, you may ask, am I concerned about? I wonder about the relationship between the technical or material aspect of public administration and its more personal side. In other words, what does it mean "to be public servants" and "how do we learn?" I submit that these are philosophical questions we need to address both in the classroom and on the job. When a profession and the individuals committed to it look beyond the tools of the trade to the deeper significance of their personal involvement, both seem to flourish. Like children who have matured, public administration must graduate from merely carrying out the mandates of legislated policy to a field that is grounded in a strong philosophical tradition.

This is the first of three challenges I believe public administration needs to face as we approach the twenty-first century. The second challenge requires insight into ways organizations can renew themselves to meet changes occurring in the postmodern world. For example, governmental agencies with their hierarchical arrangements are inappropriate structures for the egalitarian mentality common among professional administrators. The third challenge calls for an examination of the technological changes that will occur in the near future. For example, the implications of the burgeoning field of virtual reality on policymaking and program implementation deserve serious consideration. Will policy analysts and program executives be able to enter a new world and vicariously experience future public policy in action? The hair-raising adventures of Flash Gordon speeding along the futuristic super-highways of the 1950s comic pages were no less preposterous.

A philosophy of administration would provide the basic values we need if we are to meet the challenges of organizational renewal and changing technology. On the occasion of Dwight Waldo's eightieth birthday, Frank Marini (1993, 409–17) wrote a moving tribute to that great gentleman to whom we owe so much. Marini reminds us that Waldo himself has contributed to public administration's search for a philosophy. He has always favored a broad perspective for public administration because of its intimate connection with all aspects of civilization and culture. Waldo, who believes there are many avenues toward knowledge, has consistently supported multidisciplinary, as well as interdisciplinary, research.

Of particular significance to this book is Waldo's admonition against becoming "culture bound." I believe that public administration has not heeded this warning and has single-mindedly accepted the rationalistic, dichotomous thinking of western society. This book attempts to contribute toward a philosophy of administration by focusing on the level of individual persons who are committed to public service. Their need to define the professional and moral parameters within which they can function as decision makers cannot be ignored. They, like all human beings, must take a profoundly personal journey with individually designed road maps. This journey is the mystery that the book tries to penetrate. Following Waldo's advice, I have ventured outside the traditional interdisciplines and beyond the confines of western culture. I have examined ideas in analytical psychology, as defined by Carl Jung. Jung's way of thinking, like ours, is steeped in western culture. However, he was open to the rich insights of the east whose ideas are of ancient origin and have withstood the test of time.

Analytical Psychology and Eastern Philosophy

Carl Gustav Jung was born on July 26, 1875, in Kesswil, Switzerland, a village situated on Lake Constance. His father was a Protestant vicar who moved his family shortly after Jung's birth to Laufen, a small town on the Rhine River. In this lovely and peaceful setting, Jung spent the first four years of his life. His memories of that brief time recall farmland, gardens, and warm summer days bathed in sunlight. He was surrounded by the beauty of the Alps, magnificent sunsets, and the glorious colors of nature.

This idyllic setting provided Jung with a sense of harmony and peace. His boyhood was spent in Klein-Huingen, a town on the banks of the Rhine River, opposite the city of Basel. Throughout his life, Jung was influenced by the symbolic significance of water as a motif underlying spirituality and the unconscious. His affinity with water is evidenced by his decision to build a house on Lake Zurich shortly after his marriage. In his later years, Jung retired to the rural community of Bollingen, which is situated on Lake Zurich. He continued his work there, in a house on the shores of the lake, until his death in 1961 (Wehr 1988, 9–10).

Using Jungian psychology to examine eastern thought provides us with a certain degree of comfort, since it can bridge the gap that exists between our western mode of thinking and the rather different perception of the world in the east. The special gift that enables some individuals to sense major social trends years before they occur is always fascinating. Carl Jung possessed this rare ability. He referred to himself as "a man who predicts a thunderstorm when there is not a cloud in the sky." He went on to say, "Perhaps it is a storm below the horizon, and perhaps it will never reach us" (Jung 1978, 10:194). Jung prophesied the storm more than sixty years ago. Many believe it has arrived and that it roars deeply within each of us. It is a storm of psychic proportions which expresses itself in a search for spiritual growth. One need only browse through local bookstores to see the vast range of self-help paperbacks claiming to assist us in resolving the problems endemic to our times. The promise of peace and contentment these books impart soothes us as we try to cope in a world that seems not to care. There are books on all aspects of modern living, from forming lasting relationships to overcoming various addictions, or preparing for the inevitable passage from life to death. In major cities like New York, specialized stores provide a huge selection of literature steeped in the traditions of India, China, Japan, and the Middle East. Even conventional bookstores are increasingly stocking books on eastern meditative practice.

Eastern thought has generally placed a high value on the cultivation of an interior life. Introspection can provide insight into the more subtle aspects of living which are not experienced in the external world. When individuals attempt to achieve a balance between their inner striving and the demands of the outer world, they are on the path toward wholeness and integration. Appreciation and deep understanding of the human need to look within is one of the most salient differences between the eastern and western mind. In the west, the world is perceived as an objective reality which exists totally outside individuals and is under their control. A will of iron and technological strength coupled with a little good luck are all considered necessary for individuals to master most situations.

When we need to be introspective and occasionally withdraw into ourselves, we are viewed with suspicion and may even be derided by others. Consider for a moment some of the colloquialisms which so aptly define the way we approach one another. We are admired when we are "up," criticized when we are "down"; approved of when we are "go-getters," scolded when we "sit back"; praised when we "take action," condemned when we "waver"; followed when we are "convinced," blamed when we "falter"; loved when we "succeed," and abandoned when we "fail."

This tendency to see the world as a place in which extremes prevail is a distorted perception. The "take-charge" attitude that permeates our culture has led us to a narrow way of thinking in which we can be either right or wrong, succeed or fail, win or lose. Many of us respond by always being on guard and rarely taking the time to stop and weigh our choices. The time-honored respect for quiet reflection has left our consciousness and we are bereft of its benefits. We seem to have lost our sense of self and our purpose in the world. Reflection and solitude are, more often than not, considered characteristics of the unfriendly, withdrawn, and socially inept members of our families and institutions. It is through stillness that we acquire the strength to become "up," gain the insight to be "go-getters," know when to "take action," attain the wisdom that leads to "conviction," and become humble enough to "succeed."

The Search for a Greater Balance

There are signs that people are beginning to question our externally oriented way of life. Increasing attention is being paid to ways of attaining a balance between inner and outer reality. I believe this trend is our response to the psychic thunderstorm that Jung predicted so long ago. The parts of ourselves that we have ignored are not easy to access without guidance. We need to enhance our way of understanding if we are to succeed in a global world. New ways of knowing will come to us when we are able to trust our inner voice. In the west, the disciplines of psychology and psychiatry have contributed to increased psychological growth for many individuals. The psychotherapeutic setting provides an opportunity for self-expression in a safe, nonjudgmental environment.

This experience, if successful, puts individuals in touch with the innermost self. As a result, they become aware of how they have contributed to the positive and negative aspects of their lives. At its best, psychotherapy can help individuals become more responsible and mature; I believe it has made a positive contribution to the quality of life in our society. However, I am not suggesting that individuals who intend to enter the profession of public administration should rush to the couch to divulge their lives to a therapist.

I do ask readers, however, to consider the merits of a more indirect, quiet, and deliberative approach to the practice of public administration, and to living in general. If we listen to the teachings of eastern philosophy, we may change. Our profession might become less defensive and more accepting of ideas that challenge our definition of reason. This is not to suggest that we adopt a weakened approach to the practice of public administration, but rather reevaluate the assumptions upon which we define strength and weakness. Too often our actions are dysfunctional, in that the goals we seek are exactly opposite to what we achieve.

Think for a moment of the aborted attempt during the Carter administration to storm Lebanon and release American hostages, or the more recent fiasco in Waco, Texas, when the Clinton administration was responsible for poor decision making which resulted in the deaths of young children. The mountain standoff at Ruby Ridge, which also resulted in unnecessary deaths, was another example of the American tendency to rush in and control all situations.

These decisions were not made without the input of professional civil servants who were experienced and knowledgeable in the intricacies of Middle East politics and the psychological makeup of despots and cult leaders. These examples are but a few of the many instances in which public administrators fall victim to the misguided belief that action is always a sign of strength. When our inner voice whispers, "wait," the outer world shouts, "those who hesitate are lost." True to our heritage, we take action. Like our Greek and Roman ancestors, we must "seize the day." If we can keep an open mind and listen, we may evaluate different ways of reacting to complex situations and broaden our rigid world view. This book offers nothing less or more than an invitation to take a journey of professional inner discovery.

Eastern philosophy's emphasis on inner development can enlighten the west, but some argue that the gap between the eastern and western mind is so large it can never be bridged. Even Jung, who studied eastern symbolism and concepts extensively, believed that yoga and meditation techniques are not necessarily suitable to western minds (Jung 1958a, 11:875–76). For instance, it is possible for an individual practicing meditation to experience disturbing images, thoughts, or feelings from deep inside the unconscious mind. Psychological harm can result from such a confrontation with unconscious material in those who are unfamiliar with the terrain of the inner world. Jung taught that it was imperative for civilized individuals to accept the challenge of inner development. He looked toward the east for guidance, but believed that the west needed to develop its own methods of personal growth. Harold Coward suggests that one reason Jung favored eastern ideas was because he believed it is the "encounter with another way of understanding and living life which jars the Westerner loose from his own narrow-minded encapsulation" (Coward 1985, 30).

I do not agree that as westerners we cannot understand or incorporate eastern metaphysics into our way of life. In many respects, our own religions and philosophies have let us down, so we must seek guidance elsewhere. The proliferation of self-help books attests to the search for meaning in our society. Coward reminds us that, even in Jung's day, there were signs of a turning toward the east (Coward 1985, 23). Unfortunately, too many current books, often referred to as "new-age," seem to water down or trivialize the deeper significance of eastern teaching. Yet we continue to search. Jung may have been right; perhaps we do need a jolt to reach new human terrain.

Techniques for attaining inner knowledge are beyond the scope of this book and require the expertise of trained teachers. For example, meditation is the common practice of eastern philosophical and spiritual traditions. It is important in Buddhism, Hinduism, and various Zen sects. The effects of meditative practice can be quite transforming. From ancient times to the present day, individuals have used meditation to reach a place deep within themselves. This is a serious undertaking and must be pursued with care because it accesses the subconscious, which can be a frightening experience if not understood. This book intends to make the reader aware that there are other traditions, even older than those in the west, and that these teachings can provide profound truths to those who care to pursue them.

Considerable care has been taken in writing this book to avoid a shallow presentation of eastern spiritual practices. Readers who are interested in learning more about the teachings of the east are advised either to investigate the vast body of literature that exists, or find a spiritual guide who is well-versed in meditative practices. This book tries to build a bridge between eastern and western thinking by combining analytical psychology's concept of introspection with eastern metaphysics' concept of individual wholeness. While both of these orientations approach a spiritual dimension, neither rests upon a particular theistic teaching. Therefore, both may appeal to the multicultural community comprising public administration.

Analytical psychology, as conceived by Jung, probes the depths of the unconscious as well as attending to the conscious mind. As modern people living in the west, we focus our lives on what we experience through consciousness. The hidden corners of our mind are ignored because we prefer to believe that we are in control of everything. We never confront the destructive side of our nature, which causes many of the problems faced by modern civilization. Consequently, unlike more primitive human beings who were in touch with deeper levels of reality, we have cast our instincts aside like worn-out clothing.

Unlike old clothes, however, instincts come back literally to haunt us. Like the gods and demons of our less-civilized brothers and sisters, they manifest themselves in our lives. Our denial of these inner yearnings is responsible for the plethora of neuroses that continue to plague our so-called "modern civilization" (Jung 1976, 18:555). If we are to succeed in weathering the psychic storm that has cast such a long shadow on western civilization, we must find a way to unlock the mysteries that lie deeply within us and finally become whole human beings.

Aldous Huxley provides a powerful metaphor we can use in our search for greater balance. The metaphor also helps connect western and eastern thinking. He envisions a hierarchy of gates through which we pass on our way to self-knowledge. The bottom gate opens into the world of practice and morality, where practical truths are found; the middle gate into the world of human psychology, where action and morality intersect; and the uppermost gate into the world of metaphysics, where ultimate truth resides. We are free to choose which gate to open and whether to continue the journey to the summit. The path we follow once inside a particular gate does not matter; what is important is that we open the gate in the first place.

Whether we follow the ideas of the east or the teachings of the west, the business of life for each of us is to open the gates leading to truth. This is the "psychology of the Perennial Philosophy" that is found in all theological and philosophical traditions (Huxley 1970, 1).

FROM WEST TO EAST

The linkage between analytical psychology and eastern philosophy is the attention both give to the inner voice of individuals. One of Jung's most relevant ideas is the concept of individuation in which, through a process of self-examination, individuals achieve a state of personal knowledge and become fully integrated and developed people. By looking inward, individuals gain an understanding of who they really are. Consequently, they may become aware of aspects of themselves that were hidden and often expressed in inappropriate ways. Those who succeed at individuation tend to be more genuine and open in their dealings with the world than those who rely on convention to define themselves.

Most western individuals are inclined to be preoccupied with what is outside themselves and have difficulty learning to cultivate an appreciation of inner truths. Public administrators tend to look upon the world as an external object, responsive to the tools of analysis and reason that they are taught to apply to the situations they manage. Little, if any, attention is given to quiet reflection, whereby public administrators remove themselves from active involvement in a problem situation to silently look within for direction. Prevailing wisdom dictates that answers to problems can usually be found through the application of standardized solutions, such as using the findings of a needs analysis to develop criteria for a social program and predict its outcome.

What often happens is that greater significance is attached to the procedures of designing and implementing the social program than to the substance of the program itself. This emphasis on procedure over substance is but one example of where the field of public administration is today. The technical rationality that underlies the practice of modern public administration is a worthy value for practitioners and academicians to hold. However, it is not the panacea that many of us claim.

Something is amiss in our approach to administration. Our notion of what rationality means is circumscribed by the narrow parameters of western logic. If the scientific method were a cure-all, public administration would be the most successful social science experiment of the twentieth century, and it is anything but that. The truth is we are faced with a credibility crisis of massive proportions accompanied by a deep-seated lack of self-esteem. We cannot even decide whether we are a profession, a discipline, or a field. Some have argued that our strength lies more in the constitutive values of governance than in our managerial competency. Consistent with this view is the notion that public administration is a kind of vocation, a calling of sorts (Wamsley et al. 1990; Green, Kellar, and Wamsley 1993). Individuals who come to public service as to a higher calling, are inclined to listen to and trust the inner voice that led them to a career in public administration.

The advances made by technology are truly wonderful, and it is not my intention to decry the significant contribution they have made to all our lives, both personal and professional. The wonders of the computer, which serves as an extension of my arm as I write this book, enhance the quality of my professional life. And the welcome sound and delicious aroma of freshly brewed coffee dripping into my preset, automatic machine in the morning brings sheer joy! On a more serious note, technological development and scientific know-how have contributed significantly to the practice of public administration at both its comprehensive policymaking or macro-level and its more focused implementation or microlevel (Murray 1995, 44).

Scientific inquiry has brought about the unprecedented technological advances that have enhanced twentieth-century life. From the rational approach of modern science, we have learned how to develop procedures to control our government agencies, which we view as giant machines. Procedures define the functions we perform, the budgets we assign, and most disheartening, the behavior of individuals. These practices are considered rational and efficient since they provide the oil, so to speak, that lubricates the moving parts of our agencies. However, if we are to make an unbiased evaluation of our public institutions, we must admit they do not respond as efficiently as the principles of science would dictate. This is a tremendous disappointment to those who are locked into the belief that organizations are merely static entities, staffed by professionals who are held in thrall to the principles of inductive reasoning and quantitative measures.

Any attempt to represent the thinking of the west or the east is a vast undertaking. It is impossible to touch on all significant aspects of the two world views. Different aspects of eastern thought may be more relevant to different western disciplines. Likewise, there are aspects of western thought that more readily apply to particular eastern interests. Our concern in this book is to look toward the east to enrich the practice of public administration. The following strategy is designed to touch upon the representation of the west and the east in a simplified, but effective, way.

The World According to Descartes

As we depart the twentieth century, we need to reconsider some of the assumptions that have defined public administration. I refer in particular to the principle of certainty and the subject/object split which have permeated our culture since the seventeenth century when René Descartes lived. The principle of certainty holds that we can only seek truth for those things about which we are certain. In his search for truth, Descartes rejected all things that held the slightest doubt in his mind. He believed doubt implied that a thing was either false or untrustworthy. Because he believed in a God who created the world and could not deceive, Descartes concluded that absolute truth exists. He was convinced that the mind could distinguish truth from error by focusing on what it knew to be certain. The discovery of truth was proof of certainty in the world (Williams 1990, 37, 49).

Descartes credited mathematics with the ability to set standards of certainty. This idea was expressed in approximately 1628 when he penned his first work, entitled *Rules for the Direction of Our Native Intelligence*. Published posthumously, it laid the foundation for his unwavering faith in the power of reason. He spoke of experience and deduction as the only legitimate ways of attaining knowledge. Descartes believed inferences made on the basis of evidence that is observed and carefully measured are always accurate. Only those observations that can be quantitatively measured should be investigated. Mathematics, free from uncertainty and falsehood, is best exemplified by arithmetic and geometry because they " 'alone are concerned with an object so pure and simple that they make no assumptions that experience might render uncertain; they consist entirely in deducing conclusions by means of rational arguments' " (Cottingham, Stoothoff, and Murdoch 1994, 2).

Descartes' first book, *A Discourse on Method*, was published in 1637. One of his interests in writing the book was to develop a way of applying mathematical techniques to solve scientific problems. Descartes questioned the use of logic as a method of learning because it only explains what is already known. He was also critical of using geometry and algebra exclusively to attain knowledge, because they either tend to be too abstract or so laden down with rules that the mind is confused rather than stimulated (Descartes 1992a, 14–15). Descartes decided to formulate a less complicated method for seeking truth and based it upon a firm adherence to four rules.

The first precept was to accept only those things which are certain and ignore all things that are not clearly evident or that cast any doubt in the mind. Secondly, he divided every problem into as many elements as possible and included everything that might contribute to a solution. His third precept was to think sequentially, starting with the simplest element and progressively proceeding to the more complex. Finally, Descartes proposed examining every possible item to be considered and assigning each a number. His method relied on an orderly process of reasoning, in which one truth would be inferred from another. By starting with simple truths and inferring more complex ones, he sought to attain the certainty that is found in arithmetic (Descartes 1992a, 15–17).

Sounds a lot like the way public administration is practiced today, doesn't it? For example, the use of quantitative measures to evaluate the feasibility of certain policies, programs, or projects is fundamental to the practice of public administration at all levels of government. Cost benefit analysis enjoys a high status in this regard. This way of thinking is a remnant of the scientific approach to management that swept both the public and private sectors in the early days of the twentieth century. For example, Levine, Peters, and Thompson (1990, 242–43) suggest that formula-driven techniques may be appropriate for certain public sector problems, but not for all. For those situations in which it is feasible to plan before taking action, simple solutions may suffice because fewer factors can influence the outcome.

The design of a dam is a task that lends itself to the dictates of Descartes' rules. After careful analysis, engineers can develop a construction plan that will result in a suitable dam (Schmidt 1993, 525–30). On the other hand, more complex situations require a continually evolving plan designed to respond to constant changes. Solutions based upon simple arithmetic calculations give way in these instances to the more complicated practice named *disjointed incrementalism* by Charles Lindblom, in which multiple actors continually reevaluate and alter strategies and alternatives (Levine et al. 1990, 243). The simpler the problem to be solved, the more certain its outcome will be.

In the past few decades, public administration has tried to evaluate how well federal agencies implement public policy. Implementation studies have unearthed many problems. For instance, government programs are often founded upon policies tied into vague and even contradictory laws. Professional civil servants in the executive branch face the unenviable task of writing guidelines for implementing these unclear programs. Since even the goals of such policies are open to interpretation, standards for evaluating their performance are difficult, if not impossible, to set. Helen Ingram (1990, 463) suggests that not only is there confusion over which standards of performance to use and how to measure them, but even the boundaries of implementation are unclear. This raises a basic philosophical question; namely, Where does implementation begin and where does it end?

Given our lack of knowledge concerning the dynamics that contribute to the implementation of a government program and our differences of opinion on what the policy intends to achieve in the first place, public administration needs to take a good hard look at what it can expect from program evaluation. First, we need to accept the challenge posed by Ingram and decide where implementation begins. I suggest that such reassessment start with the individual civil servant in Washington, or a state capital, who is responsible for establishing the program's guidelines. Each public administrator who makes decisions concerning the daily operation of the program is responsible for its implementation. The success or failure of the program depends in large part upon the integrity of the decisions made by each of the professional administrators who contribute to its final goal.

The more imaginative literature in the field recognizes that our profession does not always comply with the rigid criteria of western rationality. The use of creative language engages our interest because it captures reality in a new and inventive way. This is important if we are to appreciate how our profession really operates in the day-to-day work place. Once we begin to think more creatively, we may pursue other explanations of how we practice public administration.

On occasion, when analyzing public policy and evaluating public programs, "simple back-of-the-envelope, analytical techniques are sometimes best" (Goodsell 1990, 501). This is a legitimate and practical way to reach conclusions that we are unable to derive from mathematical assessment. However, there is a vast difference between well-deliberated decisions made without empirical evidence and wild-eyed speculation. Whether public administrators are making decisions on the basis of factual information, through a combination of facts and experience, or through intuition alone, inner guidance is needed. I believe we always rely, to some extent, upon inner direction when we take action. We do not admit this, however, either to ourselves or anyone else; if we did, we would be looked upon as biased, lacking in technical "know-how," or worst of all, unprofessional.

In his "Principles of Philosophy," which is part of *A Discourse on Method*, Descartes perceives reality as sets of dualities composed of separate entities. For example, he argues that the mind and body can be conceived, at least in theory, as separate from one another. He submits that, because the mind contains ideas of things that may or may not exist outside itself, thought is independent of any material object (Descartes 1992b, 8:167, 13:169). He uses the same reasoning to argue that, because individuals can separate themselves physically and mentally from other objects in the material world, they are independent of one another as both thinking and material beings (60:189). Therefore, as individual persons are separate from one another, so too can the mind be conceived as separate from the body.

In his introduction to my copy of the *Discourse*, the philosopher Tom Sorrel summarizes the subject/object split, also known as the Cartesian Duality, by listing the following tenets. First, that which is essential to the mind is distinct from that which is essential to the body; hence, mind and body can be perceived as distinct substances. Second, the minds and bodies of human beings are integrated during their lifetimes. This is necessary because the mind needs a body in order to participate in life and interact with inanimate objects in the external world. Third, the body also needs the mind for its survival, but this union prevents human beings from objectively understanding both themselves and the external world. Fourth, since the mind exists prior to the body, "knowing it is a condition of knowing body" (Descartes 1992, para. 20).

Public administration abounds in examples of the trouble we get into because we have accepted the third tenet and its many implications. Before we discuss a few examples, it may be helpful to review western thinking on this point. Like Descartes, we accept that there is an objective world outside ourselves, but also that we are incapable of objectively understanding it. Therefore, we cannot trust our subjective thoughts and feelings about events in the world. This is a condition we believe needs to be rectified, especially in our professional lives, when we must make decisions about the outside world that affect other people. We think we are capable of totally repressing our personal perceptions of the problems we are asked to resolve.

We collect bits of information that can be categorized and enumerated, call them facts, and believe they are real and present an objective picture of the external world that exists outside our minds. We think of facts as if they were objects, like the objects we can see, touch, and feel in the external world. When we are able to accumulate facts, we make a decision that we believe is objective. As members of western society, we set great store on factual information, tending to discredit those times of our lives in which we either ignore the facts and rely upon inner direction, or act instinctively without bothering to get the facts. We are inclined to excuse this latter behavior more when we make decisions affecting our personal lives than when making professional decisions.

Unless we critically examine the assumptions upon which we operate, there is little hope that we will consider alternative ways of thinking, knowing, and living. As you read this book, you will discover that what I am proposing is a discerning evaluation of our profession that begins with all of us acutely evaluating ourselves. This is a difficult and lonely road to travel and is fraught with disappointments and negative discoveries. However, I believe it is the only way for modern public administration to come to terms with its more personal side.

There are times when facts cannot provide assurance that decisions made will be adequate to solve the problem at hand. We see this played out in time of war and hostage situations, when no amount of information can predict the behavior of people who are scared and out of control. In situations like these, we must take responsibility for our decisions that are not guided by objective, factual information. We must not delude ourselves into thinking that we can assume responsibility for only those events for which we can gather information that can be seen, touched, and felt.

The soldiers who crawled on their bellies in the jungles of Vietnam hardly expected women and children from the villages to lambast them with grenades; yet they were sent one after the other to be ripped apart. Military decision makers were mistaken in their assumption that only soldiers are capable of inflicting bodily harm on the enemy. Their misguided belief that the only valid interpretation of the external world is an objective one based solely on indubitable facts, caused suffering and death to countless American soldiers. One of the most disturbing aspects of our culture is the attitude that we are only accountable for those decisions whose outcome can be known with certitude. There is a subtle message in our society that we are not really responsible when we take risks with the lives or livelihoods of others, unless we have a clear notion of where our actions will lead.

Action is the driving force of the western mentality. As the first line of defense in problem solving, we tend to rely upon action before examining the facts in light of our own intuitive judgment. After all, the world is there to be controlled, isn't it? When we are unable to do so, it is merely a fluke, and no one is truly accountable for trying to resolve a problem whose solution doesn't work out as planned. Bad decisions are attributed to the absence of objective, factual information rather than personal responsibility.

The following example, borrowed from Robert Denhardt's recent book, *Public Administration, An Action Orientation* (1995, 356–57), is a classic case of a decision-making situation that could have had dire consequences. I offer a slightly different slant from Denhardt's, although we would both agree that the clear-headed response of the story's protagonist deserves praise.

The story is set in the early days of the 1960s when a British commander, responsible for a long-range radar system monitoring station, observed images on the station's screens that seemed to indicate a massive missile assault was being aimed at the United States by the Soviet Union. The commander was responsible for evaluating the situation and reporting it to officials in the United States, along with his assessment and recommendations. While he was deliberating on what to do, he remembered that Nikita Krushchev, at that time the premier of the Soviet Union, was at the United Nations in New York City. The commander reasoned that this hardly seemed the time an attack would be made on the United States. In addition, the radar system responsible for the images was a new one, and it was common for new, sophisticated equipment to harbor a few bugs. After weighing these considerations, the commander made his report stating that he felt there was no danger to the United States at that particular time.

This is a wonderful example of a decision maker who is faced with a dilemma of facts; namely, which ones to believe. One set of facts, reflected on the screen, indicated World War III was imminent. The other set of facts, intuited by the commander, indicated the system was malfunctioning. The facts that could be seen, touched, and felt were reflected on the screen. They were the measurable facts that our culture tells us we should believe. The facts that indicated the system was malfunctioning could not be seen, touched, or felt. They were the intuitive facts that western culture does not trust. And yet the commander, much to his credit, weighed both sets of facts and ultimately listened to his inner voice. In so doing, he made a decision to discount what appeared to be objective, empirical evidence, thereby averting a major disaster that could have precipitated the end of the world as we know it!

The World According to Tao

More than likely, the reader has seen the word Tao (pronounced "Dow") and wondered at its meaning. Tao embraces a variety of ideas in the eastern tradition. There is no exact translation in the western world, since no word exists for it in western languages. Consequently, it is difficult to assign it a simple meaning. The best explanation of the Tao, for purposes of this book, was developed by Jean Shinoda Bolen, who states that in ancient China there were two such notions: the uppercase Tao of the spiritual teachers and the lowercase tao of Confucius. The Confucian tao represented an ideal in which individuals attained a balance between their inner and outer lives. Those who achieved this balance were said to be psychologically developed individuals. The wisdom they gained through inner probing was made manifest in their outer lives (Bolen 1982, 86). Confucius taught that these individuals were the epitome of what public servants ought to be.

The metaphysical Tao, referred to in literature as the Great Tao, represented the spiritual way of life through which individuals attained eternal truth. Bolen points out that the differences in interpretation between Tao and tao do not necessitate conflict in meaning. The tao of everyday living reflects the spiritual development of individuals who have embraced the metaphysical Tao. How individuals live their lives indicates the degree to which they are open to Tao, which is the foundation of everything in the universe. It is Tao which connects all things, great and small. The Tao, then, becomes the philosophical basis upon which eastern teaching rests (Bolen 1982, 87). In the interest of simplicity and consistency, the uppercase Tao will be used in this book. This is in keeping with most western literature on the Tao.

I remind the reader that this book is not intended to promote or even comment on any particular religious tradition. Let me clear the air on this very important point. It is *not* a book about religious influences on public administration. If it is perceived that way, some readers who think their beliefs are not presented may feel excluded and miss what I am trying to say. It is my intention that the book not offend anyone.

Often the word Tao is translated into English as the "Way" or the "Path." Interestingly, the translation of the new testament into Chinese equates the Tao with the Greek word "Logos," which means God. For example, the gospel of St. John is translated as: "In the beginning was the Tao and the Tao was with God and the Tao was God" (Chang 1992, 15; Bolen 1982, 3). The spiritual Tao, the word Logos, and the tao of ideal living *all* connote the following qualities: creation, knowledge, life, light, logic, method, power, rational, reality, and wisdom (Chang 1992, 15). In chapter 6, when we look at how individual public administrators can benefit from the lessons of the Tao, we will meet some of these qualities again.

Looking ahead further, I discuss three concepts from eastern philosophy that provide a linkage between analytical psychology and eastern thinking. These concepts represent qualities of living based upon the Tao. Western culture, to its disadvantage, has ignored these ideas, turning a deaf ear to the inner voice and its interpretation of the external world. The concepts are: 1) silence, 2) unity, and 3) wu-wei, roughly translated as "nonaction." Each of these concepts provides an opportunity for us to listen to ideas that lie beyond the boundaries of technical rationality, while keeping sight of the advances made by modern technology and science. This book does not call for an abandonment of what is important to our culture; it merely asks for a consideration of teachings from the east, which have a long, respectable history and deserve a place in our lexicon of ideas.

Each of these three concepts is fully developed in its respective chapter later in this book. There are many ways to interpret how analytical psychology and eastern metaphysics view silence, unity, and wu-wei. Each perspective contains its own set of implications for those individuals who elect to follow the Tao by developing the qualities associated with these concepts. I conclude this chapter by providing a brief introduction to each concept, laying the groundwork for later, more systematic treatment.

Quiet and introspection allow individual administrators to hear the inner voice and attain a deeper level of understanding of the situations they face. Silence presupposes a withdrawal of sorts, in order for individuals to look within. Analytical psychology teaches that the business of life for each individual is to discover the truth that is hidden within. Jung calls this the journey toward Self. The eastern Tao teaches us that silence brings the stillness we need to find the Self and gather the truths it offers. The great Chinese sage, Lao-tze, is credited with the wisdom contained in the *Tao Teh King*, written sometime between his birth in 604 B.C. and death in 517 B.C. In this work, Lao-tze discusses the qualities of reason and virtue. Recognizing the values of nonassertion and silence, he writes, "One who knows does not talk. One who talks does not know" (Lao-tze 1991, 56, 112).

Imagine what would happen to decision making in public administration if we took those words seriously! Our meetings would become more meaningful if we weighed our thoughts before we spoke, and spoke only when we had something of significance to impart to others. Such considerate behavior would afford an opportunity for those who know to speak out and be heard.

Through silence we acquire the capacity to see beyond conventional solutions. We become more creative and less prone to flex our problem-solving muscles, relying instead upon insight. We stop complying with dictates of the external world, start listening to the inner voice, and in time, learn to discard that which is extraneous and cut to the essence of things. Out of the chaos of our endless discussions there arises a sense of order and direction. The depth of understanding we gain through silence is beautifully presented in the following words of Lao-tze (1991, 38:6–8):

> Traditionalism is the flower of Reason,
> but of ignorance the beginning.
> Therefore a great organizer abides
> by the solid and dwells not in the external.
> He abides in the fruit and dwells not in the flower.
> Therefore he discards the latter and chooses the former.

The concept of unity is an intuitive one, in that it is the principle upon which all existence rests. It is the most spiritual of the three concepts examined in this book and is found in every religious and philosophical tradition that has ever existed. In his intriguing book, *The Perennial Philosophy*, Aldous Huxley writes, "It is from the more or less obscure intuition of the oneness that is the ground and principle of all multiplicity that philosophy takes its source" (Huxley 1970, 5). Huxley refers throughout his book to the Divine Ground as the universal and transcendent basis of existence. He examines all traditions and shows that belief in the primordial unity is as true for Taoism as it is for all other eastern and western orthodoxies. We need to examine the concept of unity as we are trying to address philosophical issues in public administration.

The unity concept is one of the ideas that underlies analytical psychology. Jung states that before the seventeenth century, philosophy was "dominated" by the "original feeling of unity" that was shared by all human beings. The source of connectedness was then, and is today, the unconscious psyche. We have lost this connection because we have lost touch with the unconscious side of ourselves. The ascendancy of reason and rationality during the seventeenth century created a split between our conscious and unconscious mind (Jung 1958b, 11:443). We entered into a war between the forces of reason and instinct. It is clear which side won.

The spoils of war belong to the victor, in this case, civilization itself. Reason won the day and defines modern civilization. We have bought into the Cartesian Duality, with its externalization of reality, dichotomous assumptions, and repression of whatever is perceived to be irrational. Analytical psychology, with its internalization of reality, integrating assumptions, and focus on the psyche, presents a formidable critique of seventeenth-century philosophy. Its emphasis on the importance of turning inward and its acceptance of the unity principle correlate with the holistic nature of eastern metaphysics. Together, they can assist us in our attempt to build a philosophy that promotes the growth and development of individual public administrators.

Lao-tze wrote the following words to express how the concept of unity can lead an individual to practice the virtue of humility. This trait is particularly appropriate to public administrators because we have chosen a profession that asks us to be subordinate to political appointees and elected public officials. To do this we must be humble, a condition that is not valued in western culture. Also, humility is not necessarily inborn, and in most cases must be acquired. In this additional quote from Lao-tze, I ask the reader to substitute the word "wise" for "holy" in the first line (Lao-tze 1991, 22:2):

> The holy man embraces unity and becomes
> for all the world a model.
> Not self-displaying he is enlightened;
> Not self-approving he is distinguished;
> Not self-asserting he acquires merit;
> Not self-seeking he gaineth life.
> Since he does not quarrel, therefore no one
> in the world can quarrel with him.

The concept of wu-wei may be the most abstruse for the western mind to grasp. It translates into English as "nonaction," but is not equivalent in meaning to the word "inaction." Inaction is perceived as an inability to do something that needs to be done. It implies laziness of a sort, and is negative in its connotation. Wu-wei, to the contrary, can be interpreted as a conscious decision not to take action in a given situation. This decision is based upon an intrinsic knowing that guides us when we stop and listen to the inner voice when faced with difficult situations. In doing so, we allow the unconscious mind to exercise its power. Taoism calls this the power of "p'u."

The esteemed sinologist, Holmes Welch, provides examples of what happens when we allow p'u to do its thing, so to speak. He writes of the jade craftsman, whose sculptures attain masterpiece status only when his hands are allowed to carve freely; when the craftsman struggles, the jade becomes scarred. A writer searches in vain for the perfect word; it comes in its own time, when the author is at rest. An adoptive couple conceive a child shortly after the adoption. Welch refers to these phenomena as "ends without means" (Welch 1966, 79). This thinking is diametrically opposed to public administration, which devotes all its attention to acquiring the appropriate means to achieve the ends of government.

Again I refer to the decision to take action in Waco as a dramatic example of ill-chosen means resulting in an ill-begotten end. Officials had the need to take control of the situation, prompting them to use tanks to punch holes in the flimsy walls of the Koresh compound. Many who watched the scene on television felt the action taken was too severe to achieve a nonviolent outcome. Some referred to the decision as a classic case of overkill. Confrontations between citizens and government forces generally end in government's favor. Even when the opposition is armed and dangerous, the prodigals will eventually capitulate.

Although we claim to be impressed with the advice of Mahatma Gandhi and Martin Luther King that violence begets violence, we fail to apply these teachings when faced with difficult situations. When government intervenes, immediate resolution is the usual response, rather than restraint. Consider the action of police against students on the campus of Kent State, and at the Democratic national convention in the 1960s. This tendency to rush in and solve the problem through use of excessive force is indicative of western culture's action orientation. Insufficient regard is paid to consequences that are likely to result from strong, immediate action.

Lao-tze recognized the preeminent position the state has over its people. He compared its power to that of a cook preparing a meal. Lao-tze advises leaders to:

> Govern a great country as you would fry
> small fish: (neither gut nor scale them) (1991, 60:1)

Restraint and compassion underlie the governance of a great country. The superior power of those who govern over those who are governed requires a measured response to all situations involving citizens, however strange their behavior. Just as it is not necessary to mutilate small fish, neither is it necessary to use inordinate means to govern. The poignant words of Lao-tze add drama to any context in which a superior power imposes its will. We would do well to learn a lesson from the east and, in the Carus and Suzuki interpretation of Lao-tze, "do the not doing, practice non-practice; leave them alone and do not meddle with their affairs" (Lao-tze 1991, 180). Need I say more?

REFERENCES

Bolen, Jean Shinoda. 1982. *The Tao of Psychology*. San Francisco: Harper San Francisco.

Chang, Stephen T. 1992. *The Great Tao*. 1985. Reprint, San Francisco: Tao Publishing.

Cottingham, John, Robert Stoothoff, and Dugald Murdoch, trans. 1994. *Descartes, Selected Philosophical Writings*. 1988. Reprint, New York: Cambridge University Press.

Coward, Harold. 1985. *Jung and Eastern Thought*. New York: State University of New York Press.

Denhardt, Robert B. 1995. *Public Administration, An Action Orientation*. New York: Wadsworth Publishing Company.

Descartes, René. 1992. "Introduction." In *A Discourse on Method*. Translated by John Veitch. 1912. Reprint, Rutland, Vermont: Charles E. Tuttle Co., Inc., Everyman's Library.

————. 1992a. "Discourse on the Method of Rightly Conducting the Reason and Seeking Truth in the Sciences." In *A Discourse on Method*. Translated by John Veitch. 1912. Reprint, Rutland, Vermont: Charles E. Tuttle Co., Inc., Everyman's Library.

————. 1992b. "The Principles of Philosophy." In *A Discourse on Method*. Translated by John Veitch. 1912. Reprint, Rutland, Vermont: Charles E. Tuttle Co., Inc., Everyman's Library.

Goodsell, Charles T. 1990. "Emerging Issues in Public Administration." In *Public Administration, The State of the Discipline*. Edited by Naomi B. Lynn and Aaron Wildavsky. Chatham: Chatham House Publishers, Inc.

Green, Richard T., Lawrence F. Kellar, Gary L. Wamsley. 1993. "Reconstituting a Profession for American Public Administration." In *Public Administration Review* 53 (6).

Huxley, Aldous. 1970. *The Perennial Philosophy*. 1945. Reprint, New York: Harper and Row Publishers.

Ingram, Helen. 1990. "Implementation: A Review and Suggested Framework." In *Public Administration, The State of the Discipline*. Edited by Naomi B. Lynn and Aaron Wildavsky. Chatham: Chatham House Publishers, Inc.

Jung, Carl G. 1958a. "Yoga and the West." In *Psychology and Religion*. Vol. 11 of *Collected Works*. New York: Pantheon Books for Bollingen Foundation.

————. 1958b. "Transformation Symbolism in the Mass." In *Psychology and Religion*. Vol. 11 of *Collected Works*. New York: Pantheon Books for Bollingen Foundation.

————. 1976. "Symbols and the Interpretation of Dreams." In *The Symbolic Life: Miscellaneous Writings*. Vol. 18 of *Collected Works*. Princeton: Princeton University Press.

————. 1978. "The Spiritual Problems of Modern Man." In *Civilization in Transition*. Vol. 10 of *Collected Works*. 2d 1970. Reprint, Princeton: Princeton University Press.

Jung, Carl G. 1978. "The Spiritual Problems of Modern Man." In *Civilization in Transition*. Vol. 10 of *Collected Works*. 2d 1970. Reprint, Princeton: Princeton University Press.

Lao-tze. 1991. *Tao Teh King*. Translated by Paul Carus and D. T. Suzuki, under the title *The Canon of Reason and Virtue*. La Salle: Open Court Publishing Company.

Levine, Charles H., B. Guy Peters, and Frank J. Thompson. 1990. *Public Administration, Challenges, Choices, Consequences*. Glenview, Illinois: Scott Foresman/Little Brown Higher Education.

Marini, Frank. 1993. "Leaders in the Field: Dwight Waldo." In *Public Administration Review* 53 (5).

Murray, Nancy. 1995. "The Eastern Aesthetic in Administration." In *Public Administration Illuminated and Inspired by the Arts*. Edited by Charles Goodsell and Nancy Murray. New York: Praeger.

Schmidt, Mary R. 1993. "Grout: Alternative Kinds of Knowledge and Why They Are Ignored." In *Public Administration Review* 53 (6).

Ventriss, Curtis. 1991. "Contemporary Issues in American Public Administration Education: The Search for an Educational Focus." In *Public Administration Review* 51 (1).

Wamsley, Gary, Robert N. Bacher, Charles T. Goodsell, Philip S. Kronenberg, John
    H. Rohr, Camilla M. Stivers, Orion F. White, and James F. Wolf. 1990. *Re-
    founding Public Administration*. Newbury Park: Sage Publications.
Wehr, Gerhard. 1988. *Jung, A Biography*. Translated by David M. Weeks. Boston:
    Shambhala.
Welch, Holmes. 1966. *Taoism, The Parting of the Way*, rev. ed. Boston: Beacon Press.
Williams, Bernard. 1990. *Descartes, The Project of Pure Inquiry*. 1978. Reprint, New
    York: Penguin Books.

PART 2

The Influence of Modernism on Public Administration

CHAPTER 2

Logical Positivism and Twentieth-Century Government

TOWARD A DEFINITION OF REASON

A by-product of having a New England upbringing, with its unique use of the English language, is the storehouse of pithy sayings at my disposal. "Reason is as reason does" reflects the New England tendency to judge claims of any sort in accordance with the action that ensues.

To the traditional Yankee mind, proof must precede a promise that an outcome will follow a specific course of action. For example, a recent debate in my hometown occurred over whether the elected board of selectmen, which still managed the town business, should be replaced by a mayoral form of government. A majority of the voters thought this was a reasonable solution to assorted political problems, which they associated with power accumulated over the years by the selectmen and their designated cronies. Traditionalists replied there was no reason to change, because the town hadn't grown that much and town meetings were sufficient to hold the selectmen in check. The reformers argued there was reason to change, producing evidence that showed improvements in similar communities which adopted either a strong mayor or weak mayor/city council form of government. Although I haven't lived in the town for many years, I can see in my mind's eye what probably transpired at a typical town meeting:

A Reasonable Solution

State Senator Eleanor Gibson, daughter of one of the leading business families in the town, stands at the podium in the high school gymnasium, ready to present evidence that the town should become a city and elect a mayor as soon as possible. She adds one transparency after another to the overhead projector, while emphasizing how the facts show that efficiency and economy are dependent upon a more accountable form of government. Senator Gibson talks at length about the need to look ahead and recognize that what worked well in the past may no longer be appropriate. She concludes by buttressing her strong case with unassailable facts, and reminding the townspeople that reason is on her side.

At the conclusion of her presentation, Brett Owens, local pharmacist and scion of one of the most active political families in town (his father, grandfather, and great-grandfather served as selectmen), slowly rises from his seat. His dialogue with the senator is peppered with the aphorisms unique to small New England towns. Owens reminds the senator that the selectmen form of government made the town what it is. Grass roots government is as American as apple pie. Town meetings assure the sense of community and neighborliness that everyone values. Smiling, Owens says, "Eleanor, remember when the treetop gang decided we wanted to build a tree house in the town square? You were the one who asked my father to hold a meeting so we could get approval and finish construction before school started in three weeks. That very night, Dad convened the board in a special meeting. I'll never forget how excited we were. All the grown-ups were in favor of the idea, even those whose houses bordered the square. I, for one, do not want to lose that kind of intimacy, and we will lose it if we change our form of government. I simply cannot support your proposal, Eleanor."

Senator Gibson responds, "Of course I remember that wonderful time, Brett, but that was then and this is now. We are not children and this is not thirty years ago. Things have changed and we have an opportunity to become a part of the suburban boom. It will increase property values and make our town even more prosperous than it is now." At every turn, the senator is able to outmaneuver Owens' arguments with facts and logic. Finally, she reminds him that she has studied the matter extensively, having access to data from similar towns within the state and across the country. Her position as state senator, she argues, provides her with the latest technological advantages and working relationships with faculty in leading universities who assisted in studying the implications of the proposed change in the town's structure and governance. Therefore, she concludes, "Reason is on my side, Brett." To which Brett Owens thunders, "Reason is as reason does!"

To Brett Owens, reason is not dependent upon facts and logic; it is whatever meets the needs of the town as he perceives them. Like all good citizens of my hometown, Owens believes that "actions speak louder than words." Actions should be based upon an inner sense of what to do. Reason is not an external reality that can be weighed and measured. What is reasonable for the town cannot be detemined by numbers and so-called objective reports prepared by outsiders. Sophisticated data analysis and clever words cannot replace what Owens knows from experience and what his own judgment tells him is right for the town.

This anecdote raises a question that needs to be addressed; namely, What is reason? Is it logical thinking based upon accumulated facts, a sense of what to do based upon accumulated experience, intuition coupled with emotional feeling, or a combination of logic, experience, intuition, and emotion?

The Role of Myth

Readers may be familiar with the remarkable series of interviews Bill Moyers conducted with Joseph Campbell on the power of myth in our lives. At one point in their conversation, Moyers asked Campbell whether reason is a philosophical construct that can be understood through mythological symbols. Campbell answered in the affirmative and stated that around 500 B.C., the time of Confucius and Lao-tze, human beings stopped being guided by animal powers and the planets and began to listen to the voice of reason. The two men spoke approvingly of how familiar with the lore of ancient myths educated individuals of the eighteenth century were. Campbell praised our founding fathers because they understood the power of myth and used it to guide them in creating a new country (Campbell 1988, 28–29).

Moyers asked Campbell if there was a contradiction between his admiration for our founding fathers, who contributed to the scientific orientation of the Age of Reason, and his delight when Luke Skywalker said, "Turn off the computer and trust your feelings" in the movie *Star Wars*. Immediately, he responded, "No, no, you have to distinguish between reason and thinking." To Campbell, what we call thinking is not necessarily reason. He likens our definition of reason to a mouse who tries to break through a wall and, after bumping its nose, figures out another exit. This, according to Campbell, is "the way we figure things out. But that's not reason" (Campbell 1988, 29).

Then what is reason? We see it through its effects and know what it can accomplish, but do not know what it is. I suggest that because we have lost the knowledge that inspired our ancestors, who believed in the power of myth and ritual, we have lost the true meaning of reason.

The power of myth is the power of our unconscious mind to bring ancient truths to the surface. Through mythical stories we are able to capture the magic of intuition and imagination and apply their teachings to our everyday lives. Picture a hypothetical conversation between Joseph Campbell and Carl Jung on this subject. More than likely, Jung would agree with Campbell that reason shares in the appreciation of mystery that is common to philosophical, religious, and spiritual customs. From these traditions, the values of ritual and inner direction are accepted. Symbolism helps make connections between what is consciously experienced and what is intuitively sensed. Myths release a place deep within us that responds to our experiences. This deeper level of understanding enhances the knowledge that the senses and the intellect provide.

In defining reason, Campbell and Jung would look toward its source, which lies buried within each of us. They would concur that reason has to do with an innate sense each person has of the "fundamental structuring of order of the universe" (Campbell 1988, 29). Yet, all along in our field of public administration, we thought order came from outside ourselves, from our ability to measure, organize, and follow time-honored principles such as POSDCORB (Gulick and Urwick 1937). More recently, we have been chastised for focusing on mission at the expense of rules (Osborne and Gaebler 1992, 110).

Myths are the archetypes that Jung identified in his study of the human psyche. Because we have lost belief in their power, we are prevented from consciously incorporating them into our lives, and we fail to see the influence they have on the decisions we make. We prefer to deny them because they do not fit into our definition of what is reasonable and rational. Material that comes from our psyche is beyond conscious control and threatens our vision of ourselves as "masters of the universe."

Reason, perceived as a cookbook of formula-driven techniques, was the original dream of public administration in the Progressive Era, when the field was born. This view seems rather insipid next to the deeper, more meaningful ideas of Joseph Campbell and Carl Jung. And yet our culture, with its emphasis on technical rationality, has not been open to concepts beyond the mechanistic ones with which we are all too familiar. In my hometown, when decisions result in positive outcomes, they are considered reasonable. Facts are not the only criteria upon which reason speaks. The measure of what is reasonable lies in the results of a particular course of action, not in a rationalization of why the action was taken. In other words, "reason is as reason does." People in my hometown believe that reason emanates from an unknown source. Most of them probably would not recognize the source as the unconscious mind, but they accept its existence without hesitation.

Perhaps their acknowledgment of a hidden, though inexplicable, truth explains why standardized thinking and conventional behavior have never been highly valued in my hometown. If reason emanates from the unconscious, it is as unique as each of us. Then reason is beyond definition, and its truths can be revealed to each individual only through his or her inner voice as it integrates all thoughts, experiences, and feelings. I wonder if this analysis of the values of my hometown is what De Tocqueville saw, so long ago, when he visited the United States.

THE AGE OF REASON

Will and Ariel Durant wrote three volumes, the theme of which is the "growth of reason." In this effort, they divided civilization into three stages: *The Age of Reason Begins* (1558–1648) (1961, vol. 7); *The Age of Louis XIV* (1648–1715) (1963, vol. 8); and *The Age of Voltaire* (1715–1756) (1965, vol. 9). The growth of commerce and industry between the middle of the sixteenth and seventeenth centuries brought about a change in the kind of knowledge that was needed to meet the practical realities of a burgeoning economy. The richness of Platonic theories and ideas rediscovered by the Renaissance were of little use in a culture that was becoming more functionally oriented (Durant and Durant 1961, 163). Scholarship, literature, and the arts flourished during the Renaissance, bringing new insights into the cultures of Europe and the west. However, the arts did not address the utilitarian realities of a changing world.

The time had come for civilization to enter a new era, one grounded in the belief that what can be observed and studied is reliable and real. The Durants refer to this new era as "The Great Renewal" (Durant and Durant 1961, 172), which provided individuals with the ability to "count and calculate, measure and design, with competitive accuracy and speed" (163). The ethos of this time period was the search for certainty, which led to the development of modern science and the world as we experience it today. The theories and ideas that originated in the seventeenth century have been profoundly influential in our society.

Deduction Versus Induction

Francis Bacon, who was born in 1561 and died in 1626, possessed one of the finest minds of his time. Bacon was a practical man and, as such, sought a scientific method less theoretical than the deductive method favored by Aristotle with its emphasis on the logical syllogism (Durant and Durant 1961, 174; Kuhn 1977, 41). Some readers may have forgotten the lessons of their introductory course in logic. For them, and those who never studied logic, the following example may shed light on the fundamentals of how we reason when thinking deductively.

Private citizens construct a logical syllogism when they argue that all bureaucrats are lazy, and since John Q. Servant is a bureaucrat, John Q. Servant is lazy. They have, in effect, developed a theory based upon the assumption that all bureaucrats are, indeed, lazy. From that assumption, also called a hypothesis, they have deduced that anyone who is a bureaucrat is, of necessity, lazy. Aristotle would approve of this deduction because it is in accord with the principles of logic, which teach that it is reasonable to proceed from the universal to the particular, but not the other way around. It is acceptable to argue that John Q. Servant is lazy because every bureaucrat is lazy, and laziness is a condition of, and can logically be applied to, everyone who is a bureaucrat.

On the other hand, to argue that Mary Q. Servant is a lazy bureaucrat and therefore, all bureaucrats are lazy, is illogical. This is unreasonable because laziness is a condition of being Mary Q. Servant and cannot be logically applied to anyone else. In the first argument, a particular application was deduced from a universal condition. In the second, a universal condition was established from a particular application. This does not meet the dictates of deductive, logical reasoning.

Inductive reasoning relies on the power of experience to utilize particular situations from which generalized axioms can be constructed. Bacon's seminal work is entitled *Novum Organum*. He proposed that experimentation and experience should be the method by which science can learn about nature and the world. He argued that knowledge is induced from both experience and thought, with experience being the primary element. From experience, hypotheses or assumptions can be developed (such as your brilliance) which, in turn, need to be tested through experimentation. In order to counterbalance the inevitable bias in the hypotheses that are developed, Bacon "proposed a laborious induction by accumulation of all facts pertinent to a problem, their analysis, comparison, classification, and correlation" (Durant and Durant 1961, 176).

In other words, before an idea for a theory is proposed, information should be gathered to substantiate the experience that generated the idea in the first place. Bacon taught that what is important to understanding is not abstract principles originating in the mind, but the interpretation of what is experienced. He used a candle as a metaphor for experience and argued that it provides the light whereby observations can be made. If the information gathered from the observations supports the experience, a general assumption can be made regarding the world. This assumption is a hypothesis which is subjected to further experimentation (Magill 1990a, 218). True knowledge comes from carefully constructed experiments in which there is an "ascent to axioms educed from these particulars by a certain rule, and then descend again to new particulars" (219). In effect, Bacon suggested a series of ups and downs, not unlike a roller coaster ride.

Bacon was very impressed with the role played by our senses, providing us with the experiences we have every day. However, he realized that our senses can play tricks on us and cannot be completely relied upon. Therefore, he argued for a scientific method that would organize and arrange particular experiences so they could be tested and lead to more generalized assumptions. In ancient and medieval scientific traditions, experimentation tended to be based upon what Kuhn refers to as "thought experiments." Scientists would think of possible experiments that could be carried out, knowing full well what the outcome would be. For example, the mind would deduce that a hand placed in an open flame may suffer a burn. However, because the mind can produce mistaken thoughts, the only way to be certain is to put a hand in the flame (Kuhn 1977, 43).

Seventeenth-century scientists chose to experiment on what had not been previously examined and was not known. Through this effort, they accumulated vast amounts of data which they believed were essential to the development of scientific theory (Kuhn 1977, 43). All aspects of western culture, not just science, have been influenced by the empirical ideas of Francis Bacon and the scientists of his time. We see its effects everywhere. In the practice of public administration at the microlevel, for example, much effort is placed on improving those aspects of our work that we can be sure about, because from these experiences, we can develop rules to apply to all situations. For instance, we may study the arrangement of office space and the placing of furniture to achieve optimum efficiency and economy of movement. A particular layout that is found to work in a certain situation may become the required layout for the entire organization.

This is a relatively easy thing to do, because we are dealing with material objects that can be seen, felt, and counted. The manner in which individuals in the office interact with one another and with clients is more challenging, because we are dealing with people who have individual personalities, ambitions, and unique perceptions of what is happening at any given moment. It is difficult to develop a set of standards to measure the deeply personal way in which public employees approach organizational life, both as professionals in service to outsiders and as co-workers in cooperation with colleagues. The best possible office layout will contribute little to work accomplishment if the atmosphere is permeated by negative attitudes.

So what do we do? We pretend we need do nothing, or develop general rules of behavior that ignore the personal idiosyncracies of individuals. In other words, we write prescriptions so we can measure and control people. After all, this is the logical, and therefore reasonable, way to solve problems. It certainly works well on inanimate objects that bend to our will when we apply the strong arm of science. For example, appropriately placed desks and computers will result in greater task efficiency. A manager whose work involves sensitive issues that require private handling can be more effective in a separate office than an open system plan. These are practical solutions that contribute to the successful functioning of an office. However, when we attempt to improve the performance of people by "fixing" them with scientifically formulated standards, we objectify and categorize them, as though they were so many sticks of furniture or reams of paper.

Rationality Versus Individuality

William Scott and David Hart have written a book in which they severely criticize American organizations for what they refer to as a totalitarian approach to management. They insist this is the inevitable result of what happens when the benefits that accrue from technology supersede the values of individualism in the organizational psyche (Scott and Hart 1979, 210). The scientific method of interpreting reality that is common in industrialized nations of the western hemisphere has generated a technically rational form of management practice that equates efficiency with rationality. Individual workers and the material objects they use to do their jobs are both means to an end. There is no distinction between human and material means. Both are inputs, subjected to whatever adjustments are necessary to achieve desired outputs. The only difference between the material and human inputs is that the former depends upon technological tools of measurement and the latter depends upon behavioral tools of measurement (44).

Individuals in twentieth-century America have become subsumed in its monolithic bureaucratic structures. The "organizational imperative" determines that what is best for the organization is also best for individuals. The values of the "individual imperative," upon which our country was founded, have gone by the wayside and we have stopped being "individual America" and become "organizational America" (Scott and Hart 1979, 43, 53).

These are serious accusations levied at our institutions. Scott and Hart have been criticized for promoting a negative and bleak view of the contemporary scene in our corporations and government agencies. It is not unusual to reach that conclusion after reading their book. On the other hand, much of what they argue is convincing and consistent with the earlier warnings of Carl Jung. Jung cautioned against the development of a mass movement rooted in materialism and lower levels of consciousness resulting from strict adherence to convention. Although this book is intended to present a positive rather than negative projection for the practice of public administration in the twenty-first century, I think we need to take Scott and Hart's critique seriously. We must address the issues raised in their controversial book, and remember the admonitions of Jung, who feared that mass mindedness would smother the fires of individual exploration (Jung 1978, 10: 719):

> Just as it was necessary in America to break up the great Trusts, so the destruction of huge organizations will eventually prove to be a necessity because, like a cancerous growth, they eat away man's nature as soon as they become ends in themselves and attain autonomy. From that moment they grow beyond man and escape his control. He becomes their victim and is sacrificed to the madness of an idea that knows no master. All great organizations in which the individual no longer counts are exposed to this danger. There seems to be only one way of countering this threat to our lives, and that is the "revaluation" of the individual.

Machine Metaphor and the Ideal Type

Although Bacon did not view reason as the sole measure of human potential, he never seriously questioned its limitation as a source of gaining knowledge. For that matter, neither did Descartes. Public administration, as a creation of western culture, has accepted the seventeenth century's concept of reason and has also failed to see its limitations. At the macrolevel, we place great value on amassing data, analyzing them, and coming to conclusions that result in policies affecting the lives of every American. This process is considered scientific and therefore reasonable, since it deals only with facts. Like Bacon, we believe we can correct the biases contained in our assumptions by accumulating increasingly vast amounts of data. Of course, not all the facts can ever be collected. We ignore at worst, or underestimate at best, those influences that are neither factual nor quantifiable.

One of the most enduring metaphors in public administration likens public agencies to machines that can be controlled through technical, rational means. This analogy can be traced directly to Descartes, who equates the workings of the material world to a giant machine (Descartes 1992, 1:214). It is as if everything in the world is imprisoned "amongst the cog wheels, the pulleys, the steel castings of a relentless world-machine" (Butterfield 1965, 136). The mysterious aspects of life, the hidden truths, the phenomena, for which we have no explanation, were reduced by Descartes to mechanical interventions beyond our comprehension (Williams 1990, 276). Influenced by his thinking, our concept of reason excludes everything that cannot be explained, either through the senses, or through objects that are external to ourselves.

Our cars start when we turn the key in the ignition, go in the right direction when we turn the steering wheel, and stop when we apply pressure to the break. Likewise, we expect public agencies to respond appropriately if they have budgets, job descriptions, and program guidelines. These are the gears that operate the microlevel of the twentieth-century public administration machine. Through their machinations, modern social policy is implemented. This contemporary myth is based upon a staunch belief in the ability of reason to control social and political forces through a combination of logically consistent action, enforced order, and a sense of certitude.

The myth of the machine is not the sole arbiter of reason in public administration practice today. It is aided and abetted by the theory of the "ideal type," which was devised by the German sociologist Max Weber, who was born in 1864 and died in 1920. Most of our public agencies are still structured in accordance with the conviction that rational-legal authority, as defined by Weber, is the *only* way to assure efficiency and due process. We believe that reason lies in authority and is passed along a chain of command, assuring that the rules are obeyed and fair and equitable treatment is accorded everyone. Let us turn now to the interpretation of Weber's ideal type that was made by the eminent sociologist Talcott Parsons (Weber 1964).

Parsons tells us that Weber believed actual reality cannot be captured in broad generalizations because of their unavoidable abstraction. Therefore, he distinguished two levels of meaning: that which is experienced at the "concrete" level of the individual person, and that which is conceived at the "theoretical" level of abstraction (Weber 1964, 11–12). Weber perceived the theoretical level as a pure conception, an ideal toward which individuals may aspire. This ideal is based upon a set of values that constitute the framework upon which the theoretical level is constructed. Therefore, the individual does not merely respond to stimuli, but tries to follow a set of normative guidelines, even though this will not result in total conformance. Parsons calls the ideal type "a particular kind of abstraction," which accounts for the perfection of following the preset ideal and the irrationality of deviating from it (12).

Weberian thought has had a significant influence on the practice of public administration. The following argument seems to define how we perceive the actions taken in public agencies because of our belief in the importance of the ideal type. An action is reasonable in the extent to which it conforms to preset ideals contained in directives applicable to a jurisdiction, agency, program, or other governmental entity. This clearly implies a corollary argument. An action is unreasonable in the extent to which it deviates from preset ideals contained in directives applicable to a jurisdiction, agency, program, or other governmental entity.

Parsons reminds us that the ideal type in Weber's mind "does not describe a course of action, but a normatively ideal course" (Weber 1964, 13). This may be true, but we must not overlook the preponderance of evidence pointing to the twentieth-century preoccupation with the ideal course of action. Our mind set is locked into legally rationalized processes of behavior. I will go so far as to suggest we have made a kind of religion of rational action, having become obsessed with control and convinced that the more rational we are, the more we will be in charge of everything in the world.

Since we have established that we have norms which are translated into pure types, we can now turn to the machine metaphor which allows for the expression of these ideals. They are disseminated throughout the agency by the chain of command, which is analogous to a machine. Authority rides high in the command machine, delivering mandates designed to assist individuals in their efforts to comply with the values of the ideal. Public administrators sometimes find themselves in situations where the cost of applying the ideal to a specific case is so high they face a dilemma. Imagine the conflict experienced by a social worker faced with a troubled young man whose history is such that he does not fit the guidelines allowing the worker to either help him through the agency or refer him elsewhere! One of the reasons Weber favored generalized rules was because they assured that the ideal of impartial and consistent treatment of clients would be met. However, Parsons hints that Weber recognized the ideal may, in specific situations, fall far short of what should be done (Weber 1964, 108n, 110). When this happens, the ideal has failed to meet the challenge that "reason is as reason does."

When we expect that the practice of public administration can be reduced to a series of management principles, administrative tools, and well-designed formulas, we open ourselves to constant disappointment. Parsons argues that rationalized structures can never be inclusive of the entire social structure they are designed to accommodate. He states that " 'Reason' is, as Weber several times remarks, an inherently dynamic force subject to continual change, and hence has a strong tendency not to permit the development of settled routines" (Weber 1964, 71). If we agree with Weber and Parsons that reason must bend to change and abandon our "settled routines," we must reconsider the machine metaphor. After all, if reason must bow to dynamism, then reason is not static. A new metaphor is needed.

The end of the twentieth century has provided us with a preview of the next century. The impersonal rules that characterized a simpler time often create trouble. It is impossible for procedures and scientific formulas to meet all contingencies that may come up in either the macroworld of public administration policymaking or the microworld of policy implementation. Putting all our eggs in the rational-legal basket does not provide the solutions we need to govern effectively. This is not the world of the seventeenth century, when there seemed to be a place for everything and everything appeared to be in its place.

We now live in a charged atmosphere, filled with the dreams of the previously disenfranchised and riddled with the aspirations of ambitious politicians. Individuals will no longer accept the promises of an aloof ruling class; the United States is no longer the unopposed voice of reason in the world; the public will not readily entrust its children to war; and government services cannot be meted out in a neat and orderly fashion. The metaphor of a machine no longer applies to the making or implementation of public policy, and technical considerations can no longer be the sole determinant of our actions. The simple truth is that government decisions and the bureaucracies that carry them out operate in a complex, dynamic world in which the interdependence between technical and human needs is of prime importance (Morgan 1986, 40–44).

Those who come from a different mind set concerning what public administration's reality is, may think I am proposing a mutiny as we sail the sea of transition toward a new century. To this charge, I can only reply that we need to change course because our discipline is in very serious trouble. We have marginal credibility, at best. We are constantly berated by politicians, regardless of their ideological proclivities. Our ranks in public service are being decimated by budgetary cutbacks, attesting to how nonessential we are perceived to be as we struggle to implement public policy. I do not think we need to plug up every hole in the levee of Goodsell's river bank in order to save bureaucracy (Goodsell 1994, 158–59). As a passenger on the metaphorical "vessel at sea," I am not trying to organize a mutiny, but rather introduce different ideas for consideration if we are to take Goodsell and others seriously and charter our own course of sail into the new century.

We need to go beyond the definitions of reason that have come to us from earlier times, and must stop looking at the external world for justification of what we know innately to be reasonable. We need direction and guidance from sources outside ourselves, but to a far less degree than we think. Consider how much time and energy are spent trying to figure out how to dodge the constraints placed upon us by external forces. How many times in the course of a day do we fidget in our chairs because we have violated a rule which we know is ridiculous and preventing us from reasonable action? What is the psychic toll on us when we find it necessary to flaunt convention?

I submit that our apparent commitment to rigid thinking is destructive to our integrity as professionals. The practice of public administration is increasingly subjected to stronger methods of accountability demanded by the public, the media, and legislative bodies. This is a testament to the poor perception of our profession in the minds of the very people we are sworn to serve. As we attempt to understand how we can alter the negativity that has damaged our reputation, let us look toward the potential we have within us to rise to unprecedented levels of public service.

THE RISE OF LOGICAL POSITIVISM

Humankind has always been fascinated with the question, "Is what we experience through our sight, hearing, taste, and touch, the way things truly are?" Individuals wonder whether their particular experience of the world is unique, or shared by others. Since time began, this question has prompted thought, study, and endless speculation. It is the foundation that underlies philosophy and is as relevant today as it has always been. The great scientific and intellectual discoveries of the seventeenth century were predicated upon mathematics and the use of measurement to develop theories and test them through experimentation. Eighteenth-century Europe enthusiastically embraced the secular view of the world provided by the great minds of the sixteenth and seventeenth centuries. The rationalism promoted by Descartes, the discoveries of Isaac Newton, the pantheism of Spinoza, and the empiricism of Bacon became the bedrock of enlightened men and women.

The atmosphere in the eighteenth century was one of confidence in the ability of human reason to understand and even control the forces of nature. It was a time of great hope and certainty, built upon human knowledge and potential perfectibility. Admiration and esteem were accorded individuals of the sixteenth and seventeenth centuries who expanded the boundaries of investigation in the natural sciences. Sir Isaac Newton enjoyed wide acclaim during his lifetime and throughout the following century. His famous epitaph by Alexander Pope follows (Durant and Durant 1963, 546):

> Nature and Nature's Laws lay hid in night;
> God said, Let Newton be! and all was light.

Isaac Newton was born in 1642 and died in 1727. The recognition he achieved during his lifetime is generally reserved only for the most eminent philosophers and religious figures. Newton harbored a lifelong fascination with mathematics and mystical theory. However, he was a practical man who possessed a great deal of common sense (Durant and Durant 1963, 543, 546). In 1687 Newton published the *Principia*, in which he synthesized the two burning issues of sixteenth-century physics; namely, "How can the planets be in constant motion and not drift off into endless space?" This ground-breaking work marked the end of the scientific revolution and the beginning of modern science (Butterfield 1965, 152). The world owes much to Newton, who, while thoroughly grounded in the theoretical rationality of the classical scientific tradition, was able to appreciate the merits that can accrue through experimentation (Kuhn 1977, 50). His influence forged a connection between traditional science and the new order.

The contributions of the sixteenth and seventeenth centuries are profoundly immersed in the science of mathematics. It was as if all thought in the civilized world was motivated by the certainty that quantitative measurements could provide. The search for knowledge of the natural world was also a search for order, simplicity, and reliability; those qualities usually associated with mathematics. Great upheaval occurred when religious traditions were challenged and threatened by secular ideas and theories regarding the origin of the universe and the purpose of human beings. Through the use of geometrical reasoning, the philosopher Spinoza attempted to develop a scientific base for ethics. His pantheism was founded on the conviction that purpose and order in the universe is a response to fixed and immutable laws, designed by a perfect deity whose divinity is present in every facet of nature. Spinoza's commitment to the mechanical orientation of seventeenth-century philosophy is evidenced by his own words, "I shall consider human actions and desires in exactly the same manner, as though I were concerned with lines, planes, and solids" (Baumer 1978, 322).

The mechanical philosophy of the seventeenth century was founded upon an obsession with the workings of the external world. The customs and traditions of the ancient philosophies were cast aside, with the world of spirit yielding to the material world. The experimental method of Bacon and the mathematical approach of Descartes offered scientific discoveries that promised a better world. Intellectuals of the time were persuaded that hope for the future did not depend upon the individual spirit bringing about "change from within," but rather upon the physical world bringing about "change from without" (Baumer 1978, 250). This mind set continued into the eighteenth century and marked the completion of civilization's evolution, from ancient ideas concerning the origin of the universe and the laws governing its continued existence, to modern, scientific methods.

Toward Enlightenment

The philosophers of the eighteenth century were basically humanitarians committed to social action. Western culture was changed forever by their ideas; their influence on disciplines in the human and social sciences has survived to the present day. In previous centuries, religion was profoundly influential in shaping political and economic thought. This changed during the eighteenth century, when reason replaced religion as the source of knowledge about the world. There was an insatiable thirst to understand the workings of nature, and an unwavering desire for human and social progress. To the eighteenth-century mind, reason demanded that the world be proven. Critical evaluation, based upon evidence rather than authority or tradition, was the only acceptable method of attaining knowledge. The days of placing theoretical reason over practical experience were gone. Knowledge based solely on theory was considered too trusting of the world as it appears. A new, more critical concept of reason was deemed necessary if the truth was to be attained. The thinkers of that time asked why the laws of society could not be discovered in the same manner as the laws of nature (Baumer 1978, 367).

Eighteenth-century philosophers believed that reasoning from particulars and breaking problems down into their elemental parts would allow for making broad generalizations about reality. They were committed to inductive rather than deductive reasoning, and relied upon empirical investigation. Their empiricism, however, was not as pure as they thought. With few exceptions, they made broad generalizations about the universe which could not be substantiated through empirical research. For example, they perceived the material world as one governed by a universal law which imposes order. They also assumed that human beings can rationally comprehend the laws which support the ordered universe (Baumer 1978, 366–67). Both theoretical rationality and empirical reasoning dined at the table of truth in the eighteenth century, but empiricism sat at the head of the table.

The ideas of one era are not as neat and cleanly cut in reality as they are on the pages of history books. This is evidenced in the eighteenth century's tug-of-war between the personal and social demands of humanism and the rationalistic claims of the mechanical model of previous periods (Baumer 1978, 367). The combination of secularism and individualism (371) that characterized the Enlightenment, has become incorporated into our national psyche. Our faith in reason, science, and our capacity to understand and control the future through technology can be seen as the secular religion of the twentieth century. Its fundamental commandment requires that we become unmindful of the inner voice when it seriously questions the tenets of western culture. It is a demanding faith, because it seeks to separate us from what we intuitively know. Silence is its enemy, because it fosters a turning inward which threatens our hero worship of the external world.

Eighteenth-century individualism shattered the sovereignty of the state. Its impact is evident today in our tolerance of a messy democratic process that protects individual liberty at the cost of collective order. The Enlightenment also broke down the barriers which separated human beings into social classes. Our sense that people are the same everywhere, and cultural differences are not fundamental to human nature is a direct result of eighteenth-century humanism (Baumer 1978, 371).

Although we argue over diversity and how far we should go to preserve the integrity of individual cultures, we do not speak in terms of ranking one culture over another. If we did, we would not have the current debate over political correctness. The eighteenth century opened the mind of humankind to those values which define our society as it exists today on the cusp of a new century. The values of equality, reason, social action, and individual liberty have persevered throughout the centuries and are leading us into the millennium.

The Great Dissenter

"The cleverest reasoner in the Age of Reason" (Durant and Durant 1965, 145) was David Hume, who was born in 1711 and died in 1776. He was an important proponent of the empirical method of attaining knowledge about ethical and social issues. Hume was critical of theoretical rationality because, although it provides hypotheses, it is incapable of making causal connections. This can be done only by careful observation of what is being experienced at a given point in time. Only then, Hume argued, can scientific laws be constructed according to cause and effect. Logical explanations derived from experience form the basis of future expectations (Hume 1948, 15; Magill 1990b, 292–95). Hume's ideas on how the process of reasoning has impacted human psychology are apropos to the theme of this book. Reason and the psychological structure of individuals are not distinct from one another. Psychology and the human psyche play a significant part in the reasoning process.

Hume recognized that science could not account for "the 'real' cause of events, but for the best available probable predictions about the course of nature, founded on correlations of constant conjunctions of events and the psychological habits of human beings" (Magill 1990b, 295). Hume was ahead of his time in addressing certain aspects of human nature, such as the psychological makeup of individuals. In his earliest philosophical work, entitled *A Treatise of Human Nature*, he explains his skepticism that human beings can come to conclusions that are wholly accurate. To Hume, conclusions are not influenced by rational thought alone. The senses and psychological structure of the persons making the decision are also involved. Because we are prone to mistakes, Hume believed the inferences we make from what we call reason are, at best, only probable explanations of reality (Durant and Durant 1965, 144; Magill 1990b, 295–96).[1]

To make sense of what Hume was saying, let us again review introductory logic. The term "to beg the question" is used in argumentation when an individual assumes that what he or she is attempting to prove is true. For example, philosophers before Hume assumed that every event has a cause. This is an assumption that has always been believed, and yet Hume argued it is neither intuitively known, nor can it be proven to be true. Then where does this belief come from? Hume said it comes from our impressions and ideas which are acted upon by imagination and memory. For instance, when I hear a sound that reminds me of a doorbell, I believe someone is at the door. I have not experienced the ringing of the bell as the cause, yet I am convinced that it is. In fact, I would insist it is the only reasonable conclusion to draw. Hume would strongly disagree, arguing that I am not being logical because there is "no reason for us to think of one idea rather than another when a particular experience takes place" (Magill 1990b, 294).

What is it, then, that leads us to link events according to a causal pattern? Hume said that when events occur over and over and are connected to one another, we assume they are "conjoined" and our mind makes the connection between them. As a result, when one of the events happens, we automatically link it to the other event. We ascribe the cause to one event, and the effect to the other. Hume believed this can only be a rational conclusion if what happens is always uniform and never deviates. In other words, what we will experience in the future must be the same as a prior experience. But are the events that occur uniform, certain, and reliable (Magill 1990b, 294)? Of course not, which is why Hume said reason does not conform to the understanding of rationality that prevailed in the eighteenth century.

Just because every time I heard this particular sound in the past it was the doorbell, does not prove that is what I am hearing now. Just because every time I heard this particular sound in the past Aunt Jane was standing on the porch pressing the bell, does not mean she is there at this moment doing the same thing. I am begging the question if I assume the cause of the sound comes from the doorbell that Aunt Jane is pressing. All I can be sure of is that up to this point in time, this sound has always meant that Aunt Jane is standing on the porch pressing the doorbell. Hume would agree with this assessment. He might also add that my knowledge of what the sound is and who is causing it can only be reliable if every time I heard this sound in the past and every time I hear it in the future, Aunt Jane is pressing the doorbell.

Hume attributes our tendency to connect repeated events to one another through cause and effect to the habitual occurrence of the event rather than any rational process of reasoning. It is through our psychological processes that we assume there is uniformity in the world and that we can, because of this certainty, predict cause and effect. Our attitude toward what we experience repeatedly is such that we are convinced of its reliability and uniformity, neither of which is able to be proven. In other words, the connection is in ourselves, *not* in the events themselves. We believe what has habitually happened in the past will repeat itself in the future, even if we do not observe what is taking place. One of Hume's most famous pieces of writing emphatically argues the point just made (Durant and Durant 1965, 148).[2]

> The maxim by which we commonly conduct ourselves in our reasonings is that the objects of which we have no experience resemble those of which we have; that what we have found to be most usual is always most probable; and that where there is no opposition of arguments, we ought to give the preferences to such as are founded on the greatest number of past observations.

Hume, therefore, proposed that science engage in a method of observing and collecting information about events so some sort of "reasonable belief" about the future could be derived, based upon what transpired in the past (Magill 1990b, 295). Hume has been criticized for attempting to do two things at once: empirically analyze both the laws of psychology and the concept of "cause" (297). However, this criticism can be countered by the argument that he simply tried to show that the process by which reality is perceived is more complicated than our definition of reason allows.

Our emotions, as well as our thoughts, enable us to experience reality and interact with it so that our best interests are served. Henry Aiken, in the introduction to his edited version of Hume's philosophy, provides insight into the man's thinking. Hume believed that just as there are laws governing natural phenomena, there are also laws governing the natural processes of the human mind (Aiken 1948, 15–18). The impact of human psychology on reason was largely ignored prior to Hume. He did not disagree with his predecessors and contemporaries that reason can lead to knowledge. He simply added another dimension to the definition of reason—psychology and its emotional impact on how we perceive the world.

True to the thinking of his time, Hume recognized that knowledge without appropriate action is wasted. He argued that once knowledge is attained, a motivating power must be present if action is to occur. For knowledge to have significance, we must take action and will do so only if we have "in-terest" in a particular "end." Hume taught it is our instincts, not reason, that provide the interest we need to move knowledge into action (Aiken 1948, 23–24). His influence in this regard is evident in the words of Im-manuel Kant, "reason without passion is powerless; passion without reason is blind" (25). Hume was saying, in effect, that we need both reason and emotion if we are to take responsible action in the world. His acceptance of human emotion and the role played by instinct in the affairs of the world is an important contribution to eighteenth-century thought.

Hume was not alone in his skepticism of the power of pure reason to change the world. Like Kant, he was simply an unusually ardent critic. Other Enlightenment thinkers, such as Voltaire, Diderot, and Rousseau, recog-nized the tendency of most people to be overcome by passion at the ex-pense of reason. However, they firmly believed in the promise of reason to lead humankind away from the dogmatism of previous centuries toward a more humanistic world (Durant and Durant 1965, 607). Together with Hume, they proceeded to escort knowledge down from the ivory tower of ancient scholasticism and place it on the firm footing of modern pragmatism.

Toward a Connection

Vasilis Politis, in the introduction to his edition of the *Critique of Pure Reason*, provides a sketch of Kant's life. Kant was born in 1724 and died in 1804. Throughout his life he was engaged in the conflict between devotion to reason and devotion to experience. Although Kant lived the life of a scholar and philosopher, he read travel journals and was interested in ge-ography and anthropology. In his philosophical writings, he steered a middle course between empiricism and rationalism. He tried to reconcile the abil-ities of empiricism, which relies on sense experience; and rationalism, which relies on reason, to answer the question, "What is true in the world?" (Politis 1993, 27).

Like Hume, Kant believed that we cannot establish cause/effect relation-ships through sense experience. However, unlike Hume, he thought that even though causality cannot be proven through sense experience, the as-sumption that effects have causes is not an arbitrary one. After all, the world is not a chaotic mumble jumble. Our experience can testify to a degree of orderliness in the world. By attributing causes to effects, human beings are able to organize the various experiences they have (Magill 1990c, 329).

Kant placed great emphasis on how to validate our ideas of the world objectively. He taught there is an empirical way and a transcendental way to do this. Objective validity can be established by defining the idea in accordance with what we experience. This is what we do when we refer to material objects. Kant's empirical way of attaining objective validity is the same as that of Hume (Politis 1993, 41). For example, the concept of a doorbell ringing is empirically defined by our having heard it before. When we refer to objects, we can rely upon actual sense impressions, such as the sound of the bell ringing in the ear. When I hear the bell, I open the door and see Aunt Jane standing there, pressing the bell. I have now discovered empirical evidence that in this instance, the cause of the ringing in my ear was the noise made when Aunt Jane pressed the doorbell. This empirical experience, however, cannot account for all instances in which I may hear the same sound. It refers only to this particular experience.

To provide a general rule that explains what causes an effect, Kant turned toward an idea which he called "a priori"—a transcendental concept. He argued that an a priori cause will produce an effect that can be universally expected. This approach is independent of experience, but can be applied to it. It relies upon reason rather than the senses, and is the rationalist way of explaining the world. Kant argued that objective validity must transcend what *usually* happens in order to establish what will *always* happen. This can only be predicated upon a necessary condition (1993, 41). Kant provides an example of what he means by an a priori understanding of the concept of cause (Kant in Politis 1993, A91/B124, 95):

> For this concept demands that something, A, should be of such a nature, that something else, B, should follow from it necessarily, and according to an absolutely universal law. We may certainly collect from appearances a law, according to which this or that usually happens, but the element of necessity is not to be found in it.

For consistency's sake, let us apply Kant's a priori argument to the doorbell example, even though it makes little practical sense. The concept for the cause of the ringing in my ear demands that the doorbell (A) is of such a nature that it necessarily rings when it is being pressed by Aunt Jane (B). In other words, the ringing in my ear is conditional upon the existence of the doorbell and its being pressed by Aunt Jane. Therefore, every time I hear the ringing in my ear, I know a priori that Aunt Jane is standing on the porch, pressing the bell.

From the above argument, Kant would deduce that a ringing in my ear is always the result of Aunt Jane pressing the doorbell. A universal law can be established from this deduction. To repeat, only Aunt Jane can cause the doorbell to ring in my ear. Let's assume there is no a priori concept. Now we are back into empirical observation, which can provide evidence solely about that specific point in time when Aunt Jane is ringing the bell. After a number of repetitions of this experience, I may decide to establish a law which infers that whenever I hear the ringing sound in my ear, Aunt Jane is there and she is pressing the bell. Kant would criticize my law and argue that it is not universal. He would say it provides only limited evidence of what causes the ringing in my ear (Kant in Politis 1993, A91/B124, 95).

Through the use of deduction and induction, Kant believed he had accounted for both empirical and rationalist approaches. His critical philosophy contributed to eighteenth-century ideas because of its argument that reason transcends narrow parameters.

According to Kant, reason exists within a broad framework which encompasses theoretical reason (a priori), practical reason (empirical), reason resulting from self-reflection, and the critique of reason itself. Pure reason speculates about the events that practical reason hopes to prove. Motives and feelings belong to practical reason (Kant in Politis 1993, B129, 98), which relies upon empirical evidence to either prove or disprove the theories promulgated by pure reason. Kant was not willing to disregard those concepts that could not be measured, but which are innately present in the world. By accepting the nonmeasurable a priori concepts of ancient traditions and respecting and encouraging modern empirical research, he forged a linkage between them.

One can see a connection between Hume's recognition of the influence of psychology on scientific research and Kant's attribution of motivation and feeling to practical reason. Neither of these thinkers believed that pure reason, or pure empiricism, should be the sole arbiter of truth. Although their approaches and language differed, neither seemed as eager to break ties with the transcendental values of the ancients as their contemporaries did.

The Triumph of Logical Positivism

The more balanced views of Hume and Kant concerning the nature of reason were shattered with the rise of positivist philosophy and the modernist movement that occurred at the end of the nineteenth and beginning of the twentieth centuries. Great importance was given to immanent and pragmatic matters. The transcendental values of the ancient tradition seemed to be irretrievably lost. The power of philosophy to speculate about the world and devise abstract theories was downgraded to the status of a tool for clarifying concepts used by the empiricists. Metaphysical abstractions were considered foolish and inappropriate to an age in which science and technology held such promise. Western culture looked toward the pragmatic disciplines for answers to all questions. The twentieth century was, and has continued to be, immersed in the doctrines of scientific empiricism with little, if any, respect for those aspects of living that cannot be seen, smelled, or touched.

Thomas Luckmann sums up the effect of logical positivism on the social sciences in his book, *Phenomonology and Sociology*. He argues that twentieth-century social science has scarcely questioned the belief that we can ultimately gain knowledge about this deceptive universe. We are convinced that prescientific cultures, lacking the quantitative tools at the disposal of modern knowledge, hid behind the world of appearances. Individuals living in ancient times are believed to have been incapable of objectivity. "Despite Hume and others, they (we) cling to an apparently ineradicable push and pull notion of causality to explain how it all hangs together" (Luckmann 1978, 230). Seventeenth-century philosophy and science, transformed by the "cosmology" of the eighteenth century, became the paradigm of the physical sciences in the nineteenth century. Twentieth-century social science has been so impressed with the tools and techniques (not to mention the promises) of the paradigm, that we have made it our own.

Luckmann suggests that our stubborn adherence to a questionable paradigm has exacted a heavy price which can result in an undermining of the paradigm itself. For example, he argues that individuals have been reduced to nothing more or less than bundles of instincts, drives, and "subsystems" of a larger, action-oriented system. He refers to them, and by implication to us, as "the man machine," created by reductionists in an attempt to justify their untenable position. Sensitive individuals, disturbed by the reductionist creation, feel guilty because they cannot accept the prevailing ideology. Eventually, they become completely turned off by the "language of cybernetics, systems analysis, simulation, or even old-fashioned structural-functionalism." Luckmann refers to these people as "converts" to the "soft-belly" side of the dilemma (Luckmann 1978, 231).

This book is not intended to convert anyone to the "soft-belly" side of anything. Neither does it subscribe to the reductionist perspective. Luckmann, like Scott and Hart in their book, *Organizational America*, may offend some readers who perceive him as presenting a negative view of contemporary social science. To these readers, I ask your indulgence. I cannot speak for the authors I quote in this book, but I can tell you why I refer to their ideas. They have addressed the problems our institutions face from the perspective of the individual. This is consistent with one of the challenges this book identifies—the need for public administration to develop a philosophy of administration for individual persons.

Carl Jung warned that civilization, while providing us with a marvelous material world, was robbing us of our very essence as unique creatures. As we exit the twentieth century, we need to evaluate what we have become as individuals living in western society. Neither the writers mentioned in this book, nor you or I, single-handedly created the overall situation we are in. But we are in it, and we do participate. Only if we address the problems that effect us as individuals can we hope to solve them. After all, we are not victims, but creators of our own experience.

Modernism, grounded in the logic of positivist belief, fostered the subordination of nature to human will and the domination of practice over theory. In the process, emotion and intuitive feeling were undervalued. The human touch brings a sense of community and celebration that provides meaning to daily life. We must turn toward our own humanity if we are serious about meeting the challenges posed in chapter one; namely, the development of an administrative philosophy, restructuring of our organizations, and rethinking the implications of new technology on public administration. As we approach a new century, let us reclaim our heritage as caring, feeling, creative persons who pay attention to what our inner voice tells us.

The myth of the machine became the twentieth-century metaphor for human achievement. We ascribe greater power to the machine than to individual human endeavor. Machines cannot provide human qualities, such as courtesy and pride in accomplishment. Lacking inner direction, they respond only to the demands of the outer world. We need to remind ourselves that there is a distinction between the machines we have created and ourselves.

We cannot address the questions raised in chapter one—"What does it mean to be public servants?" and "How do we learn?"—by digging our heels in the ground of positivist certainty. Enlightenment thinking influences us to look outward. That is not what we need to do at this time in the history of our field. *We must open ourselves up to ourselves.* It is only through an interior search that we can sow the seeds of an administrative philosophy which guides our actions as we make decisions affecting organizational structure and technological development. While this book promotes a greater respect for transcendental values, it does not suggest a return to superstition or the dogmatism of previous centuries. Rather, it asks that we cast aside positivist tenets and adopt the broad perspective called for by Waldo. This requires looking toward other cultures for understanding the world that each of us harbors within ourselves. Our own culture is sadly deficient in this area of human development.

Let us not fail to cultivate an interior life. The fear of insignificance is the constant companion of those who ignore the inner voice. They have failed to connect the part of themselves that is under their conscious control with their more subtle, intuitive side. Let us follow the insight of Joseph Campbell and Carl Jung, and appreciate the importance that myths and symbols can have as we journey toward self-discovery and deeper meaning.

NOTES

1. Interpretations of book one of *A Treatise of Human Nature* are those of Frank Magill, as stated in the citations and references. For the reader who is interested in alternative interpretations, the following references may be helpful: Roland Hall, *Fifty Years of Hume Scholarship* (Edinburgh: Edinburgh University Press, 1978); Charles W. Hendel, *Studies in the Philosophy of David Hume* (Indianapolis: Bobbs-Merrill, 1963); and Terence Penelhum, *Hume* (New York: St. Martin's Press, 1975). The reader who wishes to pursue greater understanding of Hume's use of psychology to explain cause and effect should consult Barry Stroud, *Hume* (London: Routledge and Kegan Paul, 1977).

2. The original quote is from the essay "Of Miracles" found in the first *Enquiry*, section 10. This essay was refused publication in the *Treatise*.

REFERENCES

Aiken, Henry D., ed. 1948. *Hume's Moral and Political Philosophy*. New York: Hafner Press.

Baumer, Franklin LeVan., ed. 1978. *Main Currents of Western Thought*. New Haven: Yale University Press.

Butterfield, Herbert. 1965. *The Origins of Modern Science*. rev. ed. G. Bell and Sons Ltd., 1957. New York: The Free Press.

Campbell, Joseph. 1988. *The Power of Myth*. Edited by Betty Sue Flowers. New York: Doubleday.

Descartes, René. 1992. "The Principles of Philosophy." In *A Discourse on Method*. Translated by John Veitch. 1912. Reprint, Rutland, Vermont: Charles E. Tuttle Co., Inc., Everyman's Library.

Durant, Will, and Ariel Durant. 1961. *The Age of Reason Begins*. Vol. 7 of *The Story of Civilization*. Reprint, New York: Simon and Schuster.

————. 1963. *The Age of Louis XIV*. Vol. 8 of *The Story of Civilization*. Reprint, New York: Simon and Schuster.

————. 1965. *The Age of Voltaire*. Vol. 9 of *The Story of Civilization*. Reprint, New York: Simon and Schuster.

Goodsell, Charles T. 1994. *The Case for Bureaucracy*. 3d. ed. New Jersey: Chatham House Publishers, Inc.

Gulick, Luther, and Lyndall Urwick. 1937. *Papers on the Science of Administration*. New York: Institute of Public Administration.

Hume, David. 1948. *Moral and Political Philosophy*. Edited by Henry D. Aiken. New York: Hafner Press.

Jung, Carl G. 1978. "Flying Saucers: A Modern Myth." In *Civilization in Transition*. Vol. 10 of *Collected Works*. 2d 1970. Reprint, Princeton: Princeton University Press.

Kant, Immanuel. 1993. "Analytic of Concepts: The Deduction of the Pure Concepts of the Understanding." In *The Critique of Pure Reason*. Edited and translated by Vasilis Politis. Reprint, Rutland, Vermont: Charles E. Tuttle.

Kuhn, Thomas S. 1977. *The Essential Tension*. Chicago: The University of Chicago Press.

Luckmann, Thomas, ed. 1978. *Phenomonology and Sociology*. New York: Penguin Books.

Magill, Frank N., ed. 1990a. "Francis Bacon: Novum Organum." In *Masterpieces of World Philosophy*. New York: HarperCollins Publishers.

————. 1990b. "David Hume: A Treatise of Human Nature." Bk. 1. In *Masterpieces of World Philosophy*. New York: HarperCollins Publishers.

————. 1990c. "Immanuel Kant: Critique of Pure Reason." In *Masterpieces of World Philosophy*. New York: HarperCollins Publishers.

Morgan, Gareth. 1986. *Images of Organization*. Newbury Park: Sage Publications.

Osborne, David, and Ted Gaebler. 1992. *Reinventing Government*. New York: Addison-Wesley.

Politis, Vasilis, ed. and trans. 1993. *Critique of Pure Reason*. 1934, 1991. Reprint, Rutland, Vermont: Charles E. Tuttle.

Scott, William G., and David K. Hart. 1979. *Organizational America*. Boston: Houghton Mifflin.

Weber, Max. 1964. *The Theory of Social and Economic Organization*. Edited and Translated by A. M. Henderson and Talcott Parsons. 1947. Reprint, New York: The Free Press.

Williams, Bernard. 1990. *Descartes, the Project of Pure Inquiry*. 1978. Reprint, New York: Penguin Books.

CHAPTER 3

Insights into New Theories for the Twenty-First Century

THE POSTMODERN SEARCH

Our search for new ways of thinking about contemporary public administration can be stimulated, if not wholly found, by the rarefied realm of intellectual dialogue known as "postmodernism." Chuck Fox and Hugh Miller's book, entitled *Postmodern Public Administration* (1995), stimulated my own mind in this direction. Charles Goodsell's introduction to this book tells the reader that Fox and Miller are in the vanguard of postmodernism in their disdain for absolutist thinking. This means, he says, that there is no certain resolution of what is considered right and wrong. Although human beings need to have a sense of purpose, Goodsell attributes this feeling solely to the individual person (Fox and Miller 1995, xi):

> The canonical universality of that feeling is less important than how it is internally compelling as we go about the daily tasks of living or administering. Whether our belief systems as private individuals or public administrators are "true" is less important than that they are *ours*.

My insight came as I finished reading the above lines. Perhaps the most profound difference between the postmodern condition and modernism lies in exactly the point I believe Goodsell is making. In other words, the institutionalization of beliefs and values that characterized the Enlightenment and persisted throughout the nineteenth and twentieth centuries depended upon the acceptance of perceived universal truths. The result has been a world experienced as reliable, unified, unchangeable, and certain. However, as the twentieth century progressed, the absolute values of modernism lost their hold on the social psyche and the fabric of the whole cloth began to unravel. What was believed to be "true" was not based upon the inner voice of individual persons, but on the external values of the outer world.

The prevailing belief systems were indeed "ours," but in the collective, not the personal sense. In other words, we were expected to look *outside* ourselves for validation of our values, the norms by which we lived, and the ethical and moral choices we made. Decisions in personal and professional life were expected to reflect conventional mores. Carl Jung saw this happening and warned of the dire consequences that can befall a society in which the gauge that measures individual responsibility is set at the level of the average common denominator. He argued that individuals operate from a higher level of consciousness when they are either alone or few in number.

It is a less difficult struggle for people to transform themselves and attain a higher level of consciousness when alone than when they are part of a group. When alone, silence prevails and there is a greater opportunity to look within. When in a group, individuals identify with one another and share common emotions. Jung argued that there is an inevitable psychological regression within the group (Jung 1980, 9:227). He attributed this to an identification with the unconscious, and called the phenomenon the *participation mystique* (226).

Jung taught that it is easier to look outside ourselves and go along with the crowd than it is to stop and embrace the silence that will allow us to look within and discover our personal values, and in Goodsell's words, our "purposeful beliefs." Jung also reminded us that the individual psyche is in direct conflict with statistical rules designed to regulate and control as much of the world as possible. He argued that the tendency to evaluate everything statistically has a "leveling influence" on human individuality. Both science and religion discourage the "will to individuality," regarding it as "egotistic obstinacy." Science calls our attempts at self-definition "subjectivism," which is devalued in favor of a more objective rendering of reality. When personal values are in conflict with religious tenets, we are guilty of "heresy and spiritual pride" (Jung 1978, 10:529). When our inner voice is in accord with either scientific or religious doctrine, we are in tune with the collective belief system and considered to be members in good standing.

The attempt to exercise power over those who violate established beliefs has persisted throughout the ages and is not confined to scientific and religious institutions. It is endemic to modern bureaucracy, as many of us know through experience and from reading the literature on contemporary organizational practice. Bureaucratic red tape, often designed to hold individual expression in check, exemplifies Jung's criticism of statistical rules. The use of ostracism to shame renegade heretics is an effective means of exerting institutional control. It takes a very strong personality to buck the tide of negative opinion and continue to listen to the inner voice. Many apostates succumb to pressure and abandon the personal search for meaning, accepting the message of the external world in its stead. Jungian analytical psychology is highly critical of western civilization's concerted effort to hamper human development at the psychical level by leading individuals away from the inner reality each possesses: "Too much attention to externals blocks the way to immediate inner experience. Were not the autonomy of the individual the secret longing of many people it would scarcely be able to survive the collective suppression either morally or spiritually" (Jung 1978, 10:529).

If the belief systems we live by are to be *ours* and not universal dictates, we must discover who we are as individuals. Individual personhood cannot be found in the group or the collectivity. The essence of each of us is hidden within the psyche and begs to be unearthed. In our attempt to respond to the demands of the external world, we adopt arbitrary life patterns. These, in turn, become a major obstacle to the "ideal of a radically unencumbered and improvisational self" (Bellah et al. 1986, 81). The search for self is a deeply personal decision that transcends time and bridges the centuries. Ralph Hummel (1994) states that the most important issue facing late modernism is philosophical rather than psychological. He suggests that we are face-to-face with the everlasting question of what life is all about. Hummel says we must deal with "what it means to be alive today in an organized world that incorporates us into itself" (Hummel 1994, 133).

I believe more of us seem to be asking the perennial question, Why we are here? Indeed, this is a philosophically loaded issue that requires individual resolution. However, I question the distinction Hummel makes between philosophy and psychology in this context. The answer to what life is all about, while grounded in philosophy, is also deeply rooted in the soil of the unconscious. The world has incorporated us into itself because we are externally oriented and have shut ourselves off from the inner voice. As a result, we have lost our way as psychological persons and become externalized beings.

There is no definitive answer to the perennial question of what life is all about! Jung told us we should look within and discover the "wise old man (woman) who dwells in the heart" (Jung 1974, 6:370). Thomas Merton (1969) reminds us that Chuang Tzu, the great Taoist philosopher of the third and fourth centuries B.C., believed that we should "cultivate the interior life." Through this effort, he taught that we could come in contact with the "hidden 'Mother' of all life and truth" (Merton 1969, 26). Whatever the truth of life may be, it resides within, not outside ourselves.

Communitarianism

Fox and Miller (1995) begin their book with an explanation of the ortho-doxy that defined public administration in the early and mid-twentieth cen-tury. They include the belief that the practice of public administration can be separated from politics, that principles of science can be applied to man-agement, and that it is possible to control behavior through hierarchical structures (Fox and Miller 1995, 3). Later, in their presentation of alterna-tives to orthodoxy, they present the perspective of those who believe in active participation by individuals both within and outside government.[1] This approach is called communitarianism; the belief that the self is fixed in whatever cultural and historical context the individual finds himself or herself (33–35).

According to communitarianism, individuals can attain selfhood, through participating in their communities and engaging in a "give-and-take" dia-logue. This is a pragmatic way of looking at how people can work together and, through genuine human commitment, affect the world. This kind of cooperative endeavor tends to alleviate the burden of judgment and decision by moving it from the shoulders of the individual to the broader collective (Fox and Miller 1995, 34).

Some have criticized communitarianism as too idealistic and note that many citizens refuse to become involved in problems related to government, a situation the communitarians do not adequately address. Others complain that communities of individuals are not quite as altruistic as the communi-tarians would have us believe. In effect, the critics are saying that commu-nitarianism can only be effective in the "best of all possible worlds," which ours is assuredly not.

I have often wondered why idealism is considered so distasteful. Those who are idealistic are hanging out on a limb, trying not to saw themselves loose from the trunk of mainstream thinking. However, if the tree is to survive, the dead growth must be removed. Therefore, from time to time, these visionaries carefully apply their saw to a branch and hope it is not the limb upon which they stand. Idealists often perceive the present state of society as riddled with suspicion and dangerously negative. They long for a turnaround perspective to assert itself. If it is idealistic to believe things can be better than they are, let us embrace idealism.

Perhaps the communitarian idealists are onto something. Analyzing and interpreting the world we experience, accepting our intuitive sense of where we are and what we must do, and being aware of our feelings as they pertain to other human beings with whom we share responsibility for the state of the world, makes us *whole* people. The sense of connectedness that com-munitarianism promotes is a refreshing alternative to the alienation we ex-perience as a divided people.

The "practical wisdom" that Fox and Miller attribute to communitarianism (1995, 35) has the potential to respond to the needs of the external world that require people to cooperate with one another. The degree to which it can hope to fulfill its promise depends, in large part, upon the degree to which individuals have journeyed within themselves and discovered a profound inner wisdom which sustains the practical world. Considerable judgment and self-discipline are required before individuals can join others in a genuine spirit of community. It is the maturity that comes from self-knowledge, not the altruism that comes from self-effacement, that makes communitarianism practical. Since few attain self-knowledge, communitarianism is open to the charge of elitism. Critics might argue it is too hard for many people to attain the inner resources needed to fully participate in an authentically open community.

This need not be true. The great sages of ancient and modern times have all agreed that the business of life is to delve within and discover the truth upon which reality is based. From eastern metaphysical ideas to the teaching of western thinkers like Carl Jung and Aldous Huxley (1970), we learn that each individual has the capacity and even the responsibility to grow and develop in accordance with inner strivings. Thomas Moore calls this taking care of the soul (1992, 304–5):

> We know we are well on the way toward soul when we feel attachment to the world and the people around us and when we live as much from the heart as from the head. We know soul is being cared for . . . when compassion takes the place of distrust and fear. Soul is interested in the differences among cultures and individuals and within ourselves it wants to be expressed in uniqueness if not in outright eccentricity.

The Myth of Meaning

Let us return to the philosophical question raised by Hummel regarding how individual persons find meaning in life. To answer this question we need to address what is meant by human selfhood. David Kolb, in his book *The Critique of Pure Modernity* (1986), contrasts the traditional and the modern views of selfhood. The traditional view was that individuals follow a pattern based upon an external, natural force to attain a sense of who they are and how they fit into the world. Kolb attributes the modern view to the influence of Weber, who believed that meaning is created by individuals themselves. Weber taught that our beliefs and actions are based upon a shared sense of meaning which has resulted from "the elimination of logical inconsistencies" (Kolb 1986, 10).

This is Weberian rationalization in action. This modernist perspective is predicated upon a kind of reductionism in which the individual is viewed solely as a particular entity who is secondary to the shared meanings of his or her society. In other words, the beliefs that define the self and the actions that emanate from those beliefs are standardized. We see this every day in our social institutions when we allow them to define us through our acceptance of "the systematization of meaning and value into an overall consistent ethical view, and the methodical living of daily life according to rules" (Kolb 1986, 11). It is little wonder that we are beginning to question the veracity of belief systems that seem to be independent of us. Perhaps if we took ownership of ourselves more seriously, we would take the time to hear the inner voice and become, if not better men and women in the orthodox, bureaucratic sense, better men and women in the unconventional, personal sense. Authentic selfhood will improve our ability to meet the challenges facing public administration in the twenty-first century.

Weber found the source of meaning in the will of the individual who, in concert with all other individuals, follows its direction. Kant found meaning in the *categorical imperative*, "act only according to that maxim by which you can at the same time will that it should become a universal law" (McCarthy 1991, 35). This formal process of "unification, consistency, and universality" (Kolb 1986, 17) was the foundation of selfhood according to Kant. The Kantian principle provides meaning and serves as a guide to action for all individuals.

Neither Weber's nor Kant's explanation of how individuals find meaning in selfhood has been a satisfactory paradigm for the twentieth century. Both are more concerned with outer than inner reality. In Weberian terms, selfhood and the concomitant meaning it imposes on the individual is a function of logic, not inner probing. In the Kantian sense, the human self has meaning only in the context of something universal that is external to the individual.

Personal reflection is a kind of philosophizing. It allows us to deliberate on the shared meanings Weber identified as the source of modern socialization, and also to contribute to what Kant perceives as externalized universal meaning. Through the reflective process, we consciously and unconsciously evaluate these meanings and either incorporate them into our lives, or replace them with our own substitute values. When we personalize our beliefs, we change ourselves, our relations with others, and the actions we take. In other words, an individualized philosophy becomes the prime motivating force in our personal and professional lives. If this happens, we will be equipped to address the second challenge facing public administration—the renewal of its organizations. Then we will be able to intelligently decide how to structure public agencies to meet the changing needs of the new century. We can review our technology and predict future trends, thereby meeting the third challenge of our field. Only then we will be able to integrate our individually developed philosophy with organizational and technological realities, and address all three challenges.

DISMANTLING THE MACHINE

The psychoanalyst Franz Alexander argued that the sorry state of the world in the twentieth century is attributable to the "discrepancy between the development of the natural sciences and that of psychology and the social sciences" (Alexander 1978, 658). We have achieved a certain mastery over nature, but do not possess the self-knowledge and understanding of human relationships to act responsibly. He states that human nature is primarily dominated by irrational, emotional forces. For this reason, the world we long for is as much a utopian dream now as it was in the time of Plato. Having allowed ourselves to become "mechanically minded," we have also become corrupted by our own "technical accomplishments." Alexander suggests that the twentieth century is paying the price of following the maxim: "Primum vivere deinde philosophare," which translated into English means, "First live, then philosophize" (657).

Alexander became director of the Chicago Institute for Psychoanalysis in 1932. He published his book, *Our Age of Unreason*, in 1942, in which the ideas presented above were first expressed. He believed that World War II was causing the destruction of western culture as it existed at that time. His major concern was the "insecurity, fear, and distrust" that permeated society (Alexander 1978, 657). In effect, Alexander was defining what happens when individuals have lost their sense of meaning in life. Although it is difficult to refute much of what he says, we must recognize that psychology and the social sciences have made some progress since his book was written. If we are to reverse the maxim mentioned above and "First philosophize, then live," we also need to reverse our "mechanically minded" tendencies. The machine that is able to philosophize has yet to be invented. Let us allow machines to do what they do best and ourselves to do what we do best.

This is stated more eloquently in an excerpt from Karl Jaspers' landmark book, entitled *Way to Wisdom*. Jaspers, like other existentialists, believed that individuals cannot arrive at meaning in life solely through intellectual decisions based upon the objective world. He argued that we come to truth through our own subjective experiences when we recognize that there are certain ultimate realities in the human situation that cannot be denied. These include, "death, chance, guilt, and the uncertainty of the world" (Baumer 1978, 682). To come to terms with these ultimates, we need philosophy, which allows us to transcend them. We arrive at this point when we ask the perennial question, "What am I, what am I failing to do, what should I do?" Jaspers stated that modernism begot a too-busy world which has alienated the individual into a state of "self-forgetfulness." Like other critics, Jaspers bitterly attacked the mechanistic model of contemporary culture (683):

This self-forgetfulness has been aggravated by the machine age. With its time clocks, its jobs, whether absorbing or purely mechanical, which less and less fulfill man as man, it may even lead man to feel that he is part of the machine, interchangeably shunted in here and there, and when left free, to feel that he is nothing and can do nothing with himself. And just as he begins to recover himself, the colossus of this world draws him back again into the all-consuming machinery of empty labour and empty leisure.

Public administration literature is conscientious about developing theories and reporting on research concerning the organization as an object of interest and concern. This literature invariably refers to the machine metaphor as the brainchild of the scientific management school, and is often critical of its negative implications that the organization is a thing in and of itself. The metaphor is sometimes applied to individuals who work in the organization, as well. Robert Denhardt addressed this issue in his 1984 book, entitled *Theories of Public Organizations.* He makes the point that individuals often view their work as apart from themselves, with little relationship to their own creativity or vitality. As a result, they fail to satisfy the human need to produce, perceiving their work solely as a technical activity. Over time, they view themselves and others as mere instruments in the production process (Denhardt 1984, 24–25). Denhardt's analysis is similar to Jaspers' in that both see self-abnegation and a sense of emptiness.

Let us return for a moment to the ideas of Max Weber, to see if we can gain additional insight that will help us dismantle the machine and the instrumental view of ourselves it has imposed. Weber discussed the inter-connection between religion, economics, and social values in his famous book, *The Protestant Ethic and the Spirit of Capitalism.* In the introduction, Weber spoke about the means by which western industry used rational methods to develop its unique form of capitalism. He contrasted early busi-ness practices in the west with those in the east. Traditionally, in eastern cultures business was carried out as one of the functions of a household. Weber acknowledged the tradition of business activity in eastern bazaars, but argued that this was done on a small scale and was not that distinct from the functions of the household. The development of western capital-ism was unique, in that business activity was carried out apart from the household. Consequently, modern capitalistic organizations followed "a fun-damentally different, even opposite, development" from those in the east (Weber 1958, 22).

Weber attributed the success of the rational modern capitalist organization in western society to the separation of home and business, and argued that such isolation "completely dominates modern economic life" (Weber 1958, 21–22). Jaspers would probably add that the domination of the organization extends beyond economics and accounts for the emptiness felt by "self-forgetting" individuals. This phenomenon is not confined exclusively to industry. Weber also wrote that the very existence of western society is dependent on "political, technical, and economic conditions." Consequently, it has developed "a specially trained organization of officials . . . above all legally trained government officials" (16).

In some instances, work governs more than the economic needs of public administrators. What may begin as economic need can escalate to the point where work is all-consuming. The heady atmosphere that prevails in certain government positions can seduce administrators into using the job to fill the void within. Anyone familiar with the demands and power that surround high-level government jobs knows this. Those who occupy politically appointed positions or the upper levels of the civil service are particularly vulnerable to the attention they receive from legislators, the media, and other citizens. A false sense of power and control can take over and mask the inner void that is so prevalent among us.

One wonders if misplaced devotion to the mechanical organization would have occurred if the separation between home and office had not taken place. Would we instead have adopted an aesthetic approach (Goodsell and Murray 1995) to the practice of public administration? If so, perhaps Goodsell's idea of craftsmanship would have led to the alternative metaphor of the public administrator as artisan. Most of us are quite different people in our homes than in our work site. The personal creativity we exhibit in the way we design, organize, and decorate our homes speaks of who we are as individuals. It is a form of artisanship that, if cultivated at work, could manifest in ways appropriate to professional activity.

Newspaper and magazine articles frequently speculate that with the increasing availability and sophistication of home office equipment, it may be common for people to work out of their homes in the twenty-first century. While there will, inevitably, be many problems associated with this trend, it cannot help but make us feel more human and less machinelike. We professors see the difference between working from our home office and sitting in the university computer lab. At home, we can dress more comfortably, screen phone calls, enjoy the pleasant surroundings we have created, take a television or music break, and forage in the kitchen cabinets whenever we feel hungry! We do not face the pressure of making a commuter train, negotiating a crowded subway, or weaving in and out of clogged urban highways. Screeching phones and banging doors do not frazzle our nerves and test our sanity. We can talk privately to students on the phone, or personally in our home office, without fear of interruption or open ears eager to pass judgment. It is an infinitely more civilized way of working, and is conducive to an aesthetic appreciation of what the expression of our ideas means to us.

We would be amiss if, during our discussion of rationalism in twentieth-century organizations, we failed to mention at least briefly, the attention

Weber paid to the role played by western religion. Weber stated that what one culture calls rational may not be considered rational by another. He viewed western rationalism in its early stages as influenced by the ethos of organized religion, particularly Protestantism. It is beyond the scope of this book to delve into the sociological impact that religion has had on public organizations, but we need to reflect on the power it exerts over us as individuals.

I do not think we can truly rid ourselves of the hold the machine metaphor has on us, unless we address our spiritual selves. I do not promote any religious belief in this suggestion. In fact, I think we need to divest ourselves of many of the metaphors that have defined us—machine, religious, and otherwise—in order to discover who the unadulterated self really is. Surprisingly, we may find that after listening to the inner voice, our beliefs have not significantly changed. The important difference is that now they have become ours.

Our character as a nation has been based in large part upon our religious heritage. As policy advisers, we are especially affected by today's debate over the return to traditional values as a means of correcting social problems that are either real, or perceived to be. For example, citizens are raising their voices, but not in unison, about issues such as family values, sexual preferences, abortion, affirmative action, and welfare, to name a few. As professional civil servants, we are honor bound to respect the public dialogue, and contribute to and implement controversial policy, while maintaining as neutral a stance as possible. I suggest that in order to meet this Herculean responsibility, we need to know what we personally believe.

We cannot do this if we are running around like wound-up machines, responding to all situations as if they were the same. Neither can we do it if we allow forces outside ourselves to determine what is important for us. We need to take ownership of our own moral, ethical, and behavioral lives. Such an undertaking requires us to slow down, take stock, and listen carefully to the direction we receive from the voice that resides within. Then, after we have diagnosed our belief system, we will be able to carry forth the wishes of the electorate, whom we are pledged to serve, in a more liberated manner.

As public administrators who either practice in the field or study and write about it, perhaps we need to approach our work as if it were a calling—to serve others, yet inspired by an inner voice. Weber suggests that if we consider our work as our "life-task" (Weber 1958, 79), we will attain "virtue and proficiency" (54). This requires listening to the inner voice and not allowing ourselves to become the instruments of a mechanically oriented world.

The organization theory literature may also help us to dismantle the machine metaphor. Most public administration textbooks describe organizations as open to outside influences, such as citizen demands, legislative requests, and media considerations, to name a few. A machine can respond only with its mechanical parts, and therefore is closed off from everything else. If a public bureaucracy is closed off from the forces it depends upon for survival, it will lose the support it needs. Eventually, funding will end and the agency will be disassembled. The concept of organizations as open systems is part of the intellectual movement which spawned cybernetics and information theory among other quantitatively oriented disciplines, such as operations research. This movement attempted to forge a connection among the different branches of science by focusing on general concepts that could be shared among various disciplines (Scott 1981, 102).

It was eventually determined by the founder of the movement, Ludwig von Bertalanffy, and his colleagues, that all entities are composed of inter-dependent parts and can be classified as systems. However, not all systems are the same. There are mechanical, organic, and the most complex of all, social systems (Scott 1981, 103). Recent research has relied heavily on the idea of organizations as social systems, and is a radical departure from the closed, mechanical concept that dominated the traditional approach. This trend is responsible for many of the new ideas concerning how to structure organizations to meet the demands of the changing world. We need more research devoted specifically to public bureaucracies if we are to meet the challenge of organizational renewal.

General systems theory borrows a concept from the laws of thermodynamics to make a distinction between a closed and an open system. The concept is called *entropy*, which is the final outcome of all closed systems. In essence, it means that if an organization shuts itself off from the rich exchange of outside influences, it will eventually self-destruct. Entropy represents the shadow of destruction that lurks around the hierarchical corners of every closed organization. The good news is that social systems, like public bureaucracies, can enjoy the benefits of the counterpart of entropy, called *negentropy*. The idea behind this concept is that organizations become enriched when they allow themselves to open up to the complex interplay among diverse interests. The more variety there is among outside influences, the more complex and healthier the organization (Scott 1981, 109–11).

TOWARD PERSONAL RESPONSIBILITY

If the practice of public administration is conducted in open-system organizations, and there is little doubt that it is, how can we function effectively as mechanistic practitioners? The obvious answer is that we cannot. More importantly, we do not! We can become more functional as public administrators if we accept our public agencies as complex, open, and infinitely rich organizations. Also, we need to accept the simple fact that certainty does not exist. There are no sure decisions, and government organizations can never be closed off from forces beyond their control. Tradition has taught us that hierarchical structure, rigid enforcement of rules, and discouragement of innovation and change are the only ways to practice public administration. Like ostriches with our heads buried in the sand, we are encased in solid walls of denial. Structure and procedure have become defensive mechanisms through which we think we are managing the government.

In his book, entitled *Humanizing Public Organizations*, Robert Golembiewski reminds us of Richard Brown's contention that what happens in organizations is not "external to human consciousness" (Golembiewski 1985, 210). Brown states that the world we experience is our own creation. What we perceive as objectively determined reality in the work place is simply the result of "our shared forms of perception and expression." If this is true, and there is every indication that it is, the role we play and the influence we exert can hardly be compared to machinelike activity.[2]

James Fesler and Donald Kettl, in their recent book, entitled *The Politics of the Administrative Process*, argue that the responsibility we assume as public administrators is not contained in the external controls imposed by bureaucracy. They suggest that, as professionals, we need to develop internalized guidelines consistent with the standards of the profession and the obligation we have to fulfill our legitimate role. They also suggest that trust needs to be built between political and professional players in the practice of public administration. This will serve to lessen the amount of red tape required to assure that civil servants are held accountable (Fesler and Kettl 1991, 15). Few practicing administrators would disagree with Fesler and Kettl, although many may wonder where to obtain internal guidelines and how to build trust within the public sector community. To them, I would suggest slowing down and taking the time to observe, reflect, and tune into themselves so they can hear the inner voice when it speaks.

Debra Stewart and Norman Sprinthall assume a proactive stance on public sector ethics, and argue that the individual administrator, who is a moral agent, must assume responsibility. They suggest that we need to engage in more research to learn how bureaucrats react to moral dilemmas and propose the development of teaching methods to improve "moral skill and imagination" (Stewart and Sprinthall 1991, 245). While I applaud their position that the individual is responsible for his or her moral judgments, I do not believe this is something that can be taught. I am not suggesting we stop conducting courses in ethics. Administrators can benefit from exposure to the philosophical issues underlying ethical judgments. Sharing of personal experience in decision making of a moral nature can increase thought and lead to greater awareness.

However, the aspects of our lives that are the most significant are also the most personal. They define who we are as individual human beings. Our response to the deeper moments in life is dependent upon the character we possess. The source of character, embedded within, is known only to each individual. Our fundamental responsibility is to unearth unconscious material that contributes to the formation of our character and raise it to awareness. We can only accomplish this if we listen to the inner voice, which is the source. Too often we forget about the personal nature of character and think we can impose moral order on others. Our focus is always so externally oriented that we have made a god out of control. We are afraid to allow character to flourish, because if we do, we lose our influence over the actions of others.

The significant and profound moments in life are not necessarily the most dramatic. In fact, they can be quite simple and unimpressive to the outside world. For example, a public administrator fights the hierarchy to obtain a well-deserved raise for a subordinate, with no ulterior motive beyond the truth that this is the right thing to do. We are defined by the many decisions we make like this over a career and a lifetime. I don't think we recognize this as much as we could. We might be surprised at how "good" we really are, if we paid more attention to the seemingly unimportant parts of our jobs and personal lives. What we do and how we treat others are indications of whether we are listening to the voice within. The voice teaches us who we really are, and inspires us to take action or wait for a more fortuitous time.

Does the choice made by the administrator who goes out on a limb to attain a raise for an employee exemplify an ethical, moral, insignificant, stupid, or mere personnel decision? Who can answer this question? Do we have the right to even ask it? Is this decision separate from others in the administrator's life? Can we compartmentalize our actions into work, home, school, or play actions? I suggest at this stage in the development of public administration as a profession, we think we can. I also suggest this is residual dualistic thinking. In his book, *The Responsible Administrator*, Terry Cooper discusses the conflict public administrators often face as a result of the multiple roles they play in their professional and personal lives. While he distinguishes between their administrative and personal responsibilities, he acknowledges this is an artificial distinction (Cooper 1990, 84). I would like to underscore this point, and add that in the wholeness of our lives, moral responsibility and ethical action come together. From the perspective of the inner voice as the source of internal guidance, it is not possible to separate the life of an individual into isolated segments.

Let me clarify my meaning, lest the reader misinterpret my intention by thinking I am uncritically accepting the concept of individualism as it is perceived today. The American definition of individualism was provided by Alexis De Tocqueville in his book, *Democracy in America*, first published in France in 1835. De Tocqueville was sent to America by his government to study its penal system. Fascinated by the idea of a country that had never known a genuine aristocracy, he was interested in studying more than its prison system. De Tocqueville carefully and meticulously observed and recorded his experiences, and in the process created the expression *individualism* (De Tocqueville 1958, 394). His analysis of American democracy has withstood the test of time and his book is still read and discussed in college classrooms throughout the country. De Tocqueville defined individualism as "a mature and calm feeling which . . . at first only saps the virtue of public life; but in the long run it attacks and destroys all others and is at length absorbed in downright selfishness" (104).

De Tocqueville's insight is valid today. The more recent evaluation of American individualism found in *Habits of the Heart* does not advocate individualism's abandonment, but is cognizant of its weaknesses (Bellah et al. 1986, 142). The authors argue that individualism lies at the core of American identity. They distinguish between various forms of individualism and argue that those in which the individual is perceived "in relation to a larger whole, a community and a tradition—are capable of sustaining genuine individuality and nurturing both public and private life" (143). Aware of the problems of individualism, John Rohr informs readers in his book, *Ethics for Bureaucrats*, that although he emphasizes the rights of individuals, he is not condoning "the excesses of individualism" (Rohr 1989, 286).

Similarly, I hasten to assure readers that my intention is *not* to promote selfish or unchecked behavior. The assumptions underlying the search for self, promoted in this book, differ markedly from the hedonistic leanings of the "me" generation of the 1960s. The excesses of that generation, of which I am a member, were a reaction to the obsessive externalization of individual selves carried over from previous generations. I also suggest that the generation of the 1960s was seeking a genuine philosophy that emanated from within each person. Many lost their way in this search and, true to their western heritage, looked to outside sources, such as drugs and sex, for inner strength.

The Fork in the Road

The sociology of Max Weber, psychology of Carl Jung and Franz Alexander, metaphysics of Aldous Huxley, modern mysticism of Thomas Moore, existentialism of Karl Jaspers, political writing of Alexis De Tocqueville, and eastern philosophy of Chuang Tzu, along with selected writings of public administration scholars, have led us along the path toward Hummel's quest for a philosophical resolution of how to negotiate an increasingly bureaucratized world. The perspective of this book is focused at the individual level of engagement, and is therefore deeply personal. As we continue along the path toward self-knowledge, we will eventually come to a fork in the road. Readers who persist thus far will have to decide whether to take the familiar trail or follow a new route. It is an honest decision that entails no right or wrong turn. After all, the journey is personal! The poet Robert Frost movingly recounted his own choice in the beautiful poem, "The Road Not Taken" (Frost 1964, 131):

> Two roads diverged in a yellow wood
> And sorry I could not travel both
> And be one traveler, long I stood
> And looked down one as far as I could
> To where it bent in the undergrowth;
>
> Then took the other, as just as fair,
> And having perhaps the better claim,
> Because it was grassy and wanted wear;
> Though as for that the passing there
> Had worn them really about the same,
>
> And both that morning equally lay
> In leaves no step had trodden black.
> Oh, I kept the first for another day!
> Yet knowing how way leads on to way,
> I doubted if I should ever come back.
>
> I shall be telling this with a sigh
> Somewhere ages and ages hence:
> Two roads diverged in a wood, and I—
> I took the one less traveled by,
> And that has made all the difference.

The fork in the road presents each of us with an important choice that will affect the rest of our lives. We are never quite the same person after we choose which road to follow. If we decide to take the more heavily traveled road, we will be conventional in the way we act and present ourselves to others. We may be more comfortable in the world, having chosen a path that is understood. If we choose the road that has fewer travelers, we will experience periods of loneliness and insecurity. Our footing along such a path is less sure and the going can be rough. Our journey will take us to unusual places and we will see how unique our travel has been when we arrive at our destination.

Away from Groundedness

Since Descartes, philosophers have proposed many alternative ideas in their attempts to start from scratch, as it were, in reconstructing reality. Seventeenth and eighteenth-century philosophy were grounded in the absolute values of rationalism. As we come to the close of the twentieth century, we are losing the sense of rootedness that absolutism provides. Max Weber argued that rationalization, as the permeating force of modernity, allowed for the systematization of all aspects of living, including scientific, technical, moral, and everyday activities (Burger 1992, 4). In the heyday of modernist living, we basked in the certainty of a scientific, artistic, and economic climate, founded on principles of western rationality. It defined us and provided a sane and certain footing in a dangerous world. Our step is less secure now, as we slip down from the lofty heights of objectivity and universality. The days of a singular morality founded upon consensual concepts of natural law and standards of what constitutes "good living" are gone. The changes that have altered our social functioning must be taken into consideration as we develop the cultural theories which define us as a society. These changes are elemental: the western concept of the family has altered, the role of women is different, and the God we knew is dead!

David Kolb interprets the meaning behind the ideas of German philosopher Martin Heidegger in his book, entitled *The Critique of Pure Modernity*. Heidegger agrees with Weber that formal rationality dominates the modern world. He attributes this to mechanization, technological development, and the "loss of the gods" (Kolb 1986, 121). Heidegger is concerned with how human beings negotiate a world that is controlled by the calculative needs of rational planning and technological demands. He believes that individuals must be free so they may "philosophize" and "hear" what is inside themselves and experience their own sense of being (179). Self-knowledge is of paramount concern in the contemporary world in which human beings, like all other things in existence, are "standing ready" to be used (146).

Although it appears that individuals exert control and order the events in the world, Heidegger teaches that the human will is not autonomous. The individual person no longer stands in the center of an adoring world. There is no center! There is only an "open field of possibilities" (Kolb 1986, 147). Modern western culture, true to its ancient Greek heritage, accepts the essential existence or "being" of all things. What is lacking is a transcendent dimension. Hegel's idea of "mutual connection and transparency" is apparent in the modern world, but there is no depth. Augustus Comte was a nineteenth-century French philosopher who was the first to use the word *sociology*. A positivist committed to social reform, Comte would approve of the contemporary reliance on factual information to control events. He would be disappointed, however, that facts stand alone in the modern psyche, unaccompanied by a humanistic desire for harmony and well-being (148).

Heidegger argues that dependence on facts compensates for the lack of roots in modern society. Facts, and the formal rationality that gives them meaning, have replaced the former traditions that served as the bedrock of a secure society. Interestingly, Heidegger promotes neither a return to old ways of living, nor to traditional society. He seems to suggest a turning inward so we may recognize there is no certainty, no ground beneath us, and no closure. Heidegger does not defend tradition because it established a sense of grounding. To the contrary, he urges individuals to become free from metaphysical absolutism so they may discover who and what they really are (Kolb 1986, 180–81).

Kolb reminds us that Heidegger's ideas show the conditions that would lead to certain social and psychological phenomena, even though his "discussion is meant to be presocial and prepsychological" (Kolb 1986, 148–49). These conditions open the way in which individuals and the things of the world are available to one another. They provide the "space" within which individuals and institutions live (149). While he is concerned that technology has separated the modern individual from transcendental experience, Heidegger believes there is hope beyond technology. He calls for individuals to "hear" the "word of being," which then "becomes the experience of ourselves and of the world" (179).

Heidegger's interpretation of the conditions in the world that have led us into the modern "space" in which we live, provides insight into the ideas of Carl Jung. Like Heidegger, Jung perceived modern civilization as responsible for those social practices and psychological beliefs which alienate individuals from the profound experience of personhood. Both seem to be saying that modern conditions have led to awareness that a deep, substantive part of the individual person is lost. The philosophical ground upon which western individuals stood in the past was external to themselves and has now disappeared, or was never there in the first place. Bereft of roots, modern individuals turn to technology in the hope it will center their lives and provide significance.

As an existentialist, Heidegger is disturbed by the lack of meaning in human existence. In attempting to address the despair this evokes, he refers to a concept which he calls "resolve." In German, the word is "Entschlossenheit." The "resolute" individual possesses the courage to follow his or her own dictates. There is no force that can provide direction for individual action. Neither societal values, rational principles, nor an external God is responsible for individual choice. There is nothing absolute inside or outside ourselves to which we can refer for answers. We are "called" to ourselves and to our conscience, for resoluteness and courage to act in a meaningless world (Tillich 1952, 148–49).

Not all interpreters of Heidegger's philosophy perceive him as mired in unmitigated despair. Tillich argues that Heidegger, more than any other existentialist, calls for individuals to seek the courage to be fully themselves, regardless of the cost. Tillich suggests that a "mystical concept of being" lies at the foundation of Heidegger's philosophy (Tillich 1952, 149). If this is so, Heidegger's notion of individual groundlessness needs to be reinterpreted. Mysticism, while neither a religion nor an ideology, involves the search for the unifying principle in which reality is grounded. John Leavey discusses Heidegger's text, entitled "On the Essence of Truth," in which he addresses the concept of "Being." Leavey makes the point that Heidegger perceives modern individuals as living in error because of their avoidance of the "mystery." Heidegger writes, "Man's flight from the mystery toward what is readily available, onward from one current thing to the next, passing the mystery by—this is *erring* (das Irren)" (Leavey 1988, 34).

Leavey is interested in this passage for reasons other than Heidegger's possible mysticism. The passage does, however, lend credence to Tillich's assumption that mysticism has a place in Heideggerian thought. It seems reasonable to assume that since Heidegger accepts mystery as a condition of humanity and laments our tendency to ignore it, mysticism has a certain hold on his thinking. Kolb argues that Heidegger believes a new epoch is possible, in which poetic harmony can prevail. In this new world, the direct experience of living would be felt "in the deepest place of man's being" (Kolb 1986, 179). Perhaps Heidegger believes that the mysteries of life can be addressed at some future time, when the condition of the world allows for the "space" we need to experience mystical truths. However, Kolb urges us to be careful in assigning mystical intention to Heidegger, lest we become trapped in a too-romantic interpretation of what he means. His concern over the modern loss of roots does not necessarily mean he advocates a return to belief in some basic reality (190, 191).

Where does this leave the modern public administrator who is trying to understand how philosophy can help him or her attain a deeper sense of meaning and purpose in both personal and professional life? The situation need not lead to discouragement. As individuals we can look within, discover our own answer to the meaning of existence, and from this knowledge, choose how we will live in the world. Since the rise of positivism and its invalidation of metaphysics, in the mid-nineteenth century, the search for ultimate answers has largely disappeared. While espousing a positivist stance, however, Heidegger cautions modern individuals against refusing to "hear," thereby avoiding the "mystery." If Heidegger is asking us to listen to the inner voice, he is not necessarily promoting a romantic solution to the meaning of existence.

The question becomes not whether there is an inner voice, but what the inner voice says. Clearly, Heidegger does not intend to assure us by listening to the inner voice, we will hear that God is in his heaven and all is right with the world. Kolb argues that Heidegger is asking us to be open to future possibilities which may involve experiencing the world in a new way. This new way will allow us to become more aware of the finite aspect of the world and our experience in it. We will be able to see beyond technological pervasiveness, without discovering a new center to replace what we think we lost. What is grounded and what is groundless will become mere historical possibilities "rather than the essence of reality" (Kolb 1986, 199). In effect, Kolb is making a case for what he calls "deconstructive living," which is an attempt to cope in a world that no longer searches for ultimate meaning. It requires us to be consciously aware of ourselves and what is happening within us, as well as all activity that occurs inside and outside our organizations (269).

Toward Deconstruction

The search for understanding the nature of existence has been a long and arduous task which has taken bizarre twists and turns throughout the centuries. The influence of philosophical speculation on western culture began with the metaphysics of Aristotle, who used logic and syllogism as the method of arriving at first principles underlying all knowledge. In the Middle Ages, scholasticism, built upon Aristotelian logic, promoted faith and reason as the way to truth. The rationalism of the seventeenth century relied upon reason alone to provide answers to eternal questions. Kant's critical philosophy of the eighteenth century argued that scientific metaphysics was incapable of solving the mysteries of the universe. In the mid-nineteenth century, positivism focused on philosophical analysis, thereby replacing metaphysical speculation. The twentieth century has seen the culmination of positivist thinking in logical positivism, with its emphasis on mathematics and the natural sciences as the arbiters of truth.

As we approach the dawn of a new century, we need to make further adjustments to our philosophical legacies. Since we no longer engage in metaphysical speculation, we are not burdened by an overly romanticized view of existence which leads to ultimate solutions. To the contrary, we tend to engage in excessive analysis leading to inordinate rationalization and separation of everything we experience into neat and orderly categories. In this way, we convince ourselves we are in control of what happens. Because the world, at this particular point in time, is exceedingly complex and unpredictable, we feel the need to contain as much of it as possible. The problem is, we are only able to succeed in managing the elements of living that fit into conventionally approved norms.

We run into difficulty when we either defy the norms, or are excluded from deciding what they will be (Rorty 1992, 236). We can easily account for what "fits" into our conceptual framework. This includes anything we decide can be classified in an "objective" manner—for example, individuals, institutions, neighborhoods, groups, everything that is logical, consistent, and can be measured. But we also need to account for what does not "fit" into the neat categories of our objective determination. What do we do about individuals who have been excluded from deciding what the norms will be, and therefore ignore them? How do we account for bureaucratic deviancy? In what way do we handle nonlogical contradictions and dissimilarities? Postmodern philosophers attempt to "account" for these dissimilarities through a process called *deconstruction* (Gasche 1988, 4). Deconstruction takes into consideration those parts of the totality that have not been included in our rational analysis. It opposes absolute knowledge (Bennington 1992, 98), denying that such a thing is possible in this uncertain world.

Deconstruction can be applied to every aspect of modern living. It was first accepted as a viable alternative to positivism in the United States by critics who were impressed with the deconstruction of literary texts by French philosopher Jacques Derrida (Bernasconi 1992, 137). A complete discussion of the history of deconstruction and its relevance to literature and philosophy is beyond the scope of this book. Suffice it to say that deconstruction strips down the layers of thought and language underlying a literary or philosophical text.

The reader may ask, "Does deconstruction have significance to public administration as a field of practice and if so, how?" Fox and Miller state that bureaucracy, with its emphasis on control and cause/effect empiricism, requires a more sophisticated model to define what it really is. Their argument is consistent with the frequently criticized, deterministic conception of bureaucracy. They use deconstruction to suggest a more relevant model for understanding bureaucratic life as it is lived at the end of the twentieth century. In their discussion, they provide an excellent definition of what deconstruction means, stating, "It requires a tracing to the roots of a thing, a genealogy or archeology, so that they can be laid bare" (Fox and Miller 1995, 93). They proceed to give us their analysis of Weberian bureaucracy after it has been "properly" deconstructed.

Fox and Miller found, contrary to popular opinion, that bureaucracy is not neutral. As an instrument of social interaction, it legitimates our value system. What we think is concrete and objective is really nothing more or less than a series of shared ideas about the world. These ideas become habituated into our way of thinking and influence our perception of reality. Bureaucracy depends on the support of all involved parties so it can legitimize authority and assure compliance with the prevailing value system upon which it rests. Through practices such as the granting of desirable rewards, behavior is controlled and the status quo is assured. Bureaucracy does not owe its existence to objective criteria. Instead, it depends on "a shared idea—a tacitly agreed-upon set of symbols and expectations" (Fox and Miller 1995, 99).

CLOSING THOUGHTS

I was moved one day by something I read. I do not remember the source or the occasion, but it has stayed with me and is rather haunting. It said that the greatest fear of any human being is the fear of insignificance. As I mulled over in my mind why this thought disturbed me, I concluded that I must feel the threat of insignificance myself! Further introspection led me to the realization that modern life tends to reduce rather than expand my sense of who I am. I interpreted this bizarre reductionism as an attack, and saw it manifest in aspects of my life that reduce me to a calculating entity, a machine, an unfeeling being.

Given this personal assessment, I have concluded that reductionism causes more individual pain than deconstruction because it attacks us as persons and robs us of the essence of selfhood—the undefinable, unknowable, unassailable best part of who we are. It threatens our very soul! Deconstruction, on the other hand, seems more evaluative of our institutions and our belief systems. This can result in positive action, such as the constructivism proposed by Fox and Miller. However, it can also be a source of danger, in that through the process of deconstructing what we have accumulated and built, we may inadvertently discard positive elements we would prefer to keep.

I suggest we abandon our reductionist tendency and treat it with the contempt it deserves. Each of us is as far removed from possessing the characteristics of a machine as a machine is of possessing the qualities of a human being. We also need to take care in evaluating what we have learned from deconstruction. Symbolically speaking, after a building is torn down, it is important to carefully evaluate its foundation. If the foundation is determined to be weak and needs to be removed, the ground beneath, composed of compacted soil, is in danger of collapse. The builder is then faced with having to shore up the feeble soil and begin again.

The question raised by this analogy is, How deep into the structure of bureaucracy should deconstruction penetrate? If it penetrates into the root source, we may be faced with the unprecedented situation of being forced to begin anew. Through the process of deconstruction, Fox and Miller (1995, 93) suggest probabilism as more constructive than the deterministic model of bureaucracy for the practice of public administration. While probabilism is less domineering than the rigid Weberian rationality to which we are all accustomed, does it go far enough?

Fox and Miller are impressed with the statistical methodology of probabilism, which allows for "the realization that the stuff we count and measure is not so concrete as the deterministic model had supposed" (Fox and Miller 1995, 93). True as this may be, we are still faced with the "stuff" that we do *not* "count and measure." The problem, as I see it, does not lie primarily in what we examine, but rather in what we leave out. It is what we do not know that causes us to make decisions leading to the setting and implementation of public policy that is doomed to fail.

How far should deconstruction go into the root of our bureaucratic institutions, academic literature, and emerging studies in ethical behavior? Should it go so deep we actually penetrate the essence of our belief structure? I pose this as a rhetorical question that needs to be seriously discussed; otherwise, deconstruction will become just another intellectual buzzword we enjoy bantering around at academic conferences. Now that we are finally onto something with real depth, let's take Heidegger's advice and sincerely open ourselves up to a "field of possibilities!"

NOTES

1. The reader is referred to the following sources for additional reading on communitarianism: C. M. Stivers, "Active Citizenship and Public Administration." In *Refounding Public Administration*. Edited by G. L. P. Wamsley, R. N. Blacher, C. T. Goodsell, P. S. Kronenberg, J. A. Rohr, C. M. Stivers, O. F. White, and J. F. Wolf. (Newbury Park: Sage Publications, 1990, 246–273); and T. L. Cooper, *An Ethic of Citizenship for Public Administration* (Englewood Cliffs: Prentice Hall, 1991, 160), and "Hierarchy, Virtue, and the Practice of Public Administration: A Perspective for Normative Ethics," *Public Administration Review* 47, (1987): 320–328.

2. Golembiewski's reference is to the use of Action Research to solve practical problems of modern organizational life (Golembiewski 1985, 206). The reader is referred to the following citation related to the Brown article: Richard Harvey Brown, "Bureaucracy as Praxis: Toward a Political Phenomenology of Formal Organization," *Administrative Science Quarterly* 23, (September 1978): 378.

REFERENCES

Alexander, Franz. 1978. "Our Age of Unreason." In *Main Currents of Western Thought*. Edited by Franklin LeVan Baumer. New Haven: Yale University Press.

Baumer, Franklin LeVan, ed. 1978. *Main Currents of Western Thought*. New Haven: Yale University Press.

Bellah, Robert N., Richard Madsen, William M. Sullivan, Ann Swidler, and Steven M. Typton. 1986. *Habits of the Heart*. New York: Harper and Row Publishers.

Bennington, Geoffrey. 1992. "Mosaic Fragment: If Derrida were an Egyptian." In *Derrida: A Critical Reader*. Edited by David Wood. Cambridge: Blackwell.

Bernasconi, Robert. 1992. "No More Stories, Good or Bad: De Man's Criticisms of Derrida on Rousseau." In *Derrida: A Critical Reader*. Edited by David Wood. Cambridge: Blackwell.

Burger, Peter. 1992. *The Decline of Modernism*. University Park: The Pennsylvania State University Press.

Cooper, Terry L. 1990. *The Responsible Administrator*. San Francisco: Jossey-Bass Publishers.

Denhardt, Robert B. 1984. *Theories of Public Organization*. Monterey: Brooks/Cole Publishing Company.

De Tocqueville, Alexis. 1958. *Democracy in America*. Edited by Phillips Bradley. New York: Vintage Books.

Fesler, James W., and Donald F. Kettl. 1991. *The Politics of the Administrative Process*. Chatham: Chatham House Publishers Inc.

Fox, Charles J., and Hugh T. Miller. 1995. *Postmodern Public Administration*. Thousand Oaks: Sage Publications.

Frost, Robert. 1964. *Complete Poems of Robert Frost*. 1949. Reprint, New York: Holt, Rinehart and Winston.

Gasche, Rodolphe. 1988. "Infrastructure and Systematicity." In *Deconstruction and Philosophy*. Edited by John Sallis. Chicago: The University of Chicago Press.

Golembiewski, Robert, T. 1985. *Humanizing Public Organizations*. Mt. Airy, Maryland: Lomond Publications.

Goodsell, Charles, T., and Nancy Murray, eds. 1995. *Public Administration Illuminated and Inspired by the Arts*. Westport, Connecticut: Praeger.

Hummel, Ralph P. 1994. *The Bureaucratic Experience*. 4th ed. New York: St. Martin's Press.

Huxley, Aldous. 1970. *The Perennial Philosophy*. 1945. Reprint, New York: Harper and Row Publishers.

Jung, Carl G. 1974. "The Type Problem in Poetry." In *Psychological Types*. Vol. 6 of *Collected Works*. 1971. Reprint, Princeton: Princeton University Press.

————. 1978. "The Undiscovered Self." In *Civilization in Transition*. Vol. 10 of *Collected Works*. 2d ed. 1970. Reprint, Princeton: Princeton University Press.

————. 1980. "Concerning Rebirth." In *The Archetypes and the Collective Unconscious*. Vol. 9, part 1 of *Collected Works*. 2d ed. 1968. Reprint, Princeton: Princeton University Press.

Kolb, David. 1986. *The Critique of Pure Modernity*. Chicago: The University of Chicago Press.

Leavey, John P., Jr. 1988. "Destinerrance: The Apotropocalyptics of Translation." In *Deconstruction and Philosophy*. Edited by John Sallis. Chicago: The University of Chicago Press.

McCarthy, Thomas. 1991. *The Critical Theory of Jurgen Habermas*. 1981. Reprint, Cambridge: The MIT Press.

Merton, Thomas. 1969. *The Way of Chuang Tzu*. New York: New Directions.

Moore, Thomas. 1992. *Care of the Soul*. New York: HarperCollins Publishers.

Rohr, John A. 1989. *Ethics for Bureaucrats*. New York: Marcel Dekker, Inc.

Rorty, Richard. 1992. "Is Derrida a Transcendental Philosopher?" In *Derrida: A Critical Reader*. Edited by David Wood. Cambridge: Blackwell.

Scott, Richard. 1981. *Organizations: Rational, Natural, and Open Systems*. Englewood Cliffs: Prentice-Hall, Inc.

Stewart, Debra W., and Norman A. Sprinthall. 1991. *Ethical Frontiers in Public Management*. Edited by James S. Bowman. San Francisco: Jossey-Bass Publishers.

Tillich, Paul. 1952. *The Courage to Be*. New Haven: Yale University Press.

Weber, Max. 1958. *The Protestant Ethic and the Spirit of Capitalism*. Translated by Talcott Parsons. New York: Charles Scribner's Sons.

PART 3

Ideas for Administrative Theory from the East

CHAPTER 4

Lessons on the Self:
Lao-tze to Jung

One who knows others is clever, but
one who knows himself is enlightened.
One who conquers others is powerful,
but one who conquers himself is mighty. (Lao-tze 1991, 33:1–2)

THE POWER OF ALLEGORY

There are many legends surrounding the life of Lao-tze. One of the most provocative is told by Holmes Welch in his book, *Taoism, the Parting of the Way* (1996). The legend begins with the birth of Lao-tze on September 14, 604 B.C., when a woman in the village of Ch'u leaned against a plum tree and delivered her child. Her confinement was exceptional, since she did not carry an ordinary child in her womb. Lao-tze was conceived sixty-two-years prior to his birth, while his mother gazed appreciatively at a falling star. Myth has it that he was born with the ability to speak, having spent such an extended time in utero. Because his hair was as white as snow at birth, he was called Lao-tze, which means "Old Boy." As the years passed, the man attracted groups of people who longed to become disciples of his teaching. It is told that Lao-tze and Confucius, who was more than fifty years younger than he met on at least one occasion (Welch 1966, 1).

However, the two men were less than impressed with each other. Lao-tze perceived Confucius as arrogant, ambitious, and consumed with unrelenting desire for the things of the world. On his part, Confucius likened Lao-tze to an incomprehensible dragon beyond human control. When he

was 160 years old, Lao-tze despaired over the corruption of the Chou dynasty and fled to a more auspicious place. On his journey he met Yin Hsi,
who was the keeper of the Han-ku pass through which Lao-tze traveled.
Yin Hsi was concerned that Lao-tze's departure would result in the loss of
significant ideas. Therefore, he asked Lao-tze to remain with him until he
wrote a book containing his teachings, which Yin Hsi could then dissemi-
nate. Lao-tze complied, and the *Tao Teh King* was born (Welch 1966, 2).

Scholars disagree as to whether Lao-tze actually existed and if he did,
whether he and Confucius really met one another. Some believe that the
Tao Teh King was written by numerous teachers who followed a variety of
paths. Others, like Holmes Welch, are convinced that the book represents
the writings of one man. Whatever the truth, the ideas attributed to Lao-
tze are of importance, not his identity. It is generally agreed there will never
be a definitive answer to these contradictory opinions. Since we are not
experts in Chinese folklore, we will follow Welch's direction and assume
the existence and authorship of the legendary Lao-tze.

The reader may be surprised to learn that the *Tao Teh King* has been
translated into English as often as the Bible. The translations are many and
varied, owing at least in part to the similarities in the teachings of the New
Testament and Lao-tze's words. For example, in Mark 9:35 we find the
words, "If anyone would be first, he must be last of all" and in the *Tao Teh
King*, chapter 7, "The Sage puts himself last and finds himself in the fore-
most place" (Welch 1966, 6).

Lao-tze did not communicate his ideas through what westerners would
consider straightforward language. His metaphysics was presented in the
form of esoteric paradoxes. The use of paradox in presenting complex truths
is more effective than logical explanation, which can become heavy, overwhelming, and dull. The style used by Lao-tze jolts the reader loose from
conventional understanding. It is compressed and moves quickly from one
topic to another. The material itself does not elicit meaning; readers must
look within to find the significance the words express. Welch tells us that
Lao-tze, who perceived truth as possessing four corners, would provide students with one corner of a subject and expect them to unravel the other
three (Welch 1966, 9). In other words, those who read Lao-tze must stretch
beyond the limitations of their traditional thinking.

Lao-tze wrote in archaic Chinese. The difficulty of this ancient language,
and even its modern literary form, is almost unimaginable to the western
mind. For example, there are no parts of speech, singular, plural, person, or
case. There are virtually no rules that do not have many exceptions. As a
result, writing is vague, and even educated Chinese rely upon the thousands
of pages of commentaries and subcommentaries that exist to comprehend
what is meant. This explains, in part, why there are so many different English translations of the ancient Chinese teachings. It is important for the
reader to understand that a word-by-word translation of a Chinese classic

into English is impossible. What we need is a spelling out in English of what is not spelled out in Chinese" (Welch 1966, 12).

Why should we study English translations of eastern metaphyics? Holmes Welch suggests they are similar to the plays of William Shakespeare and, as such, are universally relevant. They probe deep waters and address the uncertainty of life that haunts all individuals. (Welch 1996, 13):

> It is a magic mirror, always found to reflect our concept of the truth
> . . . from person to person the sense changes, but the truthfulness remains. This Protean quality, this readiness to furnish whatever the reader needs, gives the *Tao Te Ching* an immense advantage over books written so clearly that they have only one meaning.

Perhaps the word "inspirational" comes closest to describing the writings of Lao-tze. They remind me of what happens when I experience a work of art, such as a painting, a beautiful sculpture, or a moving musical score. These aesthetic experiences evoke a deeper reaction than I am accustomed to when I encounter western metaphysics. They speak to my whole self; emotional as well as intellectual. I clearly see the parallel that Welch perceives between Picasso's tendency to draw one profile with two eyes rather than following a more conventional norm and painting two profiles with one eye. In his way, Picasso is delivering a complex truth by eschewing logical exposition. Lao-tze does the same thing using a paradox as the medium of expression (Welch 1966, 8).

When I view a Picasso painting, or read a poem by Lao-tze, I am forced to delve deep within myself to discover its meaning. Material presented in this way provides the philosopher, painter, or musician with an opportunity to penetrate the soul of his or her audience. The responsive audience is compelled to venture within and carefully peel back the corners of truth that the writer or artist has left intact.

I attempt to express some of the concepts contained in eastern metaphysics and in analytical psychology by using a similar technique in this book. While I do not necessarily use paradoxes, I do rely upon allegorical parables. Admittedly, this is an unusual approach to writing in public administration. However, the material considered here is unusual and does not lend itself to the straightforward presentation common particularly in public administration writing, and social science writing in general.

The allegories presented are not intended to instruct readers in specific cognitive skills. Rather, they are given to deepen awareness of situations, experiences, and personal perceptions. For example, the allegory presented in this chapter depicts how, through imagery and introspection, a woman becomes aware of the various aspects of her own nature. Silence and seclusion reward her with the gift of self-knowledge. Having attained this knowledge, her awareness and understanding of the strengths and weaknesses of others are heightened. This awareness is furnished by the inner voice, which exists within each of us. If we listen, we may decide to begin a dialogue that will lead to a philosophy of administration for the new century.

Traditional administrative writing that focuses on behavior recognizes the importance of individual values. Yet, the usual format for such teaching is textbook generalization or fictional and non-fictional case studies. These materials are meant to be read and interpreted literally because they deliver a clear, unambiguous message that appeals to cognitive reasoning. While this format can be very effective in presenting important findings and experiences to both academics and practitioners, it tends to discuss the qualities and virtues of effective leadership in an abstract manner that is impersonal and devoid of human warmth.

Little, if any, attention is paid to the depth of feeling individuals encounter as they try to conduct their professional lives in accordance with personal values. This oversight masks the complexity of administrative behavior by underestimating the internal dynamics that individuals experience as they attempt to integrate inner precepts with the external realities of their demanding jobs. Anyone who has either served in a public-sector position or seriously investigated the responsibility of civil servants, knows the subjective richness of governmental decision making, task functioning, human interaction, and ethical conduct.

My first parable tells the story of an old woman who, as she sifts through the events of her life as a civil servant, examines how personal values influenced certain key experiences. I present this in a style more "eastern" than "western." Its lyrical tone is intended to evoke the sensitive side of readers so they may more easily hear the whisper of their own inner voice. The lessons contained tap a level of understanding that transcends intellectual knowledge. We are asked to pass beyond the limitations of cognitive knowledge to a level of meaning both deeper and broader than that to which we are accustomed. We will not be *told* what to think by the parable. Rather, we will be invited to ponder and inwardly explore.

EMILY'S STORY—A MODERN ALLEGORY

This is the story of Emily. It begins when she is a young girl growing up on a New England farm and ends when she is an old woman living in Chicago. The story recounts how Emily was able to make connections between the values she learned as a child living in the country and some of the situations she faced as an adult working in city government.

The Story Begins

It is a bitter, cold day in northern New Hampshire. Frigid winds cut the icy shoreline of the river bank into a jagged edge. It's the kind of day that only the hardiest of folks would venture to meet. Most kids are indoors; the spirited ones argue with overprotective mothers to go outside. Something there is in the piercing cold of New England that calls to certain dispositions. Perhaps it's the opportunity to test one's mettle against the frozen hills and precipitous icicles that shouts the promise of adventure to an active, housebound child.

As the cold bores through her mittens and snow shyly inches its way down the side of her leggings into the space between sock and boot, Emily revels in it all! The icicle she longs to lick is hanging too high from the maple tree in the backyard for her to reach. Behind the barn, near last fall's cache of covered firewood, the battered old wheelbarrow sits, transformed into an interesting ice sculpture—just high enough to provide the boost Emily needs to get the sought-after icicle. As she yanks her stuck mitten from the treasured ice, she discovers a surprising drop of deeply embedded syrup. The presence of syrup in the February ice promises an early spring, with streams to jump across and squirrels to chase—an added boon to a perfect winter day.

One of Emily's favorite pastimes is to lie down in soft snow, slowly moving in rhythm with the passing clouds as though she is high in the sky looking at the world. When she's finished vicariously floating in the clouds, Emily always examines the impression her movements make in the fresh snow. The feeling of having done something important is part of the fun pretending she can climb as high as the eye can see. Today, though, the snow is too hard to make an impression, and the clouds are nowhere to be found. So Emily lies upon the frozen earth and gazes at the cold, unforgiving sky through the naked branches of the maple trees and the gossamer filter of the evergreens.

Emily is ten years old, and already the seeds of understanding are taking root. Her solitary childhood on an isolated farm intensifies an introspective bent and leads to a deep affinity with nature, its beauty, and its fury. She experiences the whole through the diversity of its parts. Fields, streams, and hilltops acquiesce to her demands in the cooperative seasons, providing her with fresh and exciting experiences. As she grows, the stamp of creativity and free expression mark her character. She respects the rules of the forest and listens when her beloved countryside is angry and full of wrath. Emily is attuned to the lessons of nature, learning when and how to graciously retreat. Her friends are the animals of the farm and forest, from the backyard gopher to the woodland lark. Even the crazy loon is Emily's friend. She sees all life as important to the totality of nature. In freedom, vitality, and practical wisdom, Emily comes of age.

The long, solitary days of Emily's country childhood are replete with the kinds of experiences that yield a rich harvest of sustaining values. The lessons of the natural world temper her high-spirited personality, and she learns the value of respecting individual differences, accepting the needs of others without imposing judgment, and maintaining perspective when life takes a scary turn. As she matures, Emily longs for broader horizons and slowly comes to accept that she has to leave the familiar pattern of country life so she can satisfy her budding ambition to contribute something to the world.

Emily attends a small, prestigious undergraduate college in the Midwest, where she is introduced to the prospect of a career in government. After college, she enrolls in graduate school and prepares for public service by earning a master's degree in public administration. Soon after graduation, she is hired as a civil servant for the city of Chicago, where she spends the remainder of her life in public service. Throughout her career, Emily is able to forge a connection between the demands of being a public servant and the lessons learned as a child on the farm.

One day, long after retirement, Emily sits by her apartment window watching bitter, cold winds blow mean off the shores of Lake Michigan. Whitecaps on the ocean lake curl around, like the churlish lips of an angry witch. Most old people are indoors; the spirited ones sit by windows, vicariously braving the howling frenzy of a wintery day. Something there is in the piercing cold of Chicago that calls to certain dispositions. Perhaps it's the opportunity to test one's mettle against remembrances of a life long-lived that whispers its promise of peace to the housebound, elderly person.

Emily winds the blanket tightly around her brittle shoulders and sinks deeply into the cushion of her chair. The pillow is placed at just the right angle between the seat of the chair and its back, allowing her to see the horizon of Lake Michigan. In her mind's eye she gazes beyond the skyline to her childhood farm in New Hampshire. From there, she revisits the campuses on which she earned her bachelor and master's degrees. Smiling as she recalls her youth, Emily allows herself to relive her days as an administrator in her adopted city.

As she recalls many of her career highlights, Emily lingers over certain events that had caused her some concern. There was that time, for example, when she had a problem with frequent absences by a talented young woman on her staff. Emily was tempted to judge her as harshly as the other managers did, until she took the time to have a long conversation with her. Emily learned that she and many other members of the staff were experiencing conflicts between job responsibilities and the demands faced by working parents of small children.

Emily tried to persuade the other managers to support her request to the commissioner to open a day-care center for agency employees. They refused, arguing that she was wasting her time. After careful deliberation, Emily put together a plan that would utilize existing space and solicit retired city employees to voluntarily staff the new day-care center as a continuing contribution to public service. After solving certain legal ramifications of the plan, the commissioner wholeheartedly endorsed it with minor modifications. As a result, both the absentee problem and employee morale improved.

Recollection of the day-care incident takes Emily back to the time on the farm when everyone said the beavers would never build a dam across the northern point of Elk Lake and cause a drought. Well, they did! Emily shivers with dread as she relives the terrible drought that awful summer so many years ago. Never again did the farmers underestimate the lengths to which the beavers would go to meet their needs. Emily sees a connection between the need of the young men and women on her staff to care for their children and the beavers need to care for their community. She wonders if the earlier experience with the beavers was a prelude to her decision to take action in favor of mothers and fathers trying to balance their parental and professional responsibilities. A sigh of satisfaction suffuses her entire being as past and present unite in her memory.

The creeping cold causes Emily to draw her blanket even closer as she recalls the time the entire office attacked Eliot Drew. From the beginning, Eliot was the office pariah because he perceived things differently from the others. He did not see most situations as negative events to be overcome through increased control and strong-armed strategies. To Eliot, problems were opportunities that should be allowed to unfold whenever possible. He took a strong, opposing stand when the team made the decision to storm the cult stronghold in Skokie and free the children held inside. His normally shy, understated demeanor gave way to a brilliant analysis of the psychodynamics being played out inside the cult headquarters. The conviction in his voice, as he tried unsuccessfully to persuade his colleagues to take the time needed to reach a peaceful solution, still resounds in Emily's ear.

Her quivering body is a response not to the cold, but to the anger she still feels at her peers who refused to listen to Eliot's impassioned and well-formulated argument. Both he and Emily, his sole supporter, were first ridiculed and then ignored. The forces of reason overtook the forces of wisdom. The sight of the bullet-ridden bodies of the dead children etched a raw notch in her heart that never quite healed.

Something shattered in Emily that day, and the world was never the same again. As she stared at the blood-soaked floor, her mind receded to the past, to the lake at the far edges of the farm's west meadow. It was a hot, sticky summer afternoon and she remembered imagining that she was swimming down, down, down deep into the waters. The dank darkness frightened her, but still she continued her descent until she was at the bottom of the lake. Emily recalls the end of her reverie that summer day when, as she tried to touch the lake bottom with her fingertips, she felt it give way and knew in horror there was no end to the depths of her descent.

Even after the terrible incident, the others regarded Eliot as too soft. They still preferred to believe the right combination of control and strategy would solve any problem, however complicated. Emily knew they could not accept what she had discovered about the way things can be that fateful summer afternoon at the lake's edge. She always felt that Eliot also approached problems differently because he saw much that the others could not fathom. He possessed a refinement of perception that contrasted sharply with the more conventional views of his colleagues. Emily tried to convince them that his tendency to examine all sides of an issue with patience and quiet determination were strong attributes that contributed to the decision-making capacity of the department. Even with her support, however, the others could not accept a person who was so different from themselves, and Eliot eventually left the agency.

Emily sees a connection between Eliot and the fine swan that appeared on the farm one day. Some said it was a whistling swan, making its way from the Arctic Circle to Mexico. Whatever it was, everyone marveled at its beauty and grace. The exquisite bird lent an air of poise and elegance to the humble farm scene, and was welcomed by all who saw it. All, that is, who were of the human persuasion—for the geese were furious that such a magnificent creature should intrude upon their territory. It was the first swan Emily had ever seen. To her child's mind, the swan was simply a lovelier version of the geese that lived on the farm. She could not understand why they turned against one of their own just because it was more beautiful.

Emily reminisces, keeping the vivid picture of the beautiful swan and the ugly geese clear in her mind. She recognizes the hidden truth in her girlhood ignorance that saw the ugly geese and the beautiful swan as related to one another. How wise of nature, she thinks, providing an opportunity for part of creation to accept what another part lacks in order to make a whole. How unfortunate that such opportunities often go unrecognized. How fortuitous it is when room is allowed for variety and change so that life is enabled to complete itself. With gratitude, Emily remembers how privileged she was to have known the gentle and intelligent Eliot. How fortunate to have had the truth revealed to her as a child on the farm and connect it to the special qualities her friend possessed.

A smile forms across the creases of Emily's face. The fabric of her life is woven from the single thread of childhood. The long, lonely days on the farm were a wonderful gift that taught her the value of paying attention to what lay within herself and not being sidetracked by outside pressures. Emily realizes that until individuals stop reacting to the incessant demands of the outer world, human institutions will not advance. Although she will never see the day when the lessons she learned on the farm would be commonly accepted, she knows it will eventually take place.

Afternoon light blends into the blue grey of dusk as the winter winds subside. Emily's mind begins an even longer journey, far beyond the horizon of Lake Michigan to a place unknown. An artist depicting the scene would paint a picture of an old woman who, while seated by a frosted window wrapped in a blanket, appears to have drifted off into a lasting sleep.

SOME COMMENTS

In the Carus/Suzuki translation that introduces this chapter, Lao-tze tells the reader that those who know others often gain power, but those who know themselves attain the wisdom that supersedes power. In his interpretation of this passage, the translator R. B. Blakney argues that Lao-tze places value on "self-mastery, quietude and acceptance of one's place in the scheme of nature" (Lao-Tzu 1983, 86). Emily's deep connection with the natural world that was forged during her childhood on the farm enabled her to accept those instances in which she would have to accede to the forces of nature and face disappointment. She learned, for example, that she could not have her way during the uncooperative seasons when nature failed to meet her demands.

This important lesson was carried into her professional life. Emily realized that at a certain point after Eliot's impassioned plea, it was as impossible to alter the decision to attack the headquarters in Skokie as it had been to prevent the fierce New England storms of her childhood. The bitter consequences of that decision continued to rankle throughout her life, but did not destroy either her personal or professional relationships. Over the years, Emily managed to maintain her friendship with Eliot, keep her job, and philosophically come to terms with the limitations of her colleagues. She accepted that her peers were as worthy of respect as Eliot. Like the geese in the presence of the swan, they simply failed to see their potential for greatness. Deep in her psyche, Emily perceived the unity of all things.

She knew that when certain events are allowed to unfold without intervention, there is no irreparable tear in the fabric of life because nature's scheme is obeyed. When there is no assertion and force, the integrity of the whole is respected and the Tao is fulfilled. Emily understood that sometimes situations are sufficiently complex to cause a rift among opposing forces. She knew that in such circumstances, a decision not to take action may be preferable. The paradox of nonaction, which in itself is a certain form of action, was not lost on Emily. Nonaction in such instances provides the necessary space for the rift to be mended. The situation in Skokie was one of these instances. Had the team listened to Eliot and not taken action, a peaceful outcome may have resulted and many lives could have been saved.

She also recognized that the scheming of modern, organizational decision making often outsmarts itself. To Emily, it was only natural that the greater the rift among opposing forces, the greater the need for standing back and allowing them to reunite. When there is deep division, no amount of intervention can force what must happen naturally. In her way, Emily understood what it meant to let go and adopt a posture of wu-wei.

The strength of Emily's vision was grounded in her appreciation of silence. Through quiet, reflective times, she gained insight into herself and began to know who she was in the hidden recesses of her psyche. Eventually, Emily discovered that what resided in her was part of everyone else. Silence brought to light the secrets of the Tao. Slowly, she began to see the connective unity everywhere and in everything. As she grew in the wisdom that silence brings, her inner voice guided her and she began to know when to let go and submit to nature's scheme.

The quiet days of New England summers taught Emily how to listen. A curious child quickly learns how to soften the sound of the canoe paddle if she wants to spot the red heron standing guard on the island grasses of the lake. Such a special sighting can add adventure to a long, hot day. The capacity to listen carefully to what others said served Emily well in her professional life. The time she took listening to the young woman who needed child care resulted in action that improved staff morale and organizational efficiency. Eliot's unique perceptions demanded full attention to be grasped. Emily was the only one who understood this and appreciated the special qualities he possessed. Childhood loneliness maturing into adult silence gave birth to an exemplary civil servant!

In his book on the teachings of Chuang Tzu, Thomas Merton argues that the great sage was "not concerned with words and formulas about reality, but with the direct existential grasp of reality in itself" (Merton 1969, 11). Chuang Tzu used parables as well as funny stories and conversations to make his point. We will meet some of his characters later. Like the personalities in the ancient fables, Emily also grasped reality as it truly is. Merton's words so aptly describe Emily that he may well have known her, for she possessed:

> a certain mentality found everywhere in the world, a certain taste for simplicity, for humility, self-effacement, silence, and in general a refusal to take seriously the aggressivity, the ambition, the push, and the self-importance which one must display in order to get along in society.

MAKING CONNECTIONS FROM EAST TO WEST

Parallels can be drawn between the eastern Tao and the western analytical psychology of Carl Jung. Recent scholarship in psychology indicates a broadening of the traditional boundaries of the discipline. For example, the writings of James Hillman and his protégé, Thomas Moore, blend conventional psychological analysis with cultural and mythological traditions. Moore addresses the consciousness that is emerging at the dawn of the twenty-first century in a way that appeals to the general reading public. The positive response to his books is an indication of the changes that seem to be occurring in the psyche of western culture. It is because of the transformation in mainstream scholarship, fostered by writers like Hillman and Moore, that we are able to make connections between the eastern concepts of silence, unity, wu-wei, and western thought.

The inner voice speaks only in the presence of silence. It is there that the truths contained within the psyche are able to break free from what Jung referred to as "the cramp in the conscious mind" (Coward 1985, 36). Without silence, individuals would not be able to look within and discover there is a principle of interconnectedness operating in the universe. When the psyche is allowed to express itself and divulge its secrets, new values come into being. According to Jung, the individual experiences a lessening in the need to control and manipulate everything that happens. The overly developed conscious mind begins to loosen its hold on psychic processes and a kind of peace can envelop the individual.

Jung would argue that in order for peace to enter the human mind, the psyche needs to achieve an integration of its conscious and unconscious aspects. When this occurs, the individual has unearthed the Self and discovered his or her uniqueness. Jung refers to this as the process of individuation, which puts the person in touch with psychic reality. This reality is both conscious and unconscious: the conscious part is that component of the psyche which the individual is aware of, and the unconscious part can be understood only through what Jung calls archetypes, which are symbolic images. The individual who has managed to achieve psychic reality is able to assimilate these images into his or her conscious life and also into "the life that transcends consciousness," becoming in the process, transformed by his higher destiny (Jung 1958a, 11:232–33).

Emily lived a life rich in imagery. She used the symbols of her childhood experiences on the farm to enhance her professional life and gain a deeper understanding of the people and events that marked her career. Possessing an inner knowledge that allowed her to accept the misjudgments of her colleagues while maintaining her own values, she was not embittered by the realities of an imperfect world.

Jung argued that the reality of the Self depends on neither logical deduction, nor conceptual constructs (Jung 1958a, 11:233). Those who attain it have lived a spiritual experience that can occur either within or beyond the conventions of organized religion. Having educated himself in eastern techniques that can lead to self-attainment, Jung felt that the west needed to develop its own counterpart. He called this "active imagination," discussed in greater detail below. Western culture's overemphasis on reason and the intellect has been at the expense of the psyche. The role the unconscious plays in human life was ignored and then dismissed. This caused the western psyche to become divided. Science replaced nature as the guiding force and reason reigned supreme. Modern western thinking became one-sided and the balance between reason and emotion was destroyed (443–44).

This resulted in a psychological split in which individuals repressed the parts of themselves that are irrational. In volume 10 of his *Collected Works*, entitled *Civilization in Transition* (1978a), Jung examined the state of contemporary humanity. Selected parts of this fascinating book should be required reading in all graduate programs which claim to prepare individuals for public life. He writes at length about the terrible results that occur when we deny the cruel and violent parts of ourselves. When we fail to look within, we do not see the underside of our nature and what we are capable of doing to ourselves and one another. Most individuals are locked into the false belief that their behavior is always reasonable and rational. This is simply not true.

Each of us is under the influence of hidden forces that erupt from the unconscious and refuse to go away. We delude ourselves into thinking that the instinctual part of our human nature has disappeared and we can rely upon reason to serve us at all times. This is nonsense and most of us do not even know it. Just think for a moment how often we are involved in a mess that we never intended! Civilization has eroded the integrated psyche of individuals in all cultures. This is not a phenomenon found only in the west. Jung is quite clear on that point. Moreover, he argues that individuals raised in the older eastern cultures are more aware of the hidden and often frightening aspects of the unconscious; consequently, they possess a deeper understanding of human nature than we do and are not as inclined to try to control the unconscious part of the psyche.

Jung feared that control is precisely what the west would try to do if it adopted eastern techniques for gaining inner knowledge. He believed that a more indirect technique for gaining insight into the hidden realms of the psyche was better suited to the sanitized western mentality. Although Jung believed the west has much to learn from the east, its conscious mind has overshadowed the unconscious to such an extent that direct confrontation could be perilous. He writes, "no insight is gained by repressing and controlling the unconscious, and least of all by imitating methods which have grown up under totally different psychological conditions" (Jung 1958b, 11: 876).

Jung worried that the western tendency to emphasize technique over substance would debase the eastern practice of yoga. Metaphysical benefits can be attained only when the contents of the unconscious are somewhat understood by the individual person who practices yoga. Such a person is sufficiently in touch with his or her primitive roots, which become incorporated into the individual's personality. He or she possesses a depth of understanding that allows freedom from attachment to the superficial aspects of life (Jung 1958b, 11:871).

Everything in western society works to discourage the development of this kind of individual. Instead, people are encouraged to focus their attention on what is happening outside themselves. Most individuals are overstimulated by a noisy, demanding culture that has little, if any, respect for silence and introspection. Many of us live our lives as members of what Jung referred to as the "mass." We want to belong, fit in, be comfortable. In the process, we overlook our own authenticity and fail to discover who we really are.

Our history, with its emphasis on science, technology, and reason, has given us a psychological orientation toward the world that differs from the east. Deeply ingrained in our western consciousness is the belief that human beings can achieve almost anything, through the exercise of will. The intellect has become so important to us that we experience a split between faith and knowledge. Control and power are the cornerstone of our belief structure. We have become alienated from our own human nature (Jung 1958b, 11:868). The sad part of this is that most of us are completely unaware of it! We live our lonely, desperate lives convinced that Thoreau's admonition to meditate at the pond does not apply to us. It refers to the person down the street, the manager in the next office, the cousin we could never tolerate, but—good grief, not us!

Emily's Escape

The story of Emily tells us how one individual maintained balance in a culture governed by autonomous intellects. Emily represents a person who was able to overcome the restrictions that our overly rationalistic culture has imposed on us. Her life seems remarkable, given Jung's warning of the harm that can come from living in a society characterized by the preponderance of reason (Jung 1958a, 11:444):

> just as the intellect subjugated the psyche, so also it subjugated Nature and begat on her an age of scientific technology that left less and less room for the natural and irrational man. Thus the foundations were laid for an inner opposition which today threatens the world with chaos. To make the reversal complete, all the powers of the underworld now hide behind reason and intellect, and under the mask of rationalistic ideology.

Often we do not recognize our tendency to retreat from the more imaginative and hidden parts of ourselves. Eliot was perceived as irrational because he saw how misguided the others were with their reliance on control and reason to solve all problems, however mild or severe. The Tao of the east had no place in the mentality of the agency in which Emily and Eliot worked. Through the patience and understanding she learned as a child in the country, Emily was able to achieve a balance between what she knew to be true and what the world preached. As an old woman in the final stages of wisdom, she accepted the world as it is and as she knew it would one day become. Hope was the hallmark of her life.

If eastern meditative techniques were embraced in the west, Jung also worried that individuals might too readily abandon their own best traditions. Lacking the special relationship with the unconscious required of eastern practices, western attempts would be superficial at best. Trying to master eastern methods could lead to rejection of their own cultural roots, and even aggravate the already existing tendency of westerners to avoid introspection. The inevitable preoccupation with technique mentioned earlier could drive the west further away from the inner life. Like the student in Faust, western men and women enamored of eastern practices might turn against science in all its manifestations and become mere imitators of this most profound human experience.

Although he had serious reservations about the adoption of eastern metaphysical techniques, Jung recognized that yoga was beginning to attract followers in the west. He attributed this development to the awakening of intuition in the western psyche. Jung believed that psychology was the means by which western men and women could take the journey within (Coward 1985, 22–23). He taught that one of the most important functions of modern psychology is to provide an understanding of the unconscious, which to the eastern mind represents reality and to the western mind mere fantasy (Jung 1978b, 11:792). This can only be accomplished, however, when there is respect for the processes by which the unconscious releases its magical powers.

The story of Emily exemplifies how a fanciful girl living a lonely life on a remote farm developed a creative approach to her childhood experiences, and how imagination flowered into wisdom in adulthood. The parable implies that Emily was left free to pursue her own psychological approach to the world. This was a great gift in a culture bent on capturing the "jewel that is coveted by all and arouses jealous strife" (Jung 1980, 9:256). Emily wrested the jewel of Self from the grasping hands of a controlling world. As a result, the natural pattern of life—the Tao—was not mere fantasy to her.

Unlike her colleagues, with the exception of Eliot, she was in touch with the deeper part of her nature. Knowledge and faith were not separated in Emily's life. She had little difficulty reconciling inner reality with the demands of the outer world. Emily saw the linkages that connect all things; her world was not compartmentalized into distinct entities. Where her colleagues perceived events as either all good or all bad, Emily saw the play of opposites as a fundamental reality. She accepted that people are neither total saints nor total sinners. Whatever she knew of herself she knew of everyone, for Emily listened and heard the inner voice.

Active Imagination

Let us speculate how Jung might have applied his method of active imagination to Emily. He believed that through symbolism the imagination of the western individual becomes activated, shutting off the conscious mind to a certain extent so new ideas and impressions can come to the surface (Coward 1985, 37). He taught that images from the unconscious, which are called archetypes or patterns of thought, are collectively shared by all human beings. They unite with material that is present in the conscious mind of the individual person so there is a synthesis between the two and the psyche becomes integrated.

Jung based his technique of active imagination on what he learned from his research in dreams. He believed that unconscious material can be elicited through imagination, as well as in dreams. The difference between the two is that the support of the conscious mind is present in active imagination and lacking when the individual is in the dream state (Jung 1973, 8:402–3).

While Jung used active imagination in a therapeutic setting, he knew it could be employed in many other ways. In considering Emily, and how she developed from the child she was to the woman she became, Jung might have added an addendum to her story more fully describing the fateful day when she discovered the underside of the human psyche:

> The summer before she left the farm for college was long and lonely. Emily passed the days pondering the depth of the lake at the far reaches of the west meadow. She became transfixed by the reflection of the old weeping willow tree, whose overarching branches seemed to rise from the murky bottom of the muddied waters. Hour after hour that anticipatory summer, Emily sat at the water's edge gazing into the depths and wondering what lay beneath. She imagined herself taking the plunge and exploring as far in the underwater as she could. Mesmerized, Emily swam side-by-side with the fish and came to feel at home there. Deeper and deeper she swam, until finally Emily knew there was no end to the depths of the lake. What she had discovered would set her apart and remain with her forever. At a tender age, Emily had taken a hero's journey. She would feel its imprint the rest of her life.[1]

This addendum to *Emily's Story*, hypothetically written by Jung, reflects his belief that the journey to the outer reaches of the human psyche is usually undertaken when an individual is in considerable conflict. We can only speculate on what was troubling Emily that summer. Perhaps she knew her life had taken an irreversible turn and she would never live on the farm again. No doubt her introspective nature had provided her with insight that the world beyond childhood pastures could be cruel and violent. Whatever motivated her to delve within and begin the process of her own individuation, the stage was set that summer for the drama that would be enacted at the Skokie stronghold many years later. Emily was prepared to encounter what Jung calls the mythological dragon that stands guard at the gates of the unconscious mind (Jung 1976, 14:756):

> In myths the hero is the one who conquers the dragon, not the one who is devoured by it. And yet both have to deal with the same dragon. Also, he is no hero who never met the dragon, or who, if he once saw it, declared afterwards that he saw nothing. Equally, only one who has risked the fight with the dragon and is not overcome by it wins the hoard, the "treasure hard to attain."

As a genuine hero, Emily remembered the dragon she met that summer day and chose not to deny its existence. Jungian scholar Robert Aziz writes that an encounter with the unconscious, through active imagination, challenges the individual to integrate knowledge gained through the experience with life as it appears every day. Emily is a true hero because she used the information from her experience at the lake to make sense of what happened in Skokie. She sought to accept the totality of the human condition, and it is this sincerity that gave her the strength to conquer the dragon and become a hero. If Emily were less a person, she might have regarded the psychic material she encountered at the lake as insignificant and discounted its value in her own search for Self. By integrating what she experienced consciously and what she knew of the unconscious, Emily transcended the limitations of a purely conscious approach to events and was able to come to terms with all the experiences of her life (Aziz 1990, 26–29).

It is not unreasonable to assume that Emily's presence may have helped Eliot express himself as the authentic and integrated individual he appeared to be in the parable. Aniela Jaffe, in her interesting book *Was C. G. Jung a Mystic?*, makes the point that one who undertakes the process of individuation and discovers the inner self contributes to the "individuation of mankind." Self-understanding shines a light seen by others. Jung referred to this phenomenon as "the real history of the world" (Jaffe 1989, 80–81).

Toward a Synthesis

The hero, in the Jungian sense and also in eastern metaphysics, is the person who has made peace with all aspects of himself or herself. The truly integrated individual does not accept the polarities the external world uses to explain reality. Good and bad, positive and negative, even right and wrong, have little meaning when human nature is understood in its totality. Most westerners repress the irrational impulses that demand to be heard. We live under the illusion that by denying the primitive part of our nature it will disappear. Jung said most individuals fit the description of "one who imagines he actually is only what he cares to know about himself" and can be compared to a "man without a shadow" (Jung 1973, 8:409).

Bereft of the truths contained in the unconscious part of themselves, most people labor under the illusions of the conscious mind. Therefore, they live the misguided lives of men and women who see themselves exactly as they wish to be, not as they truly are. They are exempt from responsibility for the experiences they have. It is always either the government or the other person who causes all the trouble in the world. They are what Jung referred to as the "common man," or the "mass man" (Jung 1973, 8:410).

Jung taught that when individuals decide to assume responsibility for what happens, they begin to examine the heretofore hidden aspects of their psychic nature. The more they reflect, the more they realize the changes they must make to become "healthier, more stable, and more efficient" (Jung 1973, 8:410). Through the process of assimilating the unconscious into the conscious mind, individuals simply become better people and, if they are in government, better public servants.

Jung was emphatic in teaching that the shadow is a part of the life of every human being. It demands to be heard and insists on living within the personality of each person. When its presence is denied, havoc ensues. This is all too evident in the craziness of the modern world. It is the shadow that defines us as human beings and we desperately need to pay heed to its presence in our lives. Jung writes (1938, 93):

> Everyone carries a shadow, and the less it is embodied in the individual's conscious life, the blacker and denser it is. If an inferiority is conscious, one always has a chance to correct it. Furthermore, it is constantly in contact with other interests, so that it is continually subjected to modifications. But if it is repressed and isolated from consciousness, it never gets corrected. It is, moreover, liable to burst forth in a moment of unawareness. At all events, it forms an unconscious snag, blocking our most well-meant intentions.

Thomas Merton provides a reading from Chuang Tzu that is so perfectly suited to what Jung taught and so beautifully written that I have quoted it here in full (Merton 1969, 155):

> There was a man so disturbed by the sight of his own shadow and so displeased with his own footsteps that he determined to get rid of both. The method he hit upon was to run away from them. So he got up and ran. But every time he put his foot down there was another step, while his shadow kept up with him without the slightest difficulty. He attributed his failure to the fact that he was not running fast enough. So he ran faster and faster, without stopping, until he finally dropped dead. He failed to realize that if he merely stepped into the shade, his shadow would vanish, and if he sat down and stayed still, there would be no more footsteps.

The time has come at the dawn of the twenty-first century for humankind of all cultures to step in the shade, shake the hand of its lurking shadow, and enter into partnership.

NOTE

1. The inspiration for this addendum to Emily's story came from an example Jung gave of active imagination as relayed to him by a young artist he treated. The story, originally told by Jung in the "Tavistock Lectures," is repeated by Harold Coward in *Jung and Eastern Thought* (New York: State University of New York Press, 1985, 36).

REFERENCES

Aziz, Robert. 1990. *C. G. Jung's Psychology of Religion and Synchronicity*. Albany: State University of New York Press.

Coward, Harold. 1985. *Jung and Eastern Thought*. New York: State University of New York Press.

Jaffe, Aniela. 1989. *Was C. G. Jung a Mystic?* Einsiedeln, Switzerland: Daimon Verlag.

Jung, Carl G. 1938. *Psychology and Religion*. New York: Yale University Press.

———. 1958a. "A Psychological Approach to the Trinity." In *Psychology and Religion: West and East*. Vol. 11 of *Collected Works*. New York: Pantheon Books for Bollingen Foundation.

———. 1958b. "Yoga and the West." In *Psychology and Religion: West and East*. Vol. 11 of *Collected Works*. New York: Pantheon Books for Bollingen Foundation.

———. 1973. *On the Nature of the Psyche*. Vol. 8 of *Collected Works*. Reprint, Princeton: Princeton University Press.

———. 1976. "The Conjunction." In *Mysterium Coniunctiones*. Vol. 14 of *Collected Works*. Princeton: Princeton University Press.

———. 1978a. *Civilization in Transition*. Vol. 10 of *Collected Works*. 2d ed. 1970. Reprint, Princeton: Princeton University Press.

———. 1978b. "Psychological Commentary on *The Tibetan Book of the Great Liberation*." In *Psychology and the East* and *Psychology and Religion*. Excerpts from Vols. 10, 11, 13, 18 of *Collected Works*. Princeton: Princeton University Press.

———. 1980. "Concerning Rebirth." In *The Archetypes and the Collective Unconscious*. Vol. 9, part 1 of *Collected Works*. 2d ed. 1968. Reprint, Princeton: Princeton University Press.

Lao-tze. 1991. *Tao Teh King*. Translated by Paul Carus and D. T. Suzuki under the title *The Canon of Reason and Virtue*. La Salle: Open Court Publishing Company.

Lao-tzu. 1983. *Tao Te Ching*. Translated by R. B. Blakney under the title *The Way of Life*. New York: Mentor Books.

Merton, Thomas. 1969. *The Way of Chuang Tzu*. New York: New Directions.

Welch, Holmes. 1966. *Taoism, the Parting of the Way*. rev. ed. Boston: Beacon Press.

CHAPTER 5

The Legacy of India: Beyond Thought Toward Silence

One who knows does not talk.
One who talks does not know.
Therefore the sage keeps his
mouth shut and his sense-gates closed. (Lao-tze 1991, 56:1)

A SOLITARY PERSPECTIVE

Aldous Huxley referred to the twentieth century as the Age of Noise (Huxley 1970, 218). When we stop to consider what noise is, we all would probably agree. There are the noises of the city, such as the sound of screaming car horns, screeching taxis, shrieking sirens, groaning jackhammers, gasping buses, and the thump of tires hitting asphalt. There are the noises of the suburbs, such as grinding road equipment, growling construction trucks, whining highway traffic, and maudlin mall "muzak." Whether we live in the city, suburbs, or country, we all are subjected to the omnipresent telephone, with its incessant ringing. While these and the many other unwelcome noises of our modern age distract us, none is as demanding as the sound of the human voice. It not only reverberates in our ear; it commands our attention.

We are constantly assaulted by the noise of televisions and radios. Garish covers of popular magazines call out to us from city newsstands and racks in suburban supermarkets. Much of our culture seems to consist of idle words, designed solely "for the sake of making a distracting noise" (Huxley 1970, 217). Noise, and the confusion it engenders, diverts us from the solitude we need to attend to our experiences and their significance in our lives. While solitary attention to life events is necessary on a daily basis, it is particularly important after a major change has occurred. At such a time, solitude and the silence that it allows can be formidable allies in our attempt to adjust to the changing circumstances. The psychiatrist Anthony Storr has written a provocative book, entitled *Solitude, A Return to the Self* (1989), in which he argues that the western preoccupation with intimate relationships has overshadowed our human need for solitude and the silence it brings. His point is that being alone is as natural to human life as being part of a loving family.

Storr proposes that there are two opposite drives that permeate the lives of all human beings: the drive for attachment to others, and the drive for independence and autonomy. Our society's overvaluation of the drive for attachment keeps us in almost constant interaction with other people, alienating us from ourselves. The drive for autonomy, which leads us to inner knowledge and our own creativity, is sadly neglected. Storr is critical of the psychoanalytic community for its insistence that the validity of the individual lies only in his or her relationships with others. And yet, he argues that many of the greatest thinkers and contributors to society gave little or nothing to particular human beings. In their search for self-fulfillment, they craved solitude and were perceived as selfish and narcissistic (Storr 1989, 13–14).

According to Storr, many individuals who possess major talent enjoy their most profound experiences when they are alone. Their creativity flourishes in the silence of their own company. He suggests that solitude and quiet are needed by all human beings, not just the highly creative (Storr 1989, 15). Each of us has a capacity for creativity which is, after all, simply self-expression. We are constantly expressing ourselves, in the work we do, the relationships we have with others, and the responses we make to situations we experience. We cannot express ourselves creatively if we are unaware of what is really going on inside us. Constant distractions from others, noise, and external time pressures, generate confusion. It is difficult to find silence and attain the peace that brings creativity in such a climate. Yet this is the prevailing condition in most public administration offices today.

So, what do we do? Shrug our shoulders and accept the status quo? Smirk and mutter some obscenity about idealism and the real world? Simply ignore the point just made? Or, do we investigate the deeper meaning of silence in the hope we can attain it and receive the personal benefits it promises? The quotation from Lao-tze that opens this chapter is a fitting place to start answering these rhetorical questions. Evidently, ancient China also had its share of inveterate talkers who expounded on nothing, while the wise remained silent. It is probably a universal human condition—the human voice commands attention, loquacious individuals cause distraction. Their words permeate our existence, making it impossible for solitude and silence to rise above the din.

According to Huxley, most of what we say in an average day is either self-serving, unkind, or silly (Huxley 1970, 217). This overstates the case, but nonetheless, many of the words that fall from the lips of our colleagues, and from our own, fit into one or more of these categories. Particularly offensive is idle talk, which may start off as an attempt to break the ice, but often degenerates into mindless chatter. We seem ill at ease in the presence of others when there is an absence of conversation.

Self-serving and unkind words are not more acceptable than idle chatter, but seem to incriminate the speaker, lowering his or her status as a person of integrity. Such words provide insight into the character of those who speak them, and are so revealing that they weaken the effect they intend to promote. The more insidious enemy in the battle of words is idle talk. It is all around us: in the conference room, on the bus, in the theater, and even in our own homes. One may ask why this is so. I believe we engage in foolish talk because we have a low tolerance for introspection. Quiet and peaceful surroundings tend to upset the western psyche, which is locked in an embrace with noise.

As Chuang Tzu said many years ago, "A dog is not considered a good dog because he is a good barker. A man is not considered a good man because he is a good talker" (Huxley 1970, 218). I wonder how many of us really agree with Chuang Tzu. We seem much impressed with barking dogs that ward off thieves in the night. Likewise, we allow the autocrat at the conference table to engage in a one-sided monologue, while we either feign listening or are genuinely impressed with his or her showmanship. Our age has seen mindlessness raised to an art form by garrulous individuals. We seem to bow to bombastic, overbearing personalities and tolerate the incessantly chattering ones.

Politics is one arena in which self-serving and unkind words seem to pay off. If we were to mention particular political figures who engage in this type of verbal bullying, the list would be excruciatingly long and would cross all ideologies. The same kind of verbal grandiosity is all too common in public agencies. Many readers will have experienced the political appointee, and even the high-ranking civil servant, who finds it necessary to remind everyone within earshot of his or her connections and past accomplishments. These are people whose speech is often self-serving, unkind, or silly.

The Meaning of Silence

The word "silence" has many connotations. If we were to think of the concept as existing along a continuum, we could distinguish degrees of silence. Huxley (1970, 218) argues that there are three:

silence of the mouth, silence of the mind, and silence of the will. To refrain from idle talk is hard; to quiet the gibbering of memory and imagination is much harder; hardest of all is to still the voices of craving and aversion within the will.

We now consider these three degrees of silence in turn, and explore how we may employ each in our daily lives and become better public administrators. A parable follows each discussion.

SILENCE OF THE MOUTH

When we are able to hold our tongue and allow ourselves to withdraw from our own self-centered concerns, we may be able to avoid the petty, self-serving behavior that seems so natural. When our mind is not engaged in what our mouths are saying, we become increasingly observant of our surroundings and can more readily experience our feelings and reactions to what is occurring at any given moment. We can enjoy a heightened sense of consciousness, with our entire being more aware and present in the moment. If we remain still, we may hear the inner voice interpreting what we experience. By listening, we open up to the words of others. This is an opportunity for us to grow in compassion and understanding. The deeper our silence, the more attention we can give to the inner voice. Our intuitive sense awakens.

We spend endless amounts of time, energy, and money trying to understand what is needed for managers to be effective communicators. Our efforts have resulted in a large body of literature and many methods for training individuals in the art of effective leadership. Seminars, training programs, and graduate courses are devoted to this subject. Corporate leaders and government officials alike go to extreme lengths to learn how to communicate with employees. Techniques such as "active listening" promise to transform office relationships from disinterested professionalism to sincere human involvement.[1] Many of these methods attract interest for a limited period of time, and are then just as quickly forgotten.

Why is this the case? Perhaps because, as westerners trained in the rationalist tradition, we are too focused on technique. As a result, we approach our development as leaders on a superficial level. Technique, while helpful, addresses the surface and not the depth of what is needed to elevate behavior from self-centeredness to a genuine concern for the needs of others. Authentic listening goes far beyond keeping one's mouth shut. It transcends the active listening technique of repeating the last words spoken by the person we are trying to understand. It involves closing out all external distractions and going to a place deep within ourselves.

In this place, the mind is quiet and we hear the other person's message through our own inner voice. It is as if the silence speaks to us of shared dreams and fears. The stillness allows us to hear and see how similar we are to one another. It is the place where we experience what psychologists call "empathy." For a moment, we partake in the feelings, thoughts, and attitudes of the other. This experience is not a common occurrence; and yet, western management would have us believe otherwise. Many management trainers are convinced that effective communication techniques are all that is required to reach this point. Perhaps they could learn from the insight of Chuang Tzu, who said that (Merton 1969, 128):

> The ears of all men seem to be alike,
> I detect no difference in them;
> Yet some men are deaf,
> Their ears do not hear.

There is no technique, however sophisticated, that can make a person hear in the way Chuang Tzu means. For he talks of the differences between us as being not of nature, but rather of capacity (Merton 1969, 128). The inner voice can be heard in each of us, provided we still our quivering tongues, quiet our restless minds, and subdue our overpowering wills. When we make the decision to genuinely communicate, we discover an unlimited capacity to listen, empathize, and experience true leadership. Individuals who are at this stage of human advancement have learned an ancient truth that goes back to the time when Plutarch taught his followers, "We learn silence from the gods, speech from men" (Eliade 1987, 13:323).

Jung taught that we learn philosophy from the gods. He compared Indian religion to a pagoda in which the gods climb over one another like ants, from the elephants carved on the base to the abstract lotus which crowns the top of the building. In the long run the gods become philosophical concepts (Jung 1978, 10:1003). The Vedas, or verses of ancient India, were a poetic tribute to the gods who resided in everything. Ingrained in the soul of India is a craving for meaning beyond the finite world. The deities who populate its religion may yield philosophical insights that help us deal with silence and listening.

The following parable is based upon a story told by Jack Kornfield in his book, entitled *A Path with a Heart* (1993). Dr. Kornfield was trained as a clinical psychologist, and is responsible for introducing Theraveda Buddhist ideas to western society. He is among a growing number of educators who believe that eastern and western philosophical traditions can come together to create a richer and more substantive human experience. This story is not a fable—it is about a real man who was responsible for the remarkable land reform movement that occurred in India after the death of Gandhi. It shows us the power and strength we gain when we truly listen to what others say. Authentic listening requires a quieting of our own speech, an opening of our heart, and a seeking after truth. For this is the path to simplicity and compassion; the hallmarks of genuine leadership.

The man in the story was Gandhi's disciple and heir apparent. As a devout Indian, he was familiar with Sanskrit literature, such as the great Hindu epic, the *Mahabarata*. In telling his story, I have taken the liberty of speculating on how the protagonist may have thought and felt after the death of his master, when he was faced with overwhelming responsibility. To this end, the reader is introduced to the "Bhagavad Gita," which is a part of the *Mahabarata*. The Gita is a poem consisting of a long dialogue in which a young man named Arjuna, son of one of the two warring factions in a large tribal family, finds himself in his chariot in the presence of the god Krishna, a very popular Hindu deity. Arjuna, crushed by the sight of the blood being spilled, throws down his arms and beseeches Krishna for answers to the horrors of the fratricidal war (Ramacharaka 1930, 11–16). The most central themes of the Gita are Light, Love, and Life. Arjuna is helped in his effort to attain these virtues by Krishna. Those quotations that are referenced are taken from the "Bhagavad Gita," as translated by Juan Mascaro.

Vinoba Bhave's Journey

It was stiflingly hot the afternoon that Vinoba made his decision. The parched soil sacrificed what moisture remained as an offering to the fiery rays of the demanding sun. As perspiration seared the deep grooves of his tanned face, Vinoba reflected on much that he had learned from Gandhi. As the master's closest disciple, he knew Gandhi better than anyone, and understood the depth and goodness of the man as no other person could. When the council asked Vinoba to lead a national conference for the purpose of establishing a plan to continue Gandhi's work, he was totally set against it. After all, he reasoned, "the past is over and cannot be resurrected, for the master is dead!"

That evening, secure in his decision not to lead the meeting, Vinoba opened the Gita and happened upon the section in which Arjuna asks Krishna to explain the meaning of renunciation and surrender. Vinoba began to question his decision when he read the familiar words, "And a man should not abandon his work, even if he cannot achieve it in full perfection; because in all work there may be imperfection, even as in all fire there is smoke" (Mascaro 1980, 18.48). Suddenly his mind was illuminated with the knowledge that he had succumbed to his own ego's demand for perfection. He had lost his capacity not to judge, and mistakenly compared himself to Gandhi. Smiling at his foolishness, Vinoba welcomed the gentle recrimination he permitted himself. He felt gratitude for the wise teachings and great secrets of living he was privileged to learn.

Free from the burden of self-aggrandizement, Vinoba prepared for the evening's rest. The peace that comes from knowledge and acceptance of the Self blanketed him in a sound sleep. Dawn arrived the following morning upon the heels of departing rain clouds which moistened the thirsty soil of India. Vinoba felt joyful and immediately called the council together for an announcement. The others were relieved to hear he had changed his mind about leading the conference. They were even pleased to accept the one condition he made, because it reminded them of what Gandhi might have done. Vinoba asked them to postpone the gathering for six months so he could walk from his home to the conference site. In the tradition of his teacher, he wanted to hear what the people had to say, and sincerely listen to their words so he could see into their hearts.

Vinoba's home was far away from the meeting place, and his journey took him halfway across India. Being the poor country it is, he visited many impoverished villages, where he met, advised, and listened to the people. The lives they led were meager and hard, with barely enough food to eat. In village after village, the people complained of hunger. Scrawny children dangled from the pointed knees of malnourished mothers. In one of the villages early in his travels, Vinoba asked the people why they did not grow their own food, and learned they were untouchables with no land of their own. After a moment's pause, he assured them that upon his return to Delhi, he would contact Prime Minister Nehru and begin the process of passing legislation to redistribute land in poor villages so the people could become self-sufficient in food production.

While sitting in silence that evening, Vinoba had a disturbing insight. He realized that his ego had lied to him again and led him astray. His sleepless night turned to morning and the final visit with the villagers to whom he promised so much. Vinoba wondered what to say. Expectant and happier faces than he had seen in many weeks greeted him as he approached the village center. Slowly, and as kindly as he could, Vinoba told the villagers that the hopes he gave them the previous day were ill-spoken. He explained that many years would go by before laws redistributing the land could be passed. He chronicled the complicated process by which the land-grant monies would eventually filter down to the village. Carefully and sensitively, Vinoba told the people there would be little, if any, land left for them and their families at the end.

As he looked upon their sad, dark eyes and witnessed their despair, Vinoba's heart sank and a feeling of heaviness almost overtook him. Injustice and the ways of the world troubled him, as it does all those who seek truth and change. His anger at the system edged toward compassion, as he recalled long discussions with Gandhi regarding the power of peace over violence. Suddenly, Vinoba felt the steady stare of dozens of eyes snapping him out of his reverie. As he met their gaze, the words of the Gita sounded in his ears and he knew what he had to do. "Think thou also of thy duty and do not waver. There is no greater good for a warrior than to fight in a righteous war" (Mascaro 1980, 2.31). Vinoba, through a firm but peaceful demeanor, would carry out the tradition of his teacher and wage a war of peace against the hunger of India's poor. Upon reflection, he felt secure that he'd come up with a way of providing land to the poorest of villages.

As he started to rise and continue on his journey across the country, he heard a loud voice asking him how much land the people needed. It belonged to a wealthy landowner, who was moved by Vinoba's honesty and compassion. Quickly multiplying the five acres required to provide food for each of the sixteen untouchable families in the village, Vinoba responded, "eighty acres." The landowner agreed to release the land, and the people cheered. Undaunted by the offer, Vinoba told the man to speak to his heirs that evening so he could be sure he was not violating the wishes of his family by giving away what belonged to them. As he prepared for sleep the last night of his extended stay in the village, Vinoba silently reflected on the hope he felt for India's forgotten people.

Morning rose calm and pink, with the promise of sun and smiles. The wealthy landowner was waiting for Vinoba with good news, which quickly spread among the forlorn families so desperately in need of help. As he passed from one village to another on his way to the conference, Vinoba relayed the tale of the good and generous man who made a gift of his fortune to those in need. By the time Vinoba reached his destination, more than 2,200 acres had been released to impoverished families throughout the country. Over the next fourteen years, Vinoba and many others inspired by his tenacity, walked through India relaying the impressive story of one family's generosity. As a result, more than ten million acres of land were turned over to poor families without government intervention!

One cool evening, long after the hot sun nestled behind the horizon, Vinoba sat reading the Gita. He came across a verse in which Krishna speaks to Arjuna of the work that one carries out in a lifetime. "The man who in his work finds silence, and who sees that silence is work, this man in truth sees the light and in all his work finds peace." Recalling the great land reform movement that he started, Vinoba raised his eyes upward in gratitude to Gandhi for teaching him the importance of silence. He gave thanks for the opportunities that enabled him to learn how to find the quiet place within himself while in the presence of others. Vinoba chuckled as he recalled how at times it had been difficult not to speak, but turn inward where answers reside. In his musings, he thought it quite remarkable how silence and introspection prepared him to listen to the needs of the people. With humility, Vinoba accepted his uncanny capacity to hear beyond the spoken word. He knew that through his work, he had captured the light and attained peace at last.

Some Comments

On two separate occasions, Vinoba Bhave came face-to-face with his demanding ego. The first occurred when he knew he could never measure up to Gandhi and refused the offer to lead. The second happened when he promised to bring about legislation that would lead to land redistribution. Later, upon silent reflection, Vinoba realized his words betrayed a need for self-promotion. He knew he had listened halfheartedly to the council and the poor people in the village. The council was not asking him to be perfect, and the people were not asking for political maneuvering. Vinoba's own words shut him off from the real meaning of what was being said by the others. His powers of observation, presence in the moment, and openness were overshadowed by the sound of his own voice. Vinoba knew that when the mouth is speaking, the ego is rarely far behind. The walk across India gave him an opportunity to be solitary and prepare himself for the difficult role that lay ahead. It also provided an opportunity for him to grow in compassion and understanding as he listened to the people.

From this story, we can learn to question our own motives when we reflect upon the decisions we make. For example, is our ego influencing us when we decide not to support a colleague who is right? Emily must have asked herself this question when she took Eliot's side in the deliberations over what to do about the situation in Skokie. The unpopular position made her look foolish to her colleagues. When the outcome supported Eliot's prediction, Emily's ego probably asserted itself again. She had to wrestle with the instinctive desire to remind everyone that she was right.

Public administrators interact with a variety of people every day. Many of these individuals are high-powered and ego-driven. Examples include: elected politicians, political appointees, chief executive officers of regulated industries, and members of the media eager for a story. The temptation is great for career civil servants to flex their ego muscles. The dynamics of these interactions are sometimes biased toward incessant conversation and one-upmanship. As a result, competing egos dance to the tune spoken at any given moment. Public administrators can grow in compassion and understanding. We do not need to follow the spiritual path of Gandhi or Vinoba Bhave to do so. Simple awareness of our own need to be recognized will go a long way toward quieting the mouth, opening the mind, and engaging the heart.

SILENCE OF THE MIND

When we decide to listen, rather than follow the western tendency to run off at the mouth, we begin the process of quieting our mind. Our perceptions are different when we are quiet; we are able to see those aspects of the world we ignore when our attention is on ourselves and what we are saying. The oft-heard expression, "take the time to smell the flowers," is an indication that we recognize this simple fact of life.

Stillness heightens awareness of our surroundings and enables us to be more open to what is happening around us. Perhaps we would see problems

sooner if we simply watched and listened to others. Potential conflict between two individuals can be observed easily in the way they interact. By
quietly observing how people speak to one another, their manner of ap-
proaching difficult situations, and how they resolve problems, public administrators can gain an understanding of how their office functions.

Good administrators realize that leadership requires constant mediation
between what is occurring in the outside world and what their inner voice
is saying. We must do more than attend to the outside world and solve
problems. We must do more than jump in and either make quick judgments
as to what the problem is or "take the bull by the horns." Silence, reflection,
and the composure they bring are simply not high on the list of American
values. We snidely smirk when it is suggested that we slow down, take some
time, and quietly appreciate the world around us. Our minds race at tremendous speed, making judgments, applying criteria, balancing alternatives,
and distancing us from ourselves. A quiet mind affords the opportunity of
examining what we observe in light of our own feelings and behaviors so
we have a greater chance of perceiving a situation accurately. Hidden in the
least likely places are the treasures of leadership.

When someone asks us to "smell the flowers," we respond that we are
too busy and must wait until we are on vacation or at rest to enjoy the finer
things in the world. Those moments when we stand atop a mountain or at
water's edge, we feel a stirring within. At times like this, we are most in
touch with who we really are, and we see things clearly. If we allow it, the
touch of the poet that resides in each of us can open our eyes to the presence
of beauty and practical wisdom. They come into our field of vision only
when we are quiet enough to see them.

Elevated Thinking

When we are silent, we elevate our thinking and become open to ideas
and realities we were unable to experience when immersed in the vagaries
of a busy mind. Appreciation of silence is part of the western literary tradition that we have ignored in the chaos of post-industrial materialism.
Through the poetry of John Keats and William Wordsworth, we see how
eastern and western thinking can complement one another. The poets sing
of the joy found in both the outer and inner worlds. Attending to the outer
world in his poem, *Ode on a Grecian Urn*, Keats rediscovered the perfection
of beauty that immortalized the inner spirit of ancient Greece. "Beauty is
truth, truth beauty—that is all ye know on earth, and all ye need to know"
(Bronson et al. 1954, 284; Mascaro 1980, 10). Like Keats, we too can quietly
observe the outer world. By attending to our surroundings and the people
we work with every day, we open ourselves to the beauty that resides in
truth.

Wordsworth found the sanctity of the inner world symbolized in his own thoughts as expressed in *Tintern Abbey*, thereby giving us a taste of the spirit of India. "And the round ocean and the living air, and the blue sky, and in the mind of man: a motion and a spirit, that impels all thinking things, all objects of all thought, and rolls through all things" (Bronson et al. 1954, 177; Mascaro 1980, 11). By listening to the inner voice and heeding its message, we begin to appreciate the connections that define the universe.

Wordsworth's poetry can inspire us to quiet our mind, and through silence see more deeply into the meaning of things. Connections we missed before suddenly become clearer, and we realize that what we experience is not unique. Inner and outer realities unite in the stillness of our inner selves, and the world becomes whole again. Silence does not come cheaply. It demands an investment of time, energy, and thought. If this investment is made by individual public administrators, the field will be in a good position to meet the challenges of organizational renewal and technological development that it faces in the twenty-first century.

The Lessons of India

As we approach the end of the twentieth century, our western culture has become increasingly interested in the practices of the east, particularly meditation as taught by the great yogis of India. While this book is not intended to promote any particular technique for personal reflection, we can gain insight from the teachings of these ancient masters. Approximately 2,300 years before the time of Confucius, Socrates, and Buddha, the first philosophical work was created. It was called *Instructions of Ptah-hotep* and dates back to 2800 B.C. Ptah-hotep lived in the land of Egypt in the fifth dynasty. As a governor and prime minister to the king, he held a position of high visibility and wielded considerable power throughout his career. Upon his retirement, Ptah-hotep decided to leave a legacy of wisdom to his son. The following is an excerpt of his instructions (Durant 1954, 194):

> Live, therefore, in the house of kindliness, and men shall come and give gifts of themselves. . . . Beware of making enmity by thy words. . . . Over step not the truth, neither repeat that which any man, be he prince or peasant, saith in opening the heart; it is abhorrent to the soul. . . . Silence is more profitable to thee than abundance of speech. . . . It is a foolish thing to speak on every kind of work. . . . If thou be powerful make thyself to be honored for knowledge and for gentleness. . . . Beware of interruption, and of answering words with heat; put it from thee, control thyself.

Ptah-hotep would be considered a wise man by any standards. His admonitions to his son are as relevant at the end of the twentieth century as they were in antiquity. We have no way of knowing how, if at all, they influenced the behavior of his son. But we do have insight into the difficulties that a modern individual would have applying his words today. It would be no easier for a member of the Federal Senior Executive Service, whose budget is being cut, to respond kindly to an analyst at the Office of Management and Budget, than it would be for a program director to remain unperturbed when testifying before a state legislative body determined to expose agency inefficiency. Both administrators may be tempted to overstep the truth and speak beyond the facts to receive what they perceive to be their fair share of the budgetary pie. The system of incrementalism underlying American public administration makes it extremely difficult to live the truth according to Ptah-hotep's wise counsel. In a world of "dog-eat-dog," we can easily become grasping rather than gentle, rude rather than respectful, arrogant rather than humble, and garrulous rather than silent.

India has always seriously addressed the great mysteries of life through a mixture of religious and philosophical ideas. Between 1000 and 500 B.C., its oldest philosophical insights into eternal truth were formed. They were based on neither dogma nor theology, but rather on the direct experience of ancient seers. They are found in the Vedas, or verses, and their authors are anonymous. (Prabhavananda and Manchester 1957, 9). Perhaps the most known of the Vedas in the west is the *Upanishads*, about which the German philosopher Schopenhauer wrote, "there is no study so beneficial and so elevating as that of the *Upanishads*. It has been the solace of my life—it will be the solace of my death" (Durant 1954, 410).[2] With the exception of the teachings of Ptah-hotep, these verses are the first philosophical and psychological attempt to understand the human mind and the world in which it exists.

The teachings in the ancient texts of India provide entree to Huxley's second metaphorical gate, which he refers to as the gateway to human psychology—the place where action and morality intersect. We enter this gate when we wish to live by Ptah-hotep's words. The member of the Federal Senior Executive Service and the program director can choose to open this gate and respond with kindness and honesty when challenged. The decision to take the high road can lead to disappointment, but as Robert Frost said, it can make all the difference.

Bridge Building[3]

An attempt to connect eastern and western thought by examining the similarities between the philosophical beliefs of Shankara and the eighteenth-century philosopher Immanuel Kant was made by Will Durant in his voluminous *The Story of Civilization*. While disclaiming an intention to establish a causal relationship between the ideas of the two philosophers, Durant was impressed at the similarity of their views (Durant 1954, 551n). Shankara, who wrote commentaries based upon his study of the *Upanishads*, lived in the eighth century. His ideas formed the basis of the Vedanta system of philosophy, which rose to a position of intellectual prominence in the country.

Predating Saint Thomas Aquinas, Shankara tried to prove the teachings in the *Upanishads* through experience and reason. Unlike Aquinas, however, he equated reason to a lawyer who, through argumentation, can show beyond doubt whatever he or she wishes. Therefore, he concluded that reason cannot provide unbiased answers to the mysteries of the universe. What we need is not the logic of reason so much as a cleansing and deepening discipline of the soul. This, perhaps, has been the secret of all profound education (Durant 1954, 547).

According to Shankara, we must begin by developing insight; for only insight can penetrate through temporal reality and grasp eternal meaning. The second step is to observe and think about the world around us; for it is through inquiry and thought that understanding comes. Thirdly, we must practice self-restraint and become tranquil; for it is through silence and patience that we overcome the temptations of the physical and material world. Finally, we must fervently seek "moksha," or freedom from ignorance; for it is through true knowledge and self-transcendence that we discover the world as a unified whole, different from what it appears to be (Durant 1954, 547). Shankara's contribution to Vedantic philosophy in the eighth century was to India what Chu Hsi's contribution to Confucianism in the twelfth century was to China, and Aquinas' contribution to Scholasticism in the thirteenth century was to Europe. Each of these philosophies was woven into the political and intellectual fabric of their respective cultures.

Lest the reader think the philosophical views of India are too esoteric for the western tradition to absorb and accept, let us join Durant and look at the views of both Kant and Shankara to see if we can find a connection between eastern and western ideas.

Kant recognized that all knowledge comes from our senses, which are bound by the constraints of time and space. Since we can never separate ourselves from what we experience with our senses, objective knowledge is impossible; the most we can learn is the world as it appears to be. However, because it exists in time and space, the world is always changing. We can know only what our senses tell us and never the foundation of experience. The appearances we experience through our senses are called "phenomena." The foundation upon which they rest are not known to us and are called "noumena."

Shankara, like Kant, believed that because the phenomena we experience are part of the material world which is constantly changing, they cannot be the foundation of reality. The Indian concept of "maya" teaches that since we experience only the appearances of a real world, we live in ignorance. Our perceptions constitute the world we experience, not an objective reality that lies outside ourselves (Durant 1954, 547–49). What is the foundation of reality, if it is not what we can see, touch, hear, smell, and experience?

To Shankara there is no personal God, but there is the Atman or "the underlying life which we feel in ourselves when we forget space and time, cause and change . . . the very essence and reality of us . . . which we share with all selves and things, and which undivided and omnipresent, is identical with Brahman, God (Durant 1954, 548).[4] To become immersed in the oneness of the ultimate reality is, to Shankara, the goal of philosophy, for it contains the "timeless and secret essence of the world" (549).

Kant argued that metaphysical speculation could never prove the existence of God. He believed that such an effort is attributable solely to reason. Furthermore, there is nothing we can experience through the senses that will confirm this idea. In other words, because the existence of God cannot be empirically supported, it is beyond our capacity to know and is therefore mere speculation (Magill 1990, 330).[5] While Kant did not see Shankara's impersonal God as the essence of the world, he was concerned about ethical and moral parameters of behavior. To solve the dilemma of behavior in a godless world, Kant turned toward reason. He argued that only goodwill, which is the same thing as rational will, is unconditionally good. Each person is duty-bound to act according to the dictates of goodwill, which include obedience to moral law. The law, which he called the "categorical imperative," should be universally applied. It states that we must always behave in a way that we can expect of others in a similar situation. In addition, we must never treat any human being as a means to an end (336–37).[6]

Although we have barely scratched the surface of Indian metaphysics by examining Shankara's teachings, we have been able to make a connection with Kantian philosophy. Can we use them in public administration? Can we acquire their deeper meanings and aspire to a more elevated life? In times past, those who sought wisdom and a higher form of living took to the mountains, where they devoted their lives to silent meditation. They were the holy men of the east and were revered, but rarely imitated. They were ascetics, who lived lives of quiet contemplation and self-denial. A great body of literature exists that expounds their discoveries and wondrous mystical experiences. They were different from their peers in the west, in that their focus was neither a single God nor doctrine. Rather, they turned their attention inward and discovered many things. Their teachings have begun to make their way into western thinking, and some of our scientists are held in thrall with many of the ancient ideas of India. In a later chapter we will discuss a conversation between the Indian philosopher Krishnamurti and the physicist David Bohm.

We cannot, of course, embark on a holy man's retreat to the hills. But, as responsible public administrators, we may simply wish to become more aware of ourselves, our colleagues, and the world in which we live. Rather than looking for a religious or mystical experience, we can look to becoming psychologically more conscious in the practice of our profession. Eastern ideas, in conjunction with our western tradition, can provide a philosophy of administration that will enable us to grow and develop as individual human beings, as well as individual public administrators. To do so, we must practice silence of the mind. Through the portals of our silent mind, we can discover the impersonal force that Shankara taught exists in each of us, and the moral goodness that Kant considered a necessary condition of life.

A Simple Conversation

There are 108 *Upanishads* in existence. Shankara authenticated sixteen of them, and wrote commentaries on ten. These are considered to be the principal *Upanishads*. There is no logic in their form, and they are written with attention to the whole of the teaching rather than isolated portions. The *Upanishads* are believed to be the highest authority in Indian metaphysics. Each of the ten has a different name (Prabhavananda and Manchester 1957, 10–11). One, called the Brihadaranyaka, is concerned with the individual discovering his or her inner self. The person who succeeds in doing this is in touch with the impersonal force; the Brahmin, of which Shankara speaks. The following parable is a verbatim excerpt from the Brihadaranyaka. It records a conversation between Janaka, the king of Videha, and Yagnavalkya, a sage who has embarked on a journey toward self-discovery so that he might see the unity of all things.

The discussion began on a day when Yagnavalkya came to the court to visit with King Janaka. Upon welcoming his visitor, the king asked him a question (Prabhavananda and Manchester 1957, 103–4).

Janaka: Yagnavalkya, what serves as the light for man?

Yagnavalkya: The light of the sun, Your Majesty; for by the light of the sun man sits, goes out, does his work, and returns home.

Janaka: True indeed, Yagnavalkya. But when the sun has set, what serves then as his light?

Yagnavalkya: The moon is then his light.

Janaka: When the sun has set, O Yagnavalkya, and the moon has set, what serves then as his light?

Yagnavalkya: The fire is then his light.

Janaka: When the sun has set, O Yagnavalkya, and the moon has set, and the fire has gone out, what serves then as his light?

Yagnavalkya: Sound is then his light; for with sound alone as his light, man sits, goes out, does his work, and returns home. Even though he cannot see his own hand, yet when he hears a sound he moves towards it.

Janaka: True indeed, O Yagnavalkya. When the sun has set, and the moon has set, and the fire has gone out, and no sound is heard, what serves then as his light?

Yagnavalkya: The Self indeed is his light; for by the light of the Self man sits, moves about, does his work, and when his work is done, rests.

Janaka: Who is that self?

Yagnavalkya: The self-luminous being who dwells within the lotus of the heart, surrounded by the senses and sense organs, and who is the light of the intellect, is that Self.

SILENCE OF THE WILL

Sit for a moment and quietly observe your thoughts. Before long, you may become uncomfortable with the realization that your mind is racing from one unconnected thought to another. Now try to control your mind, and direct it to proceed in a pattern of thought that conforms to your wishes. Soon you will find that this requires considerable focus. Once concentration is broken, the mind reverts to its aimless wandering. It appears to be controlled by a will beyond you, that must be constantly suppressed if you are to remain in charge of your own thoughts. Even when you are in control, unwelcome thoughts will creep in and divert you from rational thinking. This can be a disconcerting experiment, because it shows how undisciplined our mind really is. It is one of the reasons we tend to shy away from silent reflection. It is easier and more comfortable if we do not confront our wandering mind, and instead create increasingly noisy and hectic lives.

Discipline of the mind enjoys a rich tradition in eastern culture and is beginning to gain acceptance in the west. There are many ways this can be accomplished. We do not need to adopt eastern techniques, which are considered inappropriate for the west by some psychologists, including Carl Jung. Whichever method we employ to achieve a quiet mind must involve silent reflection, so we hear the inner voice that eastern philosophy values so highly. "When we touch beneath all the busyness of thought, we discover a sweet healing silence, an inherent peacefulness in each of us, a goodness of heart, strength, and wholeness that is our birthright. This basic goodness is sometimes called our original nature, or Buddha nature" (Kornfield 1993, 50).

We see in these words how silence can lead us to experience Shankara's teachings about the foundation of life and the true reality which we share with all things. Silence makes us aware of the essential goodness, which Kant described as residing in our rational will. The realization that we are basically good and all things in the world are connected, enables us to go forth and live ethical and moral lives. However, the further we go into the depths of our being, the more we see the totality of what we are. All is not golden in the hidden recesses of the human psyche, and it would be misleading to suggest that it is. In fact, it is the very discovery of the more unsavory aspects of ourselves that provides insight. We become more aware of our own limitations and how we need to change.

The journey within enables us to accept the totality of who we are—the negative, as well as the positive aspects of our character. We grow in our ability to understand the weaknesses of others when we meet our own face-to-face. Through silence and introspection, we seem to become better people. As prospectors panning for gold, we must sift through the sludge and stone of our lesser self before we find the "jewel that is coveted by all" (Jung 1980, 9:256). The final discovery of Shankara's "secret essence of the world" and Kant's "goodwill" yields the hero self about whom Jung writes.

Those who decide to take the journey toward self-knowledge need to be prepared for the perils it imposes. The French poststructuralist Georges Bataille (1988) wrote of his inner experience that he vacillated along a continuum from supreme joy to dreadful despair. Familiar with the eastern practice of yoga, he found it too pedantic and ascetic for him. Instead, Bataille focused on the concept of silence and wrote, "Silence is given in the sick delectation of the heart" (16). His message is simply this, the choice of silence is the choice of self-knowledge. As lonely and revealing as his journey was, Bataille was able to say that "Silence is itself a pinnacle and better yet, the saint of all saints" (68).

A commitment to introspection can bestow on an individual a subdued mind and disciplined will, which understand the Self in which they reside. This understanding is the wisdom that puts us in touch with other human beings who, after all, are part of the same impersonal force and goodwill as we are. When we truly understand what this means, we have gone beyond mere cognition. All the books in the world cannot supply this kind of knowledge, for it transcends intellectual understanding. Those who wish to attain the wisdom that self-knowledge promises must do a revolutionary thing— forgo the doubt that permeates our culture and engage in "silent grace" (Jung 1980, 9:237).

The following parable is based upon a lesson contained in the *Upanishad*, known as Chandogya (Prabhavananda and Manchester 1957, 71–72). It is about a student named Narada, who approaches Sanatkumara asking to be accepted as his pupil. The story begins when Sanatkumara questions the boy as to what he has studied.

A Lesson Learned

Narada tried to hide his frustration as he answered Sanatkumara's inquiry, because he feared the master would not accept him as his student if he appeared too nervous. He recited his studies in art, science, music, and philosophy with a steady voice and calm demeanor. It was when Sanatkumara asked why he wanted his help that Narada lost his composure. Before he could stop himself, he blurted out his sense of failure at not being able to attain inner peace. Narada admitted that because he had not been able to achieve self-knowledge, he felt his life was hopeless and that he would never know the truth of anything. Close to tears, he beseeched the master to help him.

Sanatkumara took pity on the boy. With kindness in his voice, he said, "What you have read, my son, is only name. When you meditate in silent reflection, focus your attention on name as Self." Narada, a persistent lad and anxious to advance, asked his new master, "Is there anything higher than name?" Sanatkumara replied, "Speech is higher than name. For if there were no speech, we would have no branches of learning. We would not be guided as to what is right and wrong, good and bad, true and untrue. When you meditate in silent reflection, focus your attention on speech as Self."

Feeling more secure in his position with the master, Narada pursued his line of questioning, "Dear master, is there anything higher than speech?" Sanatkumara looked deeply into the eyes of his new student, convinced he had chosen wisely. Such dedication and commitment were rare in a young man, and he would do all he could to help him. "Mind is higher than speech. As a closed fist holds two figs, or two dates, or two kiwi, so does mind hold name and speech. If you think in your mind to perform an act of kindness, you do it; if you think in your mind to be fair in your judgments, you do it; if you think in your mind to provide for your family, you do it. Mind is the inner key to the Self. When you meditate in silent reflection, focus your attention on mind as Self."

Narada was elated at having finally found a master who knew the path leading to the inner voice. With his customary persistence, he asked, "Sir, is there anything higher than mind?" Sanatkumara replied, "Will is higher than mind. For it embraces mind, speech, and name. When you will, you use your mind and its thoughts; when you engage your mind, you use speech and its words; when you speak words, you use names to express what you mean. All these are contained in will. When you meditate in silent reflection, focus your attention on will as Self."

In wonderment at what he was hearing, Narada continued to question the master, "Dear master, is there anything higher than will?" Sanatkumara, impressed with the depth of Narada's probe, decided to teach him the subtleties of the journey he was eager to take. "Discriminating will is higher than will. When you reach this stage of self-knowledge, you begin to look at your actions in the past and become aware of what you may expect of yourself in the future. Through analyzing your actions, you attain self-discrimination. Your will now leads you to right action in the present. When you meditate in silent reflection, focus your attention on discriminating will as Self."

Narada then asked his teacher if there was anything higher than discriminating will. The master replied, "Concentration is higher than discriminating will. When you are able to achieve full concentration, you will reach greatness. Common gossip, quarreling, and petty concerns will no longer tempt you. When you meditate in silent reflection, focus your attention on concentration as Self."

Finally, Narada asked Sanatkumara if there was anything higher than concentration. He was told, "Insight is higher than concentration. All branches of learning depend upon insight for knowledge. Through insight, you know right from wrong, good from bad, truth from what is false. Insight provides understanding of the world. When you meditate in silent reflection, focus your attention on insight as Self."

Through the teachings of Sanatkumara, Narada learned that knowledge of the Self is how we arrive at the truth of our experiences. He discovered this knowledge can only come from silent reflection. After many years of quiet contemplation, Narada ultimately reached his goal. He knew who he was and fully accepted his responsibility in the world. He was widely sought after by all who knew him, for his counsel and judgment were highly valued. The boy who was well versed in the arts and sciences of his time became a wise man, trained in the discipline of his mind.

Emily and Narada

We can see parallels between Emily and Narada. Throughout her life, Emily was able to focus her attention and correctly perceive what was happening. She attended to *speech* when she supported Eliot's proposal regarding the Skokie incident, and to *mind* when she refused to accept her peers' disapproval of Eliot. She attended to *will* when she continued to try to convince the others that Eliot's patience and deliberation were valuable qualities, and to *concentration* when she persisted in her efforts to obtain approval for the day-care center. She was not dissuaded by the negative reactions of the others, who told her she was wasting her time.

Emily's insight enabled her to distinguish between what was right and wrong. Both Emily and Narada valued the silence that is necessary for self-reflection. Wisdom is the gift that comes from having a quiet mind. Through their awareness of Self and the insight that knowledge brings, they were able to perceive the truth that lay at the core of their experiences.

NOTES

1. The following references may be helpful for those interested in learning more about "active listening"; Kenneth Kaye, "The Art of Listening," *HR Focus* 71 (October 1994): 24; W. J. Orlikowski and J. Yates, Genre Repertoire: Structuring of Communicative Practices in Organization, *Administrative Science Quarterly* 39 (December 1994): 541.; Andrew E. Schwartz, The Importance of Listening: It Can't be Stressed Enough . . . ," *Supervisory Management* 36 (July 1991): 7.; and Patricia Slizewski, Tips for Active Listening, *HR Focus* 2 (May 1995): 7.

2. Durant cites the following reference for this quote: Max Müller, *India, What Can It Teach Us?* (London: 1919, 254).

3. The use of bridges as a metaphor for public administration was first developed by Charles T. Goodsell and Nancy Murray, editors of *Public Administration Illuminated and Inspired by the Arts* (Westport, Connecticut: Praeger, 1995).

4. Some of Durant's sources for Shankara's concept of God are as follows: Paul Deussen, *System of the Vendanta* (Chicago, 1912, 241–44); S. Rahadkrishnan, *The Hindu View of Life* (London: 1928, 65–66); and Rudolf Otto, *Mysticism, East and West* (New York, 1932, 3).

5. Kant's refutation of proof for the existence of God can be found in *The Critique of Pure Reason*, "Transcendental Dialectic," Book 2, Section 4. "The Impossibility of an Ontological Proof of the Existence of God," A591/B619, 591–602. Edited by Vasilis Politis (Rutland, Vermont: Charles E. Tuttle, 1993).

6. The categorical imperative is based on reason alone, and does not depend upon experience in Kant's view. He argued that moral behavior is a necessary condition of life, and does not depend upon empirical proof. Additional literature on the categorical imperative can be found in "Foundations of the Metaphysics of Morals" in Frank Magill's *Masterpieces of History* (New York: HarperCollins, 1990, 340–43).

REFERENCES

Bataille, Georges. 1988. *Inner Experience*. Translated by Leslie Anne Boldt. Reprint, New York: State University of New York Press.

Bronson, Bertrand H., George W. Meyer, Walter J. Bate, William C. DeVane, Lionel Trilling, Rubin H. Brower, Elizabeth Drew, Charles W. Dunn, C. S. Lewis, G. B. Harrison, Basil Willey, Douglas Bush, Herbert Davis, and Maynard Mack, eds. 1954. *Major British Writers*. Vol. 2. New York: Harcourt Brace and Company.

Durant, Will. 1954. *Our Oriental Heritage*. Vol. 1 of *The Story of Civilization*. Reprint, New York: Simon and Schuster.

Eliade, Mircea, ed. 1987. "Silence." In *Encyclopedia of Religion*. Vol. 13. New York: MacMillan Publishing Company.

Huxley, Aldous. 1970. *The Perennial Philosophy*. 1945. Reprint, New York: Harper and Row.

Jung, Carl G. 1978. "What India Can Teach Us." In *Civilization in Transition*. Vol. 10 of *Collected Works*. 2d ed. 1970. Reprint, Princeton: Princeton University Press.

———. 1980. "Concerning Rebirth." In *The Archetypes and the Collective Unconscious*. Vol. 9, part 1 of *Collected Works*. 2d ed. 1968. Reprint, Princeton: Princeton University Press.

Kornfield, Jack. 1993. *A Path with a Heart*. New York: Bantam Books.

Lao-tze. *Tao Teh King*. 1991. Translated by Paul Carus and D. T. Suzuki under the title *The Canon Of Reason and Virtue*. La Salle: Open Court Publishing Company.

Magill, Frank N., ed. 1990. *Masterpieces of World Philosophy*. New York: HarperCollins.

Mascaro, Juan, trans. 1980. *The Bhagavad Gita*. Reprint, New York: Penguin Books.

Merton, Thomas. 1969. *The Way of Chuang Tzu*. New York: New Directions.

Prabhavananda, Swami and Frederick Manchester, trans. 1957. *The Upanishads*. Reprint, New York: New American Library.
Ramacharaka, Yogi, comp. 1930. *The Bhagavad Gita*. rev. ed. Chicago: The Yogi Publication Society.
Storr, Anthony. 1989. *Solitude, A Return to the Self*. New York: Ballantine Books.

CHAPTER 6

The Legacy of China: Perspectives on Taoism

THE MEANING OF THE TAO

Tao . . . is the ultimate reality in which all attributes are united, "it is heavy as a stone, light as a feather"; it is the unity underlying plurality. "It is that by losing of which men die; by getting of which men live. Whatever is done without it, fails; whatever is done by means of it, succeeds." (Waley 1958, 50)

As we learned in chapter one, the uppercase Tao refers to the metaphysical teachings of spiritual masters, which leads to the attainment of eternal truth. The Tao is the principle by which all things in the universe are connected. Through the Tao, the opposites of every existing thing are united into a composite whole. The Tao is the philosophical source of reality, the root and nourishment of everything that exists in this life. Lao-tze taught that all the seemingly divided things in the world come from the Tao. If he were here today, he would tell us that the Tao is reason itself, since it is the source of all that is. Those who live in accordance with the Tao are the wisest members of society. They recognize the fundamental unity of all things in the universe.

The Tao is beyond words, and for this reason, is very difficult to explain. To experience the Tao is to reach the source of one's being, the Self in Jungian terms. This reunion with "that which is" requires silence and introspection. We must move past the limits of language if we decide to embark on the journey to the Tao. When we are able to do this, we hold the key that can open the gate of metaphysical truth. Within this gate, the foundation of eastern philosophy can be found. If we choose to enter, we will discover the real meaning of reason. The following quotations of Lao-tze and ensuing discussion are cited in the Carus and Suzuki translation of the *Tao Teh King* (Lao-tze 1991, 1:1).

> The Reason that can be reasoned is not the eternal Reason. The name that can be named is not the eternal Name. The unnameable is of heaven and earth the beginning. The Nameable becomes of the ten thousand things the mother.

What we perceive to be reason is not the same as what Lao-tze calls Reason. There is no logical process by which Reason can be attained. There are neither words, nor names we can use to capture its meaning. The "ten thousand things" refer to everything that exists and appears to be divided. The "Unnameable and the Nameable" are "two aspects of one and the same thing which in Lao-tze's taoism is the Tao" (Lao-tze 1991, 132). Lao-tze's notion of Reason as leading to the acceptance of unity is evidenced in the following quotation. "Reason begets unity; unity begets duality; duality begets trinity; and trinity begets the ten thousand things" (42:1).

Lao-tze saw unity as the root of order in the universe. The following beautiful verses clarify his belief on this point. They can be compared to Plato's discussion of the oneness of things in "Parmenides." The poetry of the words sounds "like a philosophical rhapsody" (Lao-tze 1991, 166).

> From of old these things have obtained oneness:
> "Heaven by oneness becometh pure.
> Earth by oneness can endure.
> Minds by oneness souls procure.
> Valleys by oneness repletion secure.
> All creatures by oneness to life have been called.
> And Kings were by oneness as models installed."
> Such is the result of oneness. (39:1, 2)

Like the western concept of God, the Tao is transcendent and beyond human comprehension. Unlike western religious concepts of God, the Tao is not anthropomorphic. Taoism is not a religion in the western sense of being a creed from which emanate clearly defined beliefs and behaviors. While it holds certain truths, Taoism penetrates to a place that words cannot enter. There are no churches or mosques in which the faithful congregate. To the extent that it is possible to distinguish between religion and spirituality, Taoism is clearly spiritual.

The lowercase tao refers to how individuals live every day in the world. It is a reflection of the extent to which they are open to the experience of the more metaphysical Tao. The lowercase tao can be thought of as a manifestation of an individual's inner life and was used by Confucius to define perfect human behavior.

The long and complicated history of Taoism is beyond the scope of our concerns in this book. However, it does deserve at least a brief review so the reader can appreciate the philosophical and religious ideas woven through its teachings. The following history of Taoism is taken from Raymond Van Over's introduction to his edited version of *Taoist Tales* (1984). It is very difficult to separate the metaphysical from the practical aspects of the Tao, and the reader is advised not to try to distinguish them in the points being made.

The Development of Taoism

The evolution of Taoism embraced three distinct periods in the history of China. The first began in approximately 604 B.C. with the birth of Lao-tze, who was considered to be the father of Taoism. Its concepts are set down in the *Tao Teh King*, which many scholars believe was written by Lao-tze. However, there is evidence indicating it may have been penned by many hands as late as the third century B.C. The second period occurred in the fifth century B.C. with the writings of the great literary figure, Chuang Tzu, who added new dimensions to Lao-tze's original teachings. The ideas of both Lao-tze and Chuang Tzu were philosophical rather than religious. There were no deities in their conception of the Tao. This changed somewhat with the passage of time.

The infusion of religious tenets into Taoism marks the third period of its evolution. Scholars do not know exactly when this began, but the original intention behind the concept of the Tao was compromised. Attempts to apply the philosophy of Lao-tze and Chuang Tzu to religious beliefs resulted in a wide variety of interpretations, especially during the Chou Dynasty, which lasted from 1112–249 B.C. The superstitious teachings of Taoism provided relief from the miserable living conditions of the lower classes. The peasants found hope in the belief that a multitude of gods would dispense favors, asking only for loyalty in return.

More educated and socially aware citizens who had food in their stomachs and roofs over their heads enjoyed lives more suited to the elevated thinking associated with the idealism of Confucius.[1] These individuals could hope for positions in government which required men (women were excluded in those days) to exhibit traits of strong character, integrity, and impeccable manners. During the Han Dynasty (206 B.C. to A.D. 220), Indian Buddhism arrived in China. Buddhist teachings had a strong impact on Chinese thinking. Throughout the centuries, Buddhism was periodically suppressed by various Taoist sects who were jealous of its influence. In A.D. 440 Taoism gained ascendency over Buddhism and was declared the state religion.

During the Tang Dynasty (A.D. 742), Taoism reached its zenith. There were Taoist temples built across the country. Lao-tze, Chuang Tzu and their followers were canonized. Taoism finally had its hold on the Chinese mentality. It differed markedly from Confucianism's conventional attitude toward behavior, which focused on authority. The Confucian Tao was devoted to structure, regulation, and a profound sense of duty. The Tao, as perceived by Lao-tze, was concerned with insight and a literary sensitivity that was unique for its time and place. Emotions, spirit, and the stirrings of the inner voice were the central focus of life, replacing authority and tradition. Laotze's concept of the Tao was expressed through symbolism, metaphor, imagination, and poetry. There was a sense of the mysterious, even the spiritual, in nature and in men and women.

The Tao of Confucius

We see the importance of myth and lore in the east when hearing the story of the birth of Confucius. Legend has it that apparitions appeared to his young, unmarried mother, announcing the impending event. While she labored in a cave to deliver her son, dragons kept watch, and the air was sweetened with the perfume of "spirit-ladies." The child himself is said to have possessed "the back of a dragon, the lips of an ox, and a mouth like the sea" (Durant 1954, 659). Lore notwithstanding, Confucius was a man of considerable refinement and taste. He loved music and believed it had the power to perfect an individual's character. He held ceremony, courtesy, and propriety in high esteem as the mark of a gentleman. To this day, there are families in China who trace their lineage to Confucius.

The influence Confucius had on Chinese government is unique in the world. From 1313 until 1905, the basis for civil service examinations in China was the Four Books of Confucian teaching (Chan 1973, 19n).[2] Confucius was primarily concerned with establishing a good government, based upon harmony and peace among individuals. He promoted virtue over punishment, moral example over force, and righteousness over profit. He was a man of high ideals and principles.

Confucius believed in the innate goodness and perfectibility of each person. He altered the traditional Chinese preoccupation with birth status. For Confucius, superiority of one person over another was determined by moral character rather than noble birth (Chan 1973, 15). The humanistic orientation in China predated Confucius, but he is credited with bringing it to the fore in his search for a "good" society. His interest was not in metaphysical speculation, rather in how individuals could contribute to the betterment of China.[3]

The concept of *jen* is central to Chinese philosophy. Originally it meant kindness, particularly the kindness of a ruler toward the people. According to Confucius, the "man of *jen*" would work to develop his own character and also that of others; wish for the success of others, as well as his own;

and admire balance and harmony in himself and society as a whole. Conscientiousness and altruism underlie all Confucian thought and are the foundation of his "golden rule" (Chan 1973, 16–17). *Jen* cannot be translated without losing the full scope of its meaning. It has been interpreted as "humane," "altruistic," and "benevolent," all of which are inadequate. Arthur Waley translates *jen* as "good," which he believes is general enough to encompass all the meanings of the concept (Waley 1938, 29).

The contribution Confucius made to Chinese philosophy is unmatched, even though he was not a philosopher in the technical sense. He was a great teacher, and the first person in China to devote his life to full-time teaching. He believed that education should be available to everyone and focus on character development rather than vocational training. China's long literati tradition began with the gentlemen/scholars who studied with Confucius.[4] Although scholars dispute his authorship of certain writings, the *Analects* is accepted as the most reliable source of Confucian ideas (Chan 1973, 17–18).

Confucius had a deep respect for knowledge and insisted that his students develop a love for learning. Although he taught academic subjects like history, poetry, and philosophy, he was mostly concerned with rules of conduct, so that men of high moral development would govern. At one point, more than seventy of his students actually lived with him. They were fiercely loyal and affectionate, calling him "Hwuy" (Durant 1954, 659–60). Confucius believed that those who are entrusted with civic responsibilities should practice self-cultivation. His perception of government workers transcended the nitty-gritty performance of daily tasks. He viewed public servants as cultured individuals of integrity and practicality who would be loyal and considerate of others (Goodsell and Murray 1995, 49).

The "Way of Goodness" that former kings followed had been replaced by violence and aggression, and this upset Confucius. He went from state to state, accompanied by some of his disciples, hoping to convince rulers to adopt the Confucian Tao as a way of governing (Waley 1938, 14–15). Although highly respected and revered by his students and disciples, Confucius was disappointed that his perception of the Tao was not shared by the men who ruled China. There were instances, however, when he was asked to assume a high government post. He turned down these offers in administrations whose policies he considered unjust. Confucius is credited with telling his students they should adopt the attitude of a man who says, "I am not concerned that I have no place; I am concerned how I may fit myself for one. I am not concerned that I am not known; I seek to be worthy to be known" (Durant 1954, 661). Confucius followed his own advice and, although he never attained high office, he was given opportunities to put his ideas into practice.

At one point in his life, Confucius was appointed chief magistrate of the town of Chung-tu, and under his regime there was an upsurge of honesty. Legend has it that during his tenure items lost in the street would either be left there or returned to the owner. Having proven his ability to govern, Confucius was then promoted to acting superintendent of Public Works. While in this position, he conducted a survey of state lands and made agricultural improvements. He next advanced to become minister of crime. His performance in this position is recorded in Chinese records as follows, "Dishonesty and dissoluteness . . . were ashamed and hid their heads. Loyalty and good faith became the characteristics of the men, and chastity and docility those of the women. Strangers came in crowds from other states. Confucius became the idol of the people" (Durant 1954, 662–63).

While we commend his moral leadership, we can agree to disagree with him on the need for docility among the women! However, we can learn from Confucius to love learning and cultivate ourselves so that we become more cognizant of the higher pursuits of living, such as good music and good literature. Without becoming overbearing, we could also project an image of high moral development. This is best done through example, and is most effective at the ordinary level of everyday working life. For example, we can refuse to bad-mouth an ineffective boss, however much we dislike the person. When everyone is skipping out early to catch the local ball game without using vacation time, we can play it straight *without making an issue of it*, but simply because it is the right thing to do. It is surprising how our actions influence others, whether we think they are aware of what we've done or not.

Being of a practical nature, Confucius sought useful answers to the problems facing the government of his day. He preferred to leave transcendental matters to others more given to speculation than he. When asked about government, Confucius replied, "To govern is to rectify. If you lead the people by being rectified yourself, who will dare not be rectified" (Chan 1973, 40). It is appropriate to think of public administrators as individuals who govern, for that is exactly what they do. Those who attain self-knowledge through quiet reflection cultivate themselves. They are able to rectify those parts of themselves that need improvement. When we improve ourselves, we improve everyone who comes in contact with us, because we have changed. The contribution we make to situations is reflected by our attitude, behavior, and perceptions. When these characteristics are made better, we are not the only ones who benefit. This is one of the reasons why psychologists like Jung and philosophers like Confucius favor self-knowledge and self-cultivation.

Confucius responded to the chaos of his time. Constant wars were being waged between the various Chinese states. The people were governed by vindictive and tyrannical rulers. He hoped to alter these terrible conditions through educating future government officials in the importance of individual responsibility based upon ethical and moral action. One day a disciple asked the question, "What constitutes the higher man?" to which Confucius replied, "The cultivation of himself with reverential care" (Durant 1954, 669).

The essence of the Confucian Tao is contained in a few paragraphs of the Chinese classic, *The Great Learning*. It is, in effect, a prescription for living that is as relevant today as it was when it was written. Confucius argued that war existed because the natural social order was in disarray. He believed that because family structure had deteriorated, the states were also in disorder. Individuals were responsible for the decline in the family because they had failed to develop themselves. They needed to make their hearts and souls right again, and rid themselves of desiring the wrong things. China was in a state of disorder because the people hid the underside of their natures, thereby seeing themselves unrealistically. Instead of seeking knowledge before making decisions, they allowed their wishes and prejudices to prevail, regardless of the facts (Durant 1954, 668).

The wreath of social development was laid at the feet of the individual person in the Confucian Tao. Confucius primarily wanted to reach those who govern. He probably would argue in favor of the development of a philosophy for individual public administrators in the United States if he were alive today. His contribution would not be of a metaphysical nature, but practical and hands-on. Issues like character development, ethical conduct, and moral responsibility would pepper his teachings. He would probably introduce a modified version of the traditional western concept of duty in the work place. The humanism that permeates his thinking would fit in well with modern concerns about human rights throughout the world and within government organizations.

Confucius did not require his students to figure out by themselves how to develop into good government officials. He gave them a prescription called the Tao of the "higher man," which became known as the "golden rule." The kind of person Confucius envisioned as living by the "golden rule" is metaphorically described as an archer (Durant 1954, 669). "In archery we have something like the way of the Higher Man. When the archer misses the center of the target, he turns around and seeks for the cause of his failure in himself."

Individual responsibility is the bedrock of Confucius' "golden rule." However, he realized that character must be developed before human beings can assume responsibility. Character development comes from listening to the inner voice and cultivating the Self. Individuals who engage in this pursuit embody the ideal and become a combination of philosopher, saint, and sage. The virtues required to attain this state are intelligence, courage, and goodwill. Confucius taught that sincerity is the underpinning of character. Through sincerity, those who live according to the ideal act before they speak, and speak in accordance with the actions they take. Their speech is modest, but their actions are not. Ideal individuals practice moderation in all things (Durant 1954, 669–70).

Confucius, like Kant, taught that those who live in accordance with the ideal share universal maxims, such as treating others as they would expect themselves to be treated. They feel the greatest empathy toward all people. When meeting a person more worthy than they believe themselves to be, they emulate rather than compete. When they see a person who seems to be less than they are, they examine themselves because they know that all faults are shared. They do not listen to gossip or slander about others and are always courteous, but never obsequious. They are serious and dignified. Earnest in their work, they are disciplined individuals (Durant 1954, 669–70).

In his book *The Heart of Confucius*, Archie Bahm reports that Confucius once worked in a low-level position as an overseer of the fields. During this time, he practiced living in accordance with the Chinese interpretation of wisdom, called *chih*. Individuals who have *chih* willingly do whatever is required of them in any situation. *Chih* has three components, each of which must be followed exactly: *yi*, which means acting naturally; *jen* (previously discussed in this chapter), which means sincere goodwill; and *li*, which means acting according to "one's inner atttitudes" (Bahm 1992, 47).

The following parable is based upon a plate found in Bahm's book (48–49). The photograph comes from an illustrated biography of Confucius dating back to the Ming dynasty. It represents one of thirty-nine wood block print illustrations, entitled "Overseeing the Fields," in which Confucius' life as a low-level civil servant is depicted. Confucius is sitting at a makeshift table with his arms folded in the sleeves of his gown. Framing the field are background hills with slight gradations in the topography of the immediate landscape. Men and cattle are scattered throughout the scene, with some close to where Confucius is seated. The expressions on the faces of both the men and the animals are pleasant and contented.

I have taken poetic license and placed Confucius at a time in his life before he began to teach. At this juncture of his career, he is just starting to formulate ideas about how government officials should be trained.

A Job to Be Done

As his eyes swept over the broad expanse of the fields, taking in the men and the animals working together, Confucius felt a tug in his chest. He always experienced that feeling whenever he saw the interplay of nature. Men and animals, plants and trees, hills and valleys, lakes and grasses, filled him with awe for the unity of the natural world. Confucius knew that someday he would teach his students how to use the secrets of nature to create a good society. He would tell them that when the creations of the universe are allowed to follow their own inclinations freely, without interference, life is good. All things are good, and meant to exist in the way that is natural to them, he mused, preparing to make his periodic check on the men ploughing the field.

Confucius decided to tell his students that the art of governance depends upon following the course that is natural to them (*yi*). He would teach them to accept others as they are and respect their ability to do what is right. As Confucius approached, the men were watering the animals to protect them from the heat of the afternoon sun. They smiled at him, for he was kind and fair in his judgments and they were pleased to see him.

After exchanging words of encouragement for the work they were doing, Confucius sat on a rock and continued to plan a system of conduct for future government officials. Having just seen how man and beast cooperate in the field, he realized it was due to the goodwill of the men and the reciprocity of the animals (*jen*). He would teach his students to cultivate goodwill, because natural social cooperation is required between government and the people. All is well when neither man nor animal imposes its will on the other. Mutual respect is the key to good relations in all things, he concluded.

The sun began its gentle slide down the slope of the hills, far beyond the field. Rising from his seat to bid good night to the workers, Confucius marvelled at their openness and sincerity with one another. Aware of their inner feelings, they acted honestly (*li*). Confucius realized how wise the men were. Their self-knowledge allowed them to be sincere, to have goodwill toward one another, and to fulfill whatever was required of them (*chih*). Confucius felt confident that he could use what he learned from the men to teach his students the art of government. The lingering rays from the fading sun lit the path and guided his footsteps as Confucius made his way back to the tent for a long night's rest.

Taoist Literature

The stories we hear repeatedly help to define us. They become symbolic representations of all our experiences. Taoism is replete with stories. The art of storytelling touches a responsive chord in the human heart and psyche that transcends cultural differences. With this in mind, let us turn to Taoist literature.

Raymond Van Over introduces us to an interesting series of Taoist parables, anecdotes, and poems in *Taoist Tales* (1984). He speculates that the relative lack of attention to Taoist literature in the west may be because there is no cohesive body of work easily identifiable as Taoist. He also suggests that the western mentality insists on distinctions between literary, religious, and philosophical writings. Such demarcation is not possible when ideas are expressed through parables, metaphors, poetry, and anecdotes, as they are in Taoism. Also, he suggests that if the wisdom of Taoism had been established through analysis, rational argument, and logic, then it would be more palatable to the western mind.

Van Over realizes, however, that Taoism is too subtle and profound to be expressed in that manner. It is important for the westerner who reads Taoist literature not to underestimate the deep significance of what appears to be the " 'guilelessly simple' " quality of the stories. James Robert Highwater, a famed sinologist, described Taoist writings as "works marked by profound insight and poetic imagination" (Van Over 1984, 5).

The anecdote we are about to read is based upon a parable written by Chuang Tzu and relayed in Van Over's book (155–56). I have paraphrased the story, using the same conversation and examples that are contained in the parable. The anecdote tells of a hypothetical meeting between Confucius and Lao-tze. The reader may recall from chapter 4 that legend states the two men met once, but did not get along very well. Taoists who followed the teaching of Lao-tze harbored ill feelings for Confucius. They found him to be rigid and possessed of a superior attitude. Nowhere is this prejudice more evident than in Chuang Tzu's parable. He seems to take delight in treating Confucius and his ideas contemptuously.

Public administrators can learn from both Confucius and Lao-tze, so we are not taking sides here. However, there is a very important lesson contained in the story that I hope the reader will ponder. After reading the parable, I suggest that he or she stop to reflect on the lesson before continuing to read my interpretation of what is being said by each of the men.

The Meeting

Confucius worked long and hard to complete the *Twelve Classics*. When they were finished, he prepared an abstract so he could convince officials that his work was deserving of a place in the library at Chou. On a bright morning, buoyant in spirit and with his parcel in hand, Confucius journeyed west to the Cheng repository at Chou. Upon arrival he was directed to the officer in charge of such matters—a man called Lao-tze. Immediately upon introduction, Confucius felt his heart drop, for he was a perceptive man.

Lao-tze's stone eyes were set in a face locked in a disapproving grimace. They bore into Confucius like a drill penetrating the earth hardened by an early spring frost. Ah, he thought, the man knows my work, hates it, and harbors a strong dislike of me as well. I must not waver before the intimidating force of this man. Confucius unconsciously stood a bit taller, setting his mouth in a straight line, lips slightly parted, "I have an abstract of my work with me and would like to discuss it with you. For many years I have labored over my ideas and have received positive reaction from students and colleagues as well. I have divided my writing into twelve separate volumes, which I believe are worthy of inclusion in the repository here."

Lao-tze listened to Confucius present the synopsis of his ideas for a while. Suddenly, without warning, he interrupted saying, "I have time only for substance, not the vague ideas you're presenting. Cut to the quick." Confucius, without skipping a beat, retorted in a deep, resonant voice, "The qualities of benevolence and righteousness are the substance of my work." Lao-tze stared at the other man for a long time. Finally, he spoke in a measured and steady voice, as if he were holding something back. Slowly and deliberately he asked, "Is man by nature benevolent and righteous?"

Confucius responded unhesitatingly. He spoke with conviction and firm resolve, "Yes. The superior man is, indeed, benevolent. His character demands that he be so. Righteousness follows benevolence, for if it were not true, man need not be born at all. The nature of man is to be both benevolent and righteous." Lao-tze's eyes never left Confucius' face, as though he were searching for a missing part, "Tell me, what do benevolence and righteousness mean to you?" Fully confident and with a broad smile, Confucius answered, "Benevolence means to have kindness and sympathy in one's heart for all men at all times. Righteousness means never to engage in selfish thoughts or behavior. These are the qualities of benevolence and righteousness."

The hard eyes of Lao-tze tore through the heart and mind of Confucius in preparation for the words that would follow, "So, Master, you are an inferior man! For you speak of love for everyone. How vague and extravagant are your empty words. You leave no room for selfish thoughts. How selfish you are yourself to rob men of their humanity. Why, even Heaven and Earth are allowed to follow their natural course; the sun and the moon shine in all their brightness; the stars in the sky maintain their order; the beasts in the fields and the birds in the air gather in herds and flocks; the trees on the hillsides stand in their places.

"But you, Master, wish to change the Tao, to initiate your own Tao. Go ahead! It will be your undoing. It is as though you are seeking the return of a fugitive son, by beating a drum of benevolence and righteousness. In your ignorance, you are driving him further away, for you are subverting what is natural. You think you are bringing order into the affairs of men, but you do the opposite. It is disorder that you preach; you violate the nature of man and I have no use for you or for your misguided ideas."

Different Interpretations of the Tao

The discrepancy between the Tao of Lao-tze and the Confucian Tao is clearly portrayed in this parable. Confucius approaches Lao-tze full of certainty and confidence in his ability to introduce order and meaning into the world. He sees himself as a catalyst for the emergence of virtue and character in the young men destined to become government officials. He believes that by instituting codes of behavior, they will learn kindness. Through ritual and ceremony, the men will see that what is right brings its own rewards. Confucius encourages his students to be kind and good to all, including the high-born and the lowly. He focuses on the positive aspects of human nature and gives little or no attention to its underside. Confucius believes his words will convince the students that they should exercise self-control and cultivate higher pursuits, such as music.

Lao-tze had little patience for those who used words to teach. He associated language and the knowledge it imparts with complication. The search for knowledge brings false pride and the belief that the universe can be dominated by the human mind. He believed that civilization distances human beings from their natural instincts. The simplicity, peace, and inner reflection that were endemic to life prior to his time are lost forever. He taught that when people left the fields and built cities, they lost the secret of wisdom. They established laws which further alienated them, causing corruption and enervation. Trust in the workings of the natural world was replaced by artifice and human guile. Silence gave in to confusion, and humanity lost its way. Lao-tze saw a distinction between the saint and the sage. His concern was with wisdom, not goodness. It was the quiet mind, not the pious moralist that Lao-tze valued (Durant 1954, 655–56).

The similarity between the thinking of Lao-tze and Jung is quite remarkable. Both blame civilization for alienating individuals from their shadow side by forcing them to focus on the external world, to the detriment of inner stirrings. By ignoring the truths of the unconscious mind and accepting only what the conscious mind reveals, humanity lost its sense of unity and depth. Division and discord have replaced unity and balance. Seeking wisdom, Lao-tze relied upon silence. He taught that wisdom comes through example and experience, never words. The Tao is silent and does not speak. It is the path of the sage, not the provocateur. "He who knows (the Way) does not speak about it; he who speaks about it does not know it. He (who knows it) will keep his mouth shut and close the portals of his nostrils" (Durant 1954, 656).

When Confucius shows up exuding confidence in his ability to control the actions of his students, Lao-tze is scandalized. He perceives the man as the epitome of arrogance and pride. What Confucius sees as practical knowledge, Lao-tze sees as superiority and superficiality. A slightly altered account of the alleged meeting between the two men was told by a famed Chinese historian named Szuma Ch'ien. As legend has it, Lao-tze was eighty-seven when Confucius paid his visit. This account suggests that Confucius, only thirty-four at the time, sought advice from the older man. From Lao-tze's response, it is apparent that he saw Confucius as an ambitious man, eager to achieve greatness (Durant 1954, 658).

> When the hour of the great man has struck he rises to leadership; but before his time has come he is hampered in all that he attempts. . . . Get rid of your pride and your many ambitions, your affectation and your extravagant aims. Your character gains nothing for all these. This is my advice to you.

According to Ch'ien, Confucius took Lao-tze's advice to heart and vowed to follow it. Upon his return home, he allegedly spoke the following words to his students. They exemplify the "guilelessly simple" quality of Taoist stories referred to by James Highwater (Durant 1954, 658).

> I know how birds can fly, fishes swim, and animals run. But the runner may be snared, the swimmer hooked, and the flyer shot by the arrow. But there is the dragon—I cannot tell how he mounts on the wind through the clouds, and rises to heaven. Today I have seen Lao-tze, and can compare him only to the dragon.

The dragon is symbolic of the difference between the conception of the Tao by Lao-tze as compared to Confucius. Both men premised their ideas on inner reality. Confucius focused on cultivating inner virtue so the world outside the Self could be improved. He understood the world of the runner, the swimmer, and the flyer—the practical realities of life. Confucius opened the practical lower gate of the perennial philosophy, and improved practice and morality in government. Having passed through the interior leading from the lower gate, Confucius guided his followers to the threshold of the contemplative middle gate, where action and thought intersect.

Lao-tze focused on cultivating the powers of introspection so the world within the Self could be discovered. He understood the world of thought and action—the psychological realities of life. Lao-tze opened the middle gate of the perennial philosophy, and improved the capacity of individuals to understand themselves and others. Having passed through the interior leading from the middle gate, Lao-tze guided his followers to the threshold of the philosophical upper gate, where metaphysical truth resides. Like the dragon, Lao-tze was ready to soar above the clouds and reach fulfillment.

THE TAO AND PUBLIC ADMINISTRATION

Lao-tze's teachings did not impress the western mind, which prefers to fly rather than soar. Confucius, on the other hand, became one of the most renowned philosophers in both the eastern and western worlds. The values that he promoted for government officials in ancient China enhance the practice of public administration today. We expect our civil servants to be honest, righteous, loyal, and dedicated to serving others (Goodsell and Murray 1995, 49). To this end, laws have been written, commissions appointed, and agencies established.

For example, the federal government's Office of Personnel Administration, and similar agencies in states and localities throughout the country, are charged with developing and implementing policies that will attract and keep capable individuals in government work. Even a cursory examination of how civil servants are recruited, selected, given tenure, and rewarded shows that the qualities Confucius defined as appropriate for government officials in his day are valued by contemporary American public administration as well.

Shafritz, Hyde, and Rosenbloom, in their text on public personnel issues (1986) attest to the influence that federal reform measures can have on all levels of government. With the passage of the Pendleton Act in 1883, reformers succeeded in their efforts to introduce regulation and improvement into civil service. Public administration benefited from: open competition for federal job seekers; periods of probation before individuals were given tenure; and neutrality in decision making through protection from political arm twisting (Shafritz, Hyde, and Rosenbloom 1986, 28–30). These policies paved the way for a civil service system in which honesty, righteousness, and loyalty were the norm. When the doors to federal employment were opened to everyone, those who really wanted to serve had a chance. Probationary periods provided an opportunity for supervisors to look for integrity and allegiance before granting tenure. Protection of civil servants from undue political influence allowed them to make appropriate decisions and behave in an upright manner.

Over time, states and localities were influenced by the reforms the Pendleton Act brought to federal administration. Today, Shafritz and Hyde argue most jurisdictions have implemented a merit system which provides rewards for those employees who are deserving (Shafritz, Hyde, and Rosenbloom 1986, 30). The ability to recognize loyal and dedicated public administrators serves as an incentive for qualified individuals of good character to enter government service. Congress, while not always attentive to public service, enacted the Intergovernmental Personnel Act in 1970. This legislation is important because of its expectation that government service is a high calling, as revealed in the following declaration (49–50):

> since numerous governmental activities administered by State and local governments are related to national purpose and are financed in part by Federal funds, a national interest exists in high caliber public service in State and local governments.

The significance of "high caliber" public service was clearly defined in Confucian teaching. Confucius believed that the behavior, attitude, and character of those who work in government reverberate throughout the country. His ideas became the principles upon which civil service examinations were given in China for many years. The following is a translation from Confucius' work, entitled *The Great Wisdom*, also known as *The Great Learning*. The reader is advised to substitute the word "public official" for the word "man" (Bahm 1992, 143):

the selfishness and rudeness of one man can cause turmoil throughout the whole country. This is the way things work. This confirms the saying that "one slur can poison the whole atmosphere; one hero can inspire a whole country."

American public administrators can learn an additional lesson from Confucius that has not made much of an impact to-date. This concerns the aesthetics of administrative interaction. Public agencies, like most institutions in our country, have lost respect for old-fashioned manners. Far too many civil servants react in a curt and disinterested way, toward one another and the public they are sworn to serve. This well-known and unfortunate situation probably accounts for some of the "bureaucrat bashing" that is so prevalent in our country. Through the cultivation of practical virtues, individuals behave in a way that enhances the quality of life for everyone. When that quality is missing, the words of Confucius have special significance. He taught that "Uprightness uncontrolled by etiquette becomes rudeness" (Goodsell and Murray 1995, 49).

The practice of public administration can benefit immeasurably from the more profound teachings of Lao-tze, even though they are contrary to our western way. Confucius has provided the practical qualities necessary to govern successfully. Lao-tze can give us deeper insight into the philosophical qualities of governance. If we are serious about developing an administrative philosophy to be used by individuals, we cannot avoid the introspection we have ignored for so long. When commissioners, appointees, and individuals with civil service status come to terms with their inner motivating selves, public administration advances as a profession.

For too long public administration excused itself from inner probing on the grounds that it is held hostage by elected and appointed officials. The old conundrum of the politics/administration dichotomy is still debated in academic circles. Some argue that we have solved this problem through increased professionalism. However, there remain vestiges of extreme thinking, in which civil servants are perceived as mere pawns in the hands of elected officials.

THE MEANING OF WU-WEI

It is at once the beginning of all things and the way in which all things pursue their course. When this Tao is possessed by individual things, it becomes its character or virtue (*te*). The ideal life for the individual, the ideal order for society, and the ideal type of government are all based on it and guided by it. As the way of life, it denotes simplicity, spontaneity, tranquility, weakness, and most important of all, non-action (*wu-wei*). By the latter is not meant literally "inactivity" but rather "taking no action that is contrary to Nature"—in other words, letting Nature take its own course. (Chan 1973, 136)

These words are in direct opposition to western culture's emphasis on complexity over simplicity, strategy over spontaneity, stimulation over tranquility, and strength over weakness. The action orientation of the western value system is perhaps the greatest obstacle preventing us from living according to the Tao.

Wu-Wei and Creativity

Moriz Carl Cammerloher was a Viennese Sanskrit and Oriental scholar, who also consulted in analytical psychology. Writing about art (1985), he examined creativity from a psychological perspective. Cammerloher tells the story of how the great Italian operatic tenor, Enrico Caruso, trained what was arguably the greatest voice in modern operatic history. Every day he sang. Contrary to what one would assume, he did not sing arias from *Rigoletto* or other operas. He sang freely and playfully, allowing his voice to follow its own path. Caruso believed that his creativity lay in the impulsive energy of his voice. By turning over daily practice to the whims of his musical instinct, Caruso sang with gusto.

Cammerloher wrote that the "free-flowing energy" Caruso so joyfully vented "is the secret of every great achievement" (Cammerloher 1985, 430). Creative energy is not a rare commodity, reserved for those with extraordinary talent. Every human being has it. Children create games and stories which come from images in the psyche that manifest themselves through imagination. The time spent in apparent idleness is perhaps the most creative period in the lives of both children and adults. Cammerloher argued that the "free-flowing energy" that characterizes creativity emanates from long periods of rest during which no effort is exerted. During these times, we are free to peruse the corridors of the mind and listen to the inner voice.

> When we lie in the grass doing nothing, wanting nothing, and, as they say, thinking nothing, we experience this free flowing of thoughts. It is perfectly effortless. Only when we wish to hold a thought fast and pursue it does the work and exertion begin.

The free-flowing thoughts of which he speaks require silence, nonjudgment, and letting go. Introspection does not allow the inner voice to police the mind, but rather keep it flexible. The key to the gate of the psyche, where creativity and self-knowledge reside, lies in our ability to give free play to the natural flow of our thoughts. We cannot hear the inner voice that teaches us how to live creatively and in accordance with our own uniqueness, unless we leave the world behind for a while. In effect, we would do well to return to an earlier time so we may retrieve the unencumbered thoughts of childhood. Imagination, intuition, and reflection tempered by experience, are the ingredients of adult creativity. We seek not the innocence of what we were, but rather the freedom of what we may become.

Picture Emily stretched out in the long grasses of the west meadow, gazing at the cloud formations high above. It is a hot summer afternoon, and there is just enough haze for the white clouds to bleed into the blue sky like an impressionist painting. As soon as she fabricates a meaning to one of the cloud formations, it disappears and delights her active imagination. Emily learns an important lesson that long, lazy afternoon. What happens does not last for long, because life is constantly changing. She learns to make the most of what presents itself, fully accepting that all events are ephemeral. This insight helps Emily later in her career when there are downtimes, like the hostage experience. Through inner wandering and outer calm, Emily negotiates the ups and downs of a rewarding career, balancing the opposites that constantly challenge her.

Cammerloher tells us that during idle times the unconscious mind moves freely. What seems to be laziness is just a period of time in which we cast aside the constrictions of ordinary thinking and open the door to new ways of perceiving. Idleness is a kind of play that allows psychic contents to become part of the material world and, through imagination, attain form. Cammerloher writes that "Play means that the psychological process finds its expression in the physical" (Cammerloher 1985, 430–31). If we can accept these ideas, we will open ourselves to our own creativity.

Most of us admire creativity in others, whether they are artists or savvy administrators. We wonder how they got that way. We can tap into originality and inventiveness by saying to ourselves, "There is another way of looking at this situation. There are other decisions that can be made, and this may not be as it appears." All we need to do is loosen up and accept the part of ourselves that is irrational and intuitive. Our inner voice will not lead us astray. It does not obey the logic of the rational mind because it does not have to. The inner voice answers to a higher power within each of us that contains the most perceptive and accurate interpretation of our experiences. Play and introspection are the psychological underpinnings that define creative living.

> This talent for giving oneself to the free flow of one's thoughts or ideas, feelings, or intuition, this ability to play, to be lazy in the bourgeois sense, or, as Jung says, to let things happen inwardly—this action in non-action, this *wu-wei*, is the secret of the creative mind. (Cammerloher 1985, 431)

For the purpose of this book, wu-wei has a twofold meaning. Both meanings translate wu-wei as "nonaction." The first interpretation examines "nonaction" at the point of introspection; the level of awareness that enables us to seek self-knowledge. The second interpretation examines "nonaction" at the point of decision making; the level of awareness that enables us to seek innovative solutions to problems in the work place. Creativity is the reward of meaningful introspection and the hallmark of successful decision making.

Wu-Wei and Introspection

When we take the time to sit silently and examine our ideas and feelings about ourselves and our experiences at work, we begin to explore the unconscious mind. By opening ourselves to the stirrings of the psyche, we gain insight we may not have had before. We begin to see how we have influenced the actions of other people. Our contribution to the outcome of work-related activities becomes clearer as we delve deeper into the hidden recesses of our mind and listen to the message of the inner voice.

Perceiving ourselves as participants, who are responsible for every work experience, provides us with a healthy sense of personal accountability. We are less inclined to assume the role of a helpless victim when deliberating on what went wrong in a disappointing situation. Likewise, we are less prone to exaggerate our own importance in successful enterprises. We learn significant truths about human nature by seeing our own strengths and weaknesses. Through the process of inner growth we come to accept ourselves, warts and all. With self-knowledge comes a deeper understanding of others who, we begin to realize, are mirror images of ourselves. A kind of unification of self and others takes place as we continue to journey along the path toward truth. Eventually, we may experience the sense that we are deeply connected to all things.

Serious introspection automatically leads to a dialogue with our intuition. The "free-flowing energy" that is generated activates the inner voice, which can provide answers for the most intractable problems, if we only listen. When we allow ourselves to settle down and nonjudgmentally explore whatever thoughts present themselves, we gain knowledge that cannot be accessed in any other way. In effect, silent introspection is an antirational exercise, similar to eastern techniques of meditation. Paradoxically, when thoughts are allowed to freely express themselves, the mind eventually becomes quiet. Through silence and clear perception we learn to recognize both the positive and negative aspects of ourselves. From gentle acceptance of our opposing sides comes a deep understanding of the world as a place of contradictory forces seeking to establish a balance.

There is perhaps no profession that experiences the inconsistencies of the world on a daily basis as sharply as public administration. As all practitioners, students, and academics know, the dichotomy between public administration and political reality is a myth. Those who "walk-the-walk" do not "talk-the-talk" of a separation between these two opposing forces. Our democracy demands a balance between political exigencies and administrative response. This balance can be achieved only when public administrators take the time to attain the inner maturity that leads to correct perception. Maintaining this balance is the cornerstone of professionalism in public service.

Public administrators face the challenge of educating political appointees and their staffs on the nuts and bolts of government management. Unless an elected official has been in office for more than one term, there is little if any understanding by staff of the workings of government. Newly hired personnel have no history of earlier actions and the reasons why decisions were made by previous administrations. Maverick politicians and their staffs tend to think they need to change everything. This is painfully evident when there has been a landslide victory. The mandate of the people becomes the Achilles' heel of the professional civil service, which is sworn to uphold efficient and effective government.

Time for reflection is hard to come by when everything is in a state of flux. Public administrators seem, on occasion, to be at the mercy of the crises generated by city halls, gubernatorial offices, and national legislative bodies. A well-formulated philosophy for all civil servants, regardless of their position, would add a new dimension to the practice of public administration. A goal worthy of those in public service is the attainment of the highest possible level of personal maturity and psychological development. Public administrators who have mastered themselves are more capable of correctly perceiving difficult situations. Like Emily, they possess an acuity that enables them to see beyond the surface of human behavior and its consequences. For they have achieved an inner knowingness.

Wu-Wei and Decision Making

When we engage in quiet reflection, the veil of illusion that covers our perceptions slowly begins to lift. As we see situations clearly, we become more open to different ways of handling them. We use the knowledge gained from introspection to see the world as it really is, not as it appears to be. With this insight comes the wisdom to know when to hold back and allow the natural course of events to unfold. We are not as inclined to blindly jump into the fray and engage in ill-advised activity, in the mistaken belief that through intervention we can solve all problems.

Sometimes it is preferable to wait before making a decision until all aspects of a troubling situation reveal themselves. Jung warned (1974, 6:369) against misinterpreting wu-wei. The Taoist meaning of "not doing" does not imply "doing nothing." Confusion comes about when an event seems to demand immediate intervention. To the western mind, the impulsive reflex to take action and exercise control is the sensible thing to do. Failure to take action is perceived negatively as "doing nothing." To the Taoist, restraining from action and asserting no control is the appropriate response. The decision of "not doing" is perceived positively, because it allows opposing forces to reach equilibrium. The restoration of balance results in natural harmony. Through wu-wei, there is "deliverance from the cosmic tension of opposites by a return to *tao*" (370).

Wise leaders, aware that the world is filled with opposing forces, do not interfere with their interaction. They understand that human intervention is no match for the Tao. In human life, balance is achieved through the complimentary principles of yin and yang. When they are not usurped, doubt and confusion are eliminated because everyone and everything is free to follow the path of its own nature (Chan 1973, 322).

The *Book of Changes*, which contains the essence of Chinese thought, says that "the state of absolute quiet and inactivity . . . when acted on, immediately penetrates all things" (Chan 1973, 323). Thomas Merton (1969) writes that Chuang Tzu proposed wu-wei as the "secret of the way." Chuang Tzu believed it is more virtuous to choose nonaction than to consciously strive for carefully planned results. This is true, even though well-intentioned actions obey the dictates of the mind and are a form of self-aggrandizement. Chuang Tzu predicted that when human action runs contrary to the natural order of things, the result is a disharmony with the Tao (Merton 1969, 24).

Wu-wei has been interpreted as a decision not to impose one's will by taking control of a situation. This choice is more profound than a simple decision not to take charge. Rather, it is a matter of "taking no unnatural action" (Chan 1973, 791). When the opposing forces creating the situation are allowed to play themselves out without interference, the Tao is realized. Wu-wei does not mean that it is appropriate to withdraw from responsibility, but those who are wise fulfill their leadership role by not intruding in the natural chain of events. No individual will or outside control must impose itself on "the One, which is natural, eternal, spontaneous, nameless, and indescribable" (136). The One is the Tao.

When opposing forces have precipitated a situation, leaders who accept the Tao follow the course of nature. Like nature itself, they know when to bend and when to stand firm. Timeliness, consideration, and careful use of power are the means by which they govern (Chan 1973, 254). Nature, steeped as it is in uncertainty, is suspect to the western mind. The commitment to rational action tends to outweigh any inclination to bend. To the western mind, allowing a situation to evolve according to the Tao would be equivalent to welcoming chaos into the work place.

A complete rethinking of commonly held beliefs is necessary if public administrators are to relinquish control over certain events. The decision to wait for a particular situation to follow its own course must be based upon clear perception. Experienced administrators who have learned the value of reflection and who trust the natural order of things are able to make the appropriate decision. They know that without the timeliness of the seasons, there is no harvest. An ear of corn will not grow in winter. Emily knew that storming the compound in Skokie was untimely and would lead to disastrous results. She also knew that at a certain point it was counterproductive to continue arguing with her colleagues. Certain decisions have a momentum of their own, like water racing down a mountain stream after a heavy spring rain.

One of the stories written by Chuang Tzu has been cited by Thomas Merton as particularly instructive in how to live according to the Tao. The story emphasizes the important contribution wu-wei makes to Taoism. The fable concerns a man who is a disciple of one of the ancient Chinese sages, Keng Sang Chu. The disciple is a very anxious and ambitious individual, with perfectionistic tendencies. After realizing he cannot help his disciple, Keng Sang Chu sends him to Lao-tze to see if the great master can guide him toward a more peaceful accommodation with the world and his place in it. The following parable is an adaptation of Chuang Tzu's story. Direct quotations and my paraphrases of Merton's translation of the original story are referenced.

The Disciple

Chang had been with his master, Keng Sang Chu, for a long period of time. He was discouraged because he had trouble putting into practice what the master said and was therefore unable to improve himself. The master tried to teach Chang and his other disciples how to quiet their thoughts and, through the power of silent reflection, become secure in themselves. Chang tried with all his might to find meaning in Keng's teaching, but never seemed able to put his ideas into practice. The poor man was devastated when he saw how the other disciples were much more able than he to grasp the wisdom of the master and improve themselves. In desperation, he went to Keng and poured forth his frustration and disappointment. In a voice heavy with self-doubt, Chang told the master, "Tao is only a word in my ear. It does not ring any bells inside" (Merton 1969, 128).

Being the humble sage he was, Keng saw his own inadequacy as the problem. He assured Chang that he was not lacking in the qualities of the other disciples; he simply had the wrong teacher. The kindly and compassionate master suggested to his aspiring disciple that a wiser and more advanced tutor may benefit him. Keng advised Chang to visit the old master, Lao-tze. Under his tutelage, Keng felt the young man would advance and prove himself to be a worthy candidate, "Go south, my son, and speak to the old one who is well versed in such matters as transformation and enlightenment. For he, who is of the heart and the mind, will help you and guide you to your destiny."

Chang thanked his master and set about busily preparing for his journey toward the southern provinces where Lao-tze lived. For seven days and nights he traveled alone over hills and ravines until, finally, he arrived at the hut of the wise one. Lao-tze looked at the young man with narrowed eyes and set mouth. "Has Keng sent you to me?" he asked. "Yes," Chang replied. "Why did you not come alone? Who are these people with you?" Suddenly, Chang felt empty and scared! His eyes darted back and forth seeking people he could not find, "Master, there is no one with me. I traveled alone to see you." Lao-tze stared straight into Chang's eyes and said evenly, "Don't you understand?" (Merton 1969, 129). Chang was completely taken aback with confusion and doubt. In a tired, weak voice he said, "I have forgotten what you asked and how to respond." Lao-tze retorted, "Say what you mean. I do not know what you want to say."

With head lowered and eyes cast toward the ground, Chang admitted his flaws to Lao-tze, exposing his self-doubt and quiet desperation.

> When I don't know, people treat me like a fool.
> When I do know, the knowledge gets me into trouble.
> When I fail to do good, I hurt others.
> When I do good, I hurt myself.
> If I avoid my duty, I am remiss.
> But if I do it, I am ruined.
> How can I get out of these contradictions?
> That is what I came to ask you. (Merton 1969, 129)

Lao-tze, speaking quietly, told the young man his words confirmed the fear that was present in his eyes. He suggested to Chang that his dilemma was equivalent to seeking that which lies at the bottom of the ocean floor with no means of dredging it up. Lao-tze spoke.

> You have got lost, and are trying
> To find your way back
> To your own true self.
> You find nothing.
> But illegible signposts
> Pointing in all directions.
> I pity you. (Merton 1969, 130)

Chang listened carefully to these words, and after Lao-tze had spoken, he asked to be admitted for study. Lao-tze acceded to his request. Alone in his cell, Chang meditated and reflected. He spent countless hours trying to rid himself of what he perceived as his own weakness. He aspired toward attaining virtues and qualities which he admired in others and believed he lacked. After ten days of this intensive introspection, Chang was in deep despair. One morning when the sky was dark and the clouds hung low over the trees, he left his cell to talk to the old one. Immediately, Lao-tze saw how depressed his newest pupil was, and motioned to him to come inside before the rains came. In a choked voice, Chang spoke of his frustration and feelings of desolation. When he was finished, Lao-tze told him he was like a rope that is all knotted and misshapen.

Lao-tze emphathized with the misery of his student. After asking Chang whether his troubles were outside himself or came from within, Lao-tze offered the following advice.

> If your obstructions
> Are on the outside,
> Do not attempt
> To grasp them one by one
> And thrust them away.
> Impossible! Learn
> To ignore them.
> If they are within yourself,
> You cannot destroy them piecemeal,
> But you can refuse
> To let them take effect.
> If they are both inside and outside,
> Do not try
> To hold on to Tao—
> Just hope that Tao
> Will keep hold of you! (Merton 1969, 131)

In desperation, Chang compared himself to a sick farmer, "At least the farmer can tell the other farmers who visit him what his problem is. I am not so lucky. My medicine is making me sicker. This search for Tao is useless, unless you can tell me how to begin." Lao-tze breathed a long and heavy sigh. He told Chang to think overnight about the counsel he had just given, and to meet him again the following morning by the stream at the edge of the forest. Chang awoke early the next day and was surprised to find Lao-tze waiting for him at the stream.

Lao-tze motioned to Chang to sit on a tree stump perched at the edge of the water. Positioning himself on a flat stone set at an oblique angle across from the stump, Lao-tze began to speak. His voice rose in a slow cadence that was irresistible to Chang. Lao-tze kept his eyes fixed on the face of his pupil, measuring every nuance of thought and feeling. His words found their way into the mind and heart of the younger man (Merton 1969, 131–32).

> Do you have a constant knowledge and sense of the unity among all things? Are you able to rest when rest is available? Are you able to stop when it is appropriate for you to do so? Can you let others go their way without interfering? Are you in need of them reporting their actions to you so you can be sure of the progress they are making? Are you able to go your own way and be independent? Can you get out of the way when it is necessary? Can you cry all day, like an infant

without getting a sore throat? Infants can clench a fist all day without hurting their hands. Can you? Can you stare and gaze all day and not strain your eyes?

Lao-tze stopped and watched his pupil struggle to gain the significance of the words he spoke. As they sat in silence, an orange butterfly flew over Chang's head, while a fly perched on the edge of the stump. Quiet repose without effort of any kind was unusual for Chang, particularly when in company. Lao-tze noticed this, and was pleased. A cloud passed overhead, briefly dimming the bright morning sun. Lao-tze continued, "You asked how to begin to attain Tao. I suggest you consider infants. They are free from all care, and totally unaware of themselves. They are completely spontaneous, and never think about what they are going to do. They remain wherever they are placed, not knowing why they are there. Neither do they try to understand what is going on. They simply accept whatever happens as part of their lives. You might think of infants as knowing how to begin."

Chang leaned forward slightly, adjusting his buttocks on the edge of the stump. His shoulders were slightly stooped, with his right hand loosely cupped in his left palm. In a gentle, but deeper voice than usual, he queried, "Is this perfection" (Merton 1969, 132)?" Impressed with the earnestness of Chang's demeanor, Lao-tze straightened his back and slowly said, "No, my son, this is just the beginning, only a start. If you can be like an infant, you will be able to unlearn all the misleading things the ignorant have taught you. Then, and only then, will you cease being a child of the world and become a child of Tao. Effort and persistence will not provide what you seek. Trying to understand what is incomprehensible can destroy you. You must abandon all attempts to grasp the Tao. For it is a gift."

Chang rose heavily and walked along the stream, his eyes fixed ahead on the horizon. As he walked, he mulled the words of the old one over and over in his mind. How foolish I've been, he thought. While I saw myself as profound and dedicated, I was superficial and silly. I really believed I could gain the wisdom of the masters and the peace of the Tao by myself. All I needed was to take the appropriate action and my search would be rewarded. I was convinced that the harder I tried, the more I'd succeed. Those long hours of silent reflecting and meditation got me absolutely nowhere. The constant comparison I made between myself and the other disciples just made me more upset. My judgments of everything and everyone made me miserable, because all I saw were the flaws of an imperfect world. No wonder I've had problems.

Chang kicked a small pebble in the path and shifted his right foot more comfortably in his sandal before he made a complete turn, heading back to the spot where Lao-tze sat awaiting his return. The morning sun was high and yellow in the azure sky, and Chang felt relief for the first time since he began his studies with Keng Sang Chu. His step was light, befitting a young man his age, and his handsome face sported a wide smile. Chang felt good! Lao-tze did not see his approach because he was watching a small bird take a drink from a depression in a stone at the edge of the stream opposite where he sat. He was surprised when the younger man tapped his shoulder lightly, saying, "Master, I am back." "Ah, so you are, so you are! I see, from the light in your eyes, the lilt in your voice and the buoyancy in your demeanor, that you have lifted a large burden from your shoulders. It's amazing what a good night's sleep, a conversation, and a hearty walk can do to a man and his spirits!"

"Master," Chang said, "please tell me what I need to know so that I can put into practice what you taught me this morning. I hope to be able to recapture what I have lost and, like an infant, become more receptive so that I might receive the gift of Tao." Lao-tze stood and put his arm on the young man's shoulder, "I am pleased that you have learned so much so quickly. Perhaps the quiet reflection you practiced in the past prepared you for our meeting. Learn not to waste time comparing yourself with others. Do not judge the world, for it is a strange place and will never meet your expectations. The Tao rules, not the plans of men! I will leave you with words that are the greatest gift I can bestow. If you take my words seriously and live by them, you will know Tao." Chang never forgot what the old one taught him that morning as they stood at the edge of the stream, bathed in the shade of the cool forest trees.

> To know when to stop
> To know when you can get no further
> By your own action,
> This is the right beginning! (Merton 1969, 133)

Some Comments

Chang took himself and his responsibility very seriously. In his desire to achieve perfection, he lost sight of his lighter self. He tried too hard to attain his goal. The simple joys and pleasures of life passed him by, and he became totally immersed in his own desperation. Like a dog chasing its own tail, the more he tried, the more frustrated he became. Finally, with Lao-tze's guidance, he stopped grasping for perfection and began to accept his limitations. In time, Chang would gain the insight to know which things he could not alter, and the wisdom to refrain from trying.

Public administration is not the only profession that can benefit from the story of Chang and the teachings of wu-wei, but it is one of the most important. From the Watergate scandal, to the current confusion surrounding allegations in the so-called Whitewater incident, we have a history of powerful individuals imposing their wills on the course of events. Great care must be taken by those who hold the public trust in their hands. High-level elected officials, top-ranking members of the civil service, and just ordinary government employees, all have a responsibility to examine their own motives before taking action.

Holding a position in government can be a rather heady experience. Often, such jobs involve considerable discretion over the lives of other people. From the traffic cop dispensing tickets, to the motor vehicle clerk processing drivers' licenses, decisions on whether to take action are commonplace. When problems arise due to an action that should not have been taken, it is often the result of an individual's ego getting in the way of better judgment. Ego is the constant companion of ambition and success. It lurks around the corridors of power and authority. It is a seductive and dangerous mistress, misleading us into false perceptions about ourselves and others.

Public administrators can learn from the admonishments of eastern philosophy concerning the insidious nature of the ego. Time spent in quiet reflection can unearth the hidden motivation of the driven ego. When this knowledge is raised to consciousness, it is easier for western individuals to stop and consider the actions they take. One of the most acclaimed translations of the writings of Lao-tze and Chuang Tzu was written in the 1920s by the esteemed scholar, James Legge. Legge devoted his life to the study of the sacred books of China, and interpreted the following tract from Book 7 of Chuang Tzu's teaching, called "The Normal Course for Rulers and Kings" (Müller 1927, 266):

> Non-Action (makes its exemplifier) the lord of all fame; non-action (serves him as) the treasury of all plans; non-action (fits him for) the burden of all offices; non-action (makes him) the lord of all wisdom. The range of his action is inexhaustible, but there is nowhere any trace of his presence.

NOTES

1. For a synopsis of the fundamental differences between Taoism and Confucianism, see: *Encyclopedia of Religion and Ethics*. Edited by James Hastings. Vol. 9. (New York: Charles Scribner's Sons, 1917, 855).

2. These classics of Chinese thought include: *The Analects*, *The Book of Mencius*, *The Great Learning*, and the *Doctrine of the Mean*.

3. As a man of his time, Confucius was concerned with how the character of men could be developed so that society might improve. All translations of his teachings use the masculine pronoun. Therefore, direct quotes in this book also refer to the masculine pronoun. In order for women readers to feel they can benefit from the teaching of Confucius, I use the plural "they" and "individuals" or "persons" when discussing or interpreting his ideas.

4. A more detailed description of a Confucian gentleman can be found in Edwin O. Reischauer and John K. Fairbank's book, *East Asia: The Great Tradition* (Boston: Houghton Mifflin, 1962, 471–73).

REFERENCES

Bahm, Archie J. 1992. *The Heart of Confucius*. Berkeley: Asian Humanities Press.
Cammerloher, M. C. 1985. "The Position of Art and Psychology in our Time." In *Spiritual Disciplines*. Edited by Joseph Campbell. Vol. 4. Princeton: Princeton University Press.
Chan, Wing-Tsit, trans. and comp. 1973. *A Source Book in Chinese Philosophy*. Reprint, Princeton: Princeton University Press.
Durant, Will. 1954. *Our Oriental Heritage*. Vol. 1 of *The Story of Civilization*. Reprint, New York: Simon and Schuster.
Goodsell, Charles T., and Nancy Murray, eds. 1995. *Public Administration Illuminated and Inspired by the Arts*. Westport, Connecticut: Praeger.
Jung, Carl G. 1974. "The Type Problem in Poetry." In *Psychological Types*. Vol. 6 of *Collected Works*. 1971. Reprint, Princeton: Princeton University Press.
Lao-tze. *Tao Teh King*. 1991. Translated by Paul Carus and D. T. Suzuki under the title *The Canon of Reason and Virtue*. La Salle: Open Court Publishing Company.
Merton, Thomas. 1969. *The Way of Chuang Tzu*. New York: New Directions.
Müller, Max F., ed. 1927. *The Sacred Books of the East*. Vol. 39. London: Humphrey Milford, publisher to Oxford University Press.
Shafritz, Jay M., Albert C. Hyde, and David H. Rosenbloom. 1986. *Personnel Management in Government*. 3d ed. New York: Marcel Dekker, Inc.
Van Over, Raymond, ed. 1984. *Taoist Tales*. New York: New American Library.
Waley, Arthur, trans. 1938. *The Analects of Confucius*. New York: Vintage Books.
———. 1958. *The Way and its Power*. New York: Grove Weidenfeld.

CHAPTER 7

A Meeting of the Minds: Beyond
Isolation Toward Unity

A human being is part of the whole.... He experiences himself, his
thoughts and feelings as something separated from the rest, a kind of
optical delusion of his consciousness (Weber 1986, 203).

ACROSS THE GREAT DIVIDE

The above quotation is attributed to Albert Einstein, who represents the
epitome of rational thought in western science. Einstein is saying that the
way in which we experience reality is illusory. This assertion is counter to
commonly held views of rationality. The idea that the world is based upon
a fundamental oneness is foreign to Cartesian dualism and its influence on
western thought. The perception of the universe as a unified whole has
persisted throughout the centuries among eastern peoples. Modern scientific
discoveries in quantum physics support the seemingly irrational idea that
everything in the universe is united. What appear to be separate entities
are simply manifestations of the same thing.

The parallels between modern physics and eastern metaphysics cannot
be ignored. The view that the world we see and experience is an illusion
is counterintuitive. To follow such thinking requires a stretching of the
western mind beyond traditional concepts of reality (Zukav 1989, 282):

That which is, is that which is. That which is not is that which is.
There is nothing which is not that which is.... We are part of that
which is. In fact, we are that which is.

David Bohm was one of the leading physicists of the twentieth century who saw a connection between quantum physics and eastern philosophy. Lecturing at the University of California at Berkeley in 1977, he called for a new order in the way science perceives the universe. He argued that science needs to reexamine its tradition of focusing on the parts of a problem in order to fit them together and make a whole. Bohm saw reality as an "unbroken wholeness" that includes the fundamental unity, which he referred to as "that-which-is" (Zukav 1989, 306).

The very fabric of the universe is enclosed in an "enfolded or implicate order," which is not easily seen or intuited. The "unbroken wholeness" that is the essence of reality is found here. It is impossible to describe the implicate order, beyond saying that at this level of reality everything is connected to everything else (Bohm 1983, 172):

> in the implicate order the totality of existence is enfolded within each region of space (and time). So, whatever part, element, or aspect we may abstract in thought, this still enfolds the whole and is therefore intrinsically related to the totality from which it has been abstracted. Thus, wholeness permeates all that is being discussed, from the very outset.

Whether it exists as matter or consciousness, everything in the universe is united at its source. This source provides a hidden order that defines our experiences in the world; it is folded inward, and has infinite depth. It is the most subtle and profound level of the world in which we live. This inward enfolded source is the implicate order which encompasses everything, including physical, psychological, and spiritual existence (Weber 1986, 25).

The most obvious and superficial level of our experience is the world of matter, which is composed of objects that appear to have autonomous existence. These objects comprise the "unfolded or explicate order." Bohm argued that our experience on this level is misleading, because it reflects only a portion of reality. The wholeness that is enfolded in the implicate order is never made totally manifest in the external world. We misinterpret reality when we assume that the visible world contains the entire picture of the multidimensional universe. Reality is made up of multiple phenomena, some of which are unfolded and become part of our daily lives. Other dimensions of reality exist but are not revealed to our consciousness. All aspects of reality are present in the implicate order in which everything in the universe is united (Weber 1986, 24–26).

The apparent scientific validation of the concept of unity, traditional to eastern metaphysics, is a significant contribution to western philosophy. The inner voice that strains to be heard resides within the implicate order. Ancient religious traditions likened it to a tiny flame that flickers and refuses to die. It is the source of all spiritual teaching and philosophical speculation. Intuition, imagination, and creativity are tightly woven into the implicate order. All aspects of our experience can be grasped at this level of profundity. Through the inner voice we learn of unity. We discover that we are not unique, but part of a larger reality.

Albert Einstein wrote a remarkable little book, called *The World As I See It* (1991), in which he presents his thoughts about the universe and our place in it. Einstein discusses that certain sense which lies within, believing it to be a cosmic feeling, equivalent to religion but without its theistic connotation. He states that the most profound scientists enjoy this cosmic feeling, recognizing there is a superior intelligence at work in the universe. They perceive nature as a harmonious blending of natural laws which reflect an underlying rationality (Einstein 1991, 28–29).

Einstein proposed that "it is the most important function of art and science to awaken this feeling and keep it alive in those who are capable of it" (Einstein 1991, 27). Public administration has the characteristics of both an art and a science. A philosophy appropriate for the practice of this art can encourage public administrators to tap into the cosmic feeling by engaging in silent reflection and listening to the message of the inner voice.

The implicate order and Jung's conception of the unconscious seem to be similar. When we experience the hidden recesses of the psyche and begin to understand our experiences in the unfolded world of everyday living, we discover much about ourselves and others. The unconscious is the key to the gate of metaphysical truth. When we enter its portals, we are able to hear the inner voice and encounter the hidden dimensions of ourselves—the source of all our actions in the outside world.

As we discover the covert truth of our connection to one another, responsibility takes on a new dimension. We begin to see ourselves reflected in the actions of others, and understanding replaces judgment. When we accept the fundamental unity that defines existence, we realize that our actions have significant impact on others. This realization increases our sense of accountability for what we do.

Unity and the Inner Voice

Vinoba Bhave relied on his own counsel the night prior to his scheduled departure from the village where he promised the poor people he would speak to Prime Minister Nehru about reforming the laws regarding land ownership. Prior to retiring for the night, Vinoba quietly reflected on the day's events. His mind was able to transcend the rush of activity he had engaged in and achieve a state of inner awareness. Vinoba acknowledged that his own ego was reflected in the rash promise. By listening to the inner voice he was able to overcome his desire for recognition. He saw the connection between himself and the villagers. Their needs became his needs, and he was able to identify with them. The silence of the night brings truth when we take the time to listen.

Bohm believed that western individuals can raise their consciousness and experience the truths contained in the implicate order (Zukav 1989, 308). He came to this realization after many conversations with eastern sages about sophisticated psychologies that evolved over thousands of years. Meditation practices focus on introspection, allowing individuals to hear the inner voice and experience the "pure undifferentiated reality which is that-which-is." Bohm's lectures on the Berkeley campus were addressed to physics students and professional physicists. He made the following statement at one of these lectures (309):[1]

> The word "reality" is derived from the roots "thing" (res) and "think" (revi). "Reality" means "everything you can think about." This is not "that which is." No idea can capture "truth" in the sense of that-which-is.

Emily's Voice

Emily recognized how limited the common perception of truth is. She fully accepted the value of ideas and knowledge as necessary adjuncts to successful functioning as a public administrator. She also fulfilled a deep-seated need to spend time in quiet reflection. During silent moments, Emily was able to place the demands of the outside world into perspective. Because she understood the connection among all things, her perception of what was happening in a given situation transcended the obvious. Neither the superficial nor the profound level of reality was lost to her. She often returned to a place deep within herself and experienced each event in her life in its totality.

As a child, Emily stood at the metaphorical fork in the road. She chose the path "less traveled by," which made all the difference in her life. While traveling the circuitous and sometimes treacherous pathways of the unconscious, Emily stopped at each of the gates of truth. She opened the gate where morality begins—the place where thought and action intersect. She also entered the gate leading to the site where the mystery of human psychology is revealed. Finally, Emily arrived at the gate leading to metaphysical truth. She chose to enter, and found the place where the inner voice reveals its secrets.

The incident in Skokie rocked the confidence of her colleagues. Emily, on the other hand, was empowered with the strength of complete understanding. She knew how to avert the bloodshed that always attends violence, but her colleagues refused to listen. They were convinced they could control the situation through the power of their superior force. Emily understood their response, because she saw herself reflected in their assessment of the situation; every time she looked upon another person, whether a colleague or client, she saw herself. She understood the actions of those who held the unfortunate hostages captive, as well as the hostages themselves.

All human characteristics, good or bad, positive or negative, were mirrored in each person Emily encountered. There was no human action, however heinous, that she could not understand. She had pondered the depths of the human psyche and integrated all aspects of the Self. Emily knew she did not stand apart. The optical delusion of consciousness that Einstein said makes us experience ourselves as separate was apparent to her. Emily was able to incorporate the wisdom of the inner voice into her experience as a public administrator. She possessed an unusual sensitivity to others and perceived the subtleties inherent in every situation.

Emily's sense of identification with everyone was total. Through years of experience with the actions of her family, friends, and colleagues, she developed a kind of fatalistic acceptance. She recognized her role as a partner in the dance of life, who sometimes was able to take the lead. During those times when she had to watch others orchestrate the dance, Emily acquiesced. Such was the situation she experienced that fateful day in Skokie.

Emily learned through silence and introspection what David Bohm learned through science: "inseparable quantum interconnectedness of the whole universe is the fundamental reality, and that relatively independently behaving parts are merely particular and contingent forms within this whole" (Capra 1991, 138). The universe is not made up of distinct physical objects as it appears to be. Rather, it is composed of complicated sets of interactions which are constantly changing. Complexity, ambiguity, interconnectedness, continual motion, and mutual dependence describe the essential nature of the universe.

Newton's Assumptions

Early physicists attempted to explain how the solid bodies we see and experience in the world move and relate to one another. The philosophical basis of classical physics was the Cartesian assumption that there is a division between the individual person and everything that exists. True to Descartes' legacy, physicists believed there is an objective world outside ourselves that can be observed, explained, and predicted. They believed that the objects composing the world are separate and distinct from one another. In the eighteenth century, an English philosopher and mathematician named Sir Isaac Newton made two assumptions about the nature of the universe: that the objects outside ourselves are composed of solid matter, and these objects move in empty space. Following these assumptions, Newton concluded that the multiple objects making up the universe are tightly controlled and remain fundamentally unchanged during their existence. This is certainly a useful belief for everyday living. No one will dispute that a brick thrown from the top of a building will probably kill a passerby on the sidewalk below, if the person is hit.

The law of gravity assures us we will not be bombarded by objects flying out of control. The reality we experience every day is one in which separate objects exist simultaneously in a relationship that assures they have the space they need. There was little evidence available in the eighteenth century to dispute the assumptions of Newtonian physics. Physicists believed that immutable laws applied to every type of physical system in the universe. After the discovery of electric and magnetic phenomena, scientists concluded that Newton's model "could be applied only to a limited group of phenomena, essentially the motion of solid bodies" (Capra 1991, 41).

The discovery of electromagnetic forces opened a Pandora's box of creativity in physics. The research prompted by this finding implies that physics and eastern philosophy belong together like a hand in a well-fitting glove. Both physicists and philosophers act on the natural sense of wonder that we all share. They pursue their questions relentlessly, until they arrive at an explanation that satisfies the mind. Scientists were eager to study why Newton's laws apply only to solid matter and large objects. Philosophers began to reexamine traditional ideas concerning the foundation of reality. Thinking people everywhere wondered if there was more to appearances than met the eye. Long-held intuitive impressions began to surface, which contradicted scientific explanations of the composition of the universe, how it operates, and the purpose of life.

A Quantum Leap

In the 1920s physicists from all over the world discovered that certain phenomena regarding the structure of atoms could not be explained by classical physics. Highly acclaimed scientists, such as Niels Bohr from Denmark, Louis DeBroglie from France, Austrian physicists Erwin Schrödinger and Wolfgang Pauli, Werner Heisenberg from Germany, and the English physicist Paul Dirac, simultaneously studied the reality of the subatomic world. Their findings were bizarre, for they learned that atomic physics is filled with paradoxes that could not be resolved by applying traditional descriptions to what they observed. After trial and error, the scientists developed a mathematical theory that addressed the phenomena they were studying (Capra 1991, 66).

The citations in the next two sections refer to Gary Zukav's book, *The Dancing Wu Li Masters*. Unlike Newtonian physics, which is based upon preexisting separate parts, quantum theory relies solely upon observation and is unconcerned with relationships or what occurs between observations. Something happens only when it is observed. For example, a scientist observes an electron at point A. The same scientist observes an electron at point B. In no way does the physicist assume that an electron traveled from point A to point B. The only conclusion the scientist makes is that an electron was observed at point A and at point B (Zukav 1989, 305).

Quantum physics shows there is a genuine relationship between a person who is making an observation and the item being observed. In effect, it means we do not experience external reality, but rather our interaction with it. Niels Bohr, the Danish physicist, called this phenomenon the principle of complementarity, and used it to explain the observations made by scientists studying the behavior of light (Zukav 1989, 305).

Experiments have shown that light has two aspects, mutually exclusive of one another. Sometimes light manifests particle-like behavior; other times it exhibits wave-like properties. Light cannot be a wave and a particle at the same time. One must always exclude the other. If these two behaviors are mutually exclusive, how can they both be properties of light? The answer is that they are not properties of light. They are properties of the interaction of the observer with light. In other words, the presence of the scientist is required for light to exhibit either wave- or particle-like properties (Zukav 1989, 93).

It appears, then, that light has no properties independent of the human observer. "To say that something has no properties is the same as saying that it does not exist. The next step in this logic is inescapable. Without us, light does not exist" (Zukav 1989, 95). Bohr argued that since light needs "agencies of observation" to exist, these agencies also require light for their existence. By use of the term "agencies of observation," it is unclear whether Bohr was referring to the instruments used in measuring the waves and particles, or to the human observers. Whichever he had in mind, his implication is clear—without light we do not exist. This is an inevitable conclusion when we consider that the wave-particle duality is found in everything. Zukav argues that Bohr has solved the wave-particle duality by showing that properties belong to interactions and not to independent objects. In a philosophical sense, it appears that the universe is composed of interactions, not things.

The German physicist, Werner Heisenberg, argued that it is not possible for someone to observe a phenomenon without changing it. What we experience in the physical world outside ourselves is integrally connected with our psychological and philosophical perceptions (Zukav 1989, 305). Heisenberg learned through many experiments that it is impossible for scientists to study anything without exerting an influence on the outcome. He observed that at the level of subatomic particles there appears to be no objective reality. The scientist observing subatomic activity is not distinct from what he or she is seeing. The observer and that which is being observed are one and the same. At the level of particle physics, we create the world we see. "If the new physics has led us anywhere, it is back to ourselves, which of course, is the only place that we could go" (114).

Heisenberg also proved that science is not exact, but riddled with uncertainties. The natural world imposes limits upon the ability of scientists to measure phenomena accurately. For instance, it is impossible to measure the position and momentum of a particle at the same time. The more that is learned about one, the more obscure the other becomes. It is like trying to adjust a moving picture that is not focused. When the left side is clear, the right side clouds over. When the image on the right side of the screen is clarified, the clarity on the left disappears. Each time scientists achieve accuracy in momentum, they lose it in position. With this in mind, Heisenberg concluded that at the subatomic level of reality, the very act of measuring and observing alters the phenomena being studied. There is no such thing as an independent observer who can stand on the sidelines watching nature run its course without influencing it (Zukav 1989, 112).

Therefore, there are no external certainties that we can rely upon as causes for what happens. Zukav asks us to conduct an easy experiment to verify our capacity to influence events. He suggests that we stare at a person's back. After a period of time, it is almost assured that the individual will turn around and look. Many of us have had a similar experience, but discounted it because it contradicts what we've been conditioned to believe. We think what occurs is completely outside ourselves and our thoughts. We look for causes in the external world to explain what happens (Zukav 1989, 113).

Quantum physics was born in an atmosphere of excitement and bewilderment because it ran contrary, not only to classical physics, but also to common sense. Common sense tells us everything has a cause and if we isolate the cause, we can influence the outcome. Causality is firmly rooted in our consciousness and extremely difficult to discard. It provides assurance that the apparent chaos in the world rests upon a foundation of order and control.

Science is based upon the perfection of our ability to observe and measure what we see so we can elicit causes and affect greater control over nature and the working of the universe. Our everyday experience with solid bodies of matter moving at slow velocities presents a picture of reality that is the opposite of what happens at the subatomic level of existence, which is defined by the activities of ever-changing particles.

There is no cause and effect at the level of particle behavior; there is only probability. In 1964 the Scottish physicist, J. S. Bell, developed mathematical proof that if the probability predictions of quantum theory are correct, common sense is wrong. Zukav argues that "the statistical predictions of quantum mechanics are always correct" (Zukav 1989, 290). The implication of this fact is events that occur are not independent of one another, however distant they may be in either space or time. This is a direct contradiction of common sense, which presents a world in which all events seem to be independently caused and separate. It further implies that everything we do, think, or say has repercussions that transcend distance and time.

In 1975 Henry Stapp, a physicist at the prestigious Lawrence Berkeley Laboratory in California, secured a grant from the U.S. Energy Research and Development Administration. After studying Bell's work, Stapp argued that the probability predictions of quantum theory violate common sense because they apply both to events in the macroscopic world of everyday experience and to subatomic reality (Zukav 1989, 290). Stapp further concluded that Bell's theorem may be the most significant scientific discovery to-date (294).

If the physicists are correct, everything in the universe is united in the fundamental oneness that eastern metaphysics has taught since ancient times. What appear to be separate entities are simply manifestations of the same thing. Because the oneness that unites us all with one another and with every other object is beyond space and time, it cannot be measured. There is not, nor can there ever be, final proof of a primordial unity that forever lies at the source of the universe.

Due to the influence of Descartes and the conditioning of twentieth-century science, we are convinced that duality is the law of the universe. We believe our mind is separate from our body. We experience our feelings, intellects, thoughts, and abilities as distinct from everything else that defines us. As a result of all this division, we have become alienated from ourselves, one another, and the mysteries and glories of the natural world. This dualistic thinking is in marked contrast to the idea of unity that formed the basis of early Greek and eastern ideas (Zukav 1989, 22–23).

Unity and an Open Mind

Eastern metaphysics teaches that an open mind is necessary if an individual is to attain ultimate truth. The discipline of physics demonstrates the value of being open to fresh ideas. If modern physicists had failed to keep an open mind, the startling discoveries of quantum mechanics would not have been made. In the early 1900s, physicists believed that Newtonian physics had solved almost all the mysteries of the universe, and their discipline would soon disappear. By the late 1920s, the cornerstone of quantum mechanics and relativity theory had been laid, and a new era was born in modern physics.

Wherever today's physicists stand in their conception of the universe, their thinking is qualitatively different in that they recognize the unity that lies at the root of existence. It is no longer taken for granted that the world we experience every day is the only reality there is. Modern physics has become intellectually open with the discoveries of the twentieth century. However, as a science that demands proof, it differs from the more intuitive tradition of eastern metaphysics (Zukav 1989, 311–12).

Although the new physics and eastern philosophy share similar insights into what reality is, they differ in the manner in which they discern the truth. This distinction was recognized by the father of quantum mechanics, Max Planck who wrote the following words (Zukav 1989, 313): "Science . . . means unresting endeavor and continually progressing development toward an aim which the poetic intuition may apprehend, but which the intellect can never fully grasp."[2]

The aim toward which science and intuition aspire is the attainment of "the higher dimensions of human experience" (Zukav 1989, 313). Silence, reflection, and openness to the message of the inner voice can lead us to such heights of awareness. We can reach these heights if we keep our minds receptive to possibilities that are not part of our belief system. Most individuals raised in the traditions commonly found among the diverse components of western culture are unaware of their full potential.

Unity, Science, and Intuition

On June 11, 1983, a conversation was held in Brockwood Park, England, between David Bohm and the great Indian teacher Jiddu Krishnamurti. Three years prior to this meeting, the western physicist and eastern metaphysician engaged in thirteen similar dialogues. I have taken the liberty of quoting relevant sections of this particular conversation to show the reader how the power inherent in our thoughts affects the world. If we recognize that separation is misguided perception and embrace the concept of unity, our influence can contribute to a changed world. Each of the following excerpts is preceded by a brief explanation of the context in which it occurs (Krishnamurti and Bohm 1986).

CONTEXT: Krishnamurti and Bohm are discussing the fact that suffering continues to exist in the world. Krishnamurti argues that as human beings we delude ourselves into thinking that suffering is an individual experience. Because of this misperception, we do not take steps to eliminate suffering unless it directly affects us. Bohm, interested in Krishnamurti's concept of consciousness, raises interesting questions (Krishnamurti and Bohm 1986, 43–44):

JK: Suffering is common to all humanity.

DB: But the fact that it is common is not enough to make it all one.

JK: It is actual.

DB: Are you saying that the suffering of mankind is all one, inseparable?

JK: Yes, that's right.

DB: That when anybody suffers, the whole of mankind is suffering.

JK: Suffering is part of our consciousness.

DB: But one doesn't get the feeling immediately that this suffering belongs to the whole of mankind, you see.

JK: The world is me: I am the world. But we have divided it up into the British earth, and the French earth, and all the rest of it!

DB: Do you mean by the world, the physical world, or the world of society?

JK: The world of society, primarily the psychological world.

DB: So we say the world of society, of human beings, is one, and when I say I am that world, what does it mean?

JK: The world is not different from me.

DB: The world and I are one. We are inseparable.

CONTEXT: Having established that as human beings we are united, the two men now discuss the implications of that unity (Krishnamurti and Bohm 1986, 45):

JK: Yes. And that is real meditation, you must feel this, not just as a verbal statement: it is an actuality. I am my brother's keeper.

DB: Before we go on, let's clear up a point about "me" . . . it seems that you are still defining an individual. Is that right?

JK: Yes. I am using the word "I" as a means of communication.

CONTEXT: Having established that human beings are both united and responsible for one another, Krishnamurti and Bohm ponder the effect our misperception of separation from one another has on the human condition (Krishnamurti and Bohm 1986, 47):

DB: Yes, we have to say that in some ways the consciousness of mankind has divided itself, it is all one but it has divided itself by thought. And that is why we are in this situation.

JK: *That* is why. All the problems that humanity has now, psychologically, as well as in other ways, are the result of thought. And we are pursuing the same pattern of thought, and thought will never solve any of these problems. So, there is another kind of instrument, which is intelligence.

CONTEXT: After a prolonged dialogue on the mind and brain, Krishnamurti and Bohm arrive at the conclusion that the intelligence that can solve humanity's problems resides in the mind (Krishnamurti and Bohm 1986, 67):

DB: Yes, I understand that we have here two things which can be somewhat independent. There is the brain and the mind, though they make contact. Then we say that intelligence and compassion come from beyond the brain. Now I would like to go into the question of how they are making contact.

JK: Ah! Contact can only exist between the mind and the brain when the brain is quiet.

DB: Yes, that is the requirement for making it. The brain has got to be quiet.

JK: Quiet is not a trained quietness. Not a self-conscious, meditative, desire for silence. It is a natural outcome of understanding one's own conditioning.

DB: And one can see that if the brain is quiet it could listen to something deeper?

JK: That's right. Then if it is quiet it is related to the mind. Then the mind can function through the brain.

CONTEXT: Krishnamurti has argued that the brain is conditioned *while the mind is not*. Both he and Bohm agree that through silence the brain can achieve the quiet necessary for contact with mind. They are saying, in effect, that the brain is used as an instrument through which mind can be expressed. Mind and brain are in contact and not divided, but there must be space for mind to enter. Space comes when the brain is quiet and free from conditioning. It seems they are equating mind with psyche. Referring to psyche, Krishnamurti says, "It is what it is" (Krishnamurti and Bohm 1986, 71–72):

DB: You are using the word mind; not *"my"* mind.

JK: Mind. It is not "mine."

DB: It is universal or general.

JK: Mind is universal—if you can use that ugly word.

DB: Unlimited and undivided.

JK: You cannot call it *your* mind. You only have *your* brain which is conditioned. You can't say "It is *my* mind."

DB: But whatever is going on inside I feel is mine, and it is very different from what is going on inside somebody else.

JK: No, I question whether it is different.

DB: At least it seems different.

JK: My thought has created the belief that I am different from you because my body is different from yours, my face is different from yours. We extend that same thing into the psychological area.

DB: But now if we said that division is an illusion, perhaps?

JK: No, not perhaps! It is.

DB: It is an illusion. All right. Although, it is not obvious when a person first looks at it.

JK: Of course.

DB: In reality even brain is not divided, because we are saying that we are all not only basically similar but really connected. And then we say beyond all that is mind, which has no division at all.

JK: It is unconditioned.

Here we see how modern scientific thinking and eastern metaphysics can exist side by side, and together interpret the meaning of reality.

Emily's Connectedness

Emily was sensitive to the suffering of the captors as well as the hostages in the Skokie incident because she shared with them the pain that anger generates. Her journey to the gates of truth taught her she was psychologically connected to all human beings. In a psychological sense, she was inseparable from the men and women holed up in Skokie, and possessed a deep understanding of how the experience was affecting them all.

Through her personal identification with their predicament, Emily was able to relate to them at a level beyond the capacity of her colleagues. She could not adequately express in words how the situation affected her, because her response was rooted in intuitive knowing, not in reason. The ability to feel the suffering of others *in a manner conducive to the maintenance of one's own psychological well being* in no way lessens one's capacity to think of a solution. To the contrary, it enhances thought processes. Emily was able to weigh the solutions her thoughts provided against the deep feelings she was experiencing. The *psychological balance* she sustained provided her with a carefully deliberated solution, tempered by a profound comprehension of the nature of the drama that was unfolding.

The response of Emily's colleagues to the hostage situation was rooted in reason, not feeling. Certainly, they shared the expected human reaction of sympathy and concern for the hostages, but they were not capable of feeling anything other than anger at the captors. Their emotional reaction to the situation was qualitatively different from Emily's. They simply lacked the depth of psychological involvement that she possessed. They would not have been capable of preserving their own psychological health had they experienced the degree to which Emily identified with the plight of all the individuals involved. Eliot was the only other person who understood the situation as thoroughly as she did.

The definition of intelligence that Krishnamurti proposed in his conversation with David Bohm is foreign to western concepts of rationality. To Krishnamurti, intelligence lies in the mind, not the brain, where the powers of reason are found. Krishnamurti distinguished between the brain and the mind. When the brain is quiet, it is able to understand the biases of the culture in which it is immersed. When the noise of its conditioning has been stilled, the brain is able to hear the whisper of the inner voice, which resides in the mind.

The long, lonely days spent on the farm as a child, coupled with her introspective nature, enabled Emily to see through the conditioning that was a part of her life. Silence and reflection were her constant companions. Her busy brain quieted during the days when Emily lost herself investigating the wonders of the farm. She became engrossed in the efficiency of the insects and antics of the animals that lived there. The mind that is shared by all of humanity entered the space vacated by her preoccupied brain.

Deep within her mind the inner voice raised its pitch, and Emily heard the message.

Once she possessed the intuitive knowing that accompanies the intelligence of the mind, Emily became aware of her connection with all things in the universe. She understood that what appeared to be a world of division was only the superficial level of reality. Having experienced the truths of the inner voice, Emily knew the significance of genuine intelligence. She would always be a person of deep insight, requiring silent times for reflection, and a person of uncommon compassion and understanding.

MAKING A DIFFERENCE

> He will rest in his eternal place
> Which is no place.
> He will be hidden
> In his own unfathomable secret.
> His nature sinks to its root
> In the One.
> His vitality, his power
> Hide in secret Tao.
> When he is all one,
> There is no flaw in him
> By which a wedge can enter. (Merton 1969, 105–06)

Chuang Tzu's words help explain Emily's character. She was unaware that her feeling of connection with all of life could be traced to ancient eastern teachings. Neither was she interested in amassing power. The vitality and power of which Chuang Tzu speaks is not the self-aggrandizing public display usually associated with the term in western culture. Emily's power lay in her realization that because she was united with all human beings, she was neither superior nor inferior to any of them. She was somehow a part of every thought and action. The secret truth of unity that the inner voice shared with Emily enabled her to accept life on its own terms.

Unity and the Public Administrator

Emily's experience with the unconscious and the message of the inner voice may be difficult for many public administrators to accept, let alone apply to themselves. We have been conditioned to doubt there is such a thing as a reality that knows no division. In western society we are encouraged to live according to our senses. Only what we can see and feel is real to us. Intuitive knowledge is held in suspicion in our sensate culture. Our lives are filled with thoughts of differences and separation, not identification and unity.

For example, a common practice in government human resource offices is to trace the patterns of behavior that a troublesome employee exhibits, to determine the cause of his or her disturbance. The pattern is assumed to define whatever problem is motivating the individual. Actually, patterns of behavior simply trace the progression of an individual's need to act out. They do not explain the motivation behind the behavior. A more effective way of understanding a disgruntled employee is to view that person as no different from the rest of us. When we see ourselves in others, however uncomfortable that may make us feel, we come closer to a realization of why there is a problem and what can be done to alleviate it. In other words, we touch a place in ourselves that enables us to identify with the individual who is experiencing the problem.

Emily exemplifies this in her handling of the situation involving high absentee rates among young parents in her agency. Through silent reflection, she was able to put herself in the situation of a working parent, responsible for the care and well-being of young children. Her capacity to identify with others without losing her own sense of Self made Emily a vital force in her profession. Her value also lay in her ability to see each situation in the context of the whole. She knew that everything is interdependent and does not exist in isolation.

Not only does our Cartesian heritage with its doctrine of duality affect human relationships, it also affects many aspects of public administration practice. Many administrators pay considerable attention to detail, viewing things in terms of the particular rather than the general. This is a difficult habit to overcome because of our preoccupation with efficiency. It is widely believed among contemporary public administrators that problems can be solved when their cause is determined. Once the source of a problem is found, an appropriate outcome can be managed. Efficiency, therefore, is the result of separating cause from effect and controlling both.

However, it is not always possible to pinpoint the cause of something. We think we know, but upon further study we find we have been mistaken. Remember Aunt Jane pressing the doorbell back in chapter two? We are always limited by our own perspective. Our location in time and space affects what we perceive to be the cause of any effect we wish to understand. It is impossible to remove ourselves from the cause of any effect we are studying.

For instance, analysts trying to recommend government programs to curb drug use in high schools have differing opinions about why teenagers use drugs. Some argue that the cause lies in dysfunctional families; others believe it is the result of dire poverty; and some are convinced it is due to conditions prevalent in a pathological society. We mislead the inquiry and jeopardize the solution to our social problems when we try to reduce them to single, manageable causes, thereby separating them from their effects.

Quantum physics has revealed that the universe operates according to probability, not causation. No matter how much we improve our ability to make accurate measurements, the natural world will always behave in an unpredictable manner. Scientists are starting to see the universe as a series of profoundly interconnected events. When we find an apparent cause of a particular event, it is due to certain conditions which have focused on a single factor. This factor operates in conjunction with many interconnected and inextricably woven phenomena which contribute to the probability that the event will either occur or not. Causation, as an independent element in explaining why an event happens, seems to be another delusion of western consciousness.[3]

When we lose our guarantee that causation can provide irrefutable answers to the dilemmas we face as public administrators, we become like small boats adrift in an endless sea of ever-receding horizons. Where do we go from here? If the observations and measurements made by the so-called hard sciences are unreliable, where do the social sciences stand? What do we do with the sophisticated formulas and models we use to rationalize policymaking?

We should not abandon our advanced measurement techniques, but continue to improve them. Because we lack the highly evolved mental faculties we could potentially rely upon as a replacement, we need to use what we have devised at this stage in human development. We can also be wiser in our expectations. Instead of reducing all data to formula-driven certainties, we can admit we are dealing with endlessly changing phenomena that are beyond our control. Each situation is unique and subject to its own set of circumstances.

When we are implementing a new program, we must be careful that the "conditions under which the operations are to be executed must be stated precisely. Operations implemented at one order of magnitude may not provide the same outcome when repeated at another" (Siu 1991, 34). By looking within and listening to the inner voice, we can fill in the blank spaces that exist between what science provides and our instincts command. Our decisions can then be consistent with what we learn from the objective world, tempered by our own subjective reality. A certain sense that lies deep within allows us to see beyond the limits of outside knowledge.

Public administrators can learn from eastern teaching and quantum theory to accept cause and effect as mysteriously linked together. The delusion of consciousness is misleading, because it gives us false hope that we can reduce all problem situations to an elemental source, and through rational means affect solutions. Our failure to recognize there is a unity that connects all things and events has caused many mistakes to be made. The most serious are those which have separated individuals and groups from the rest of humanity.

The most heinous example of such a mistake in the twentieth century is the Holocaust. This blot on the face of humankind speaks of the unimaginable degree to which government policy can alienate human beings from one another. More recent examples include the regimes of Baby Doc in Haiti, Saddam Hussein in Iraq, and the bloody slaughter in Rwanda and Bosnia. These examples bear witness to the evils that can befall humanity when we do not see the face of another as a mirror of our own.

As Americans dedicated to the preservation of human rights, we may consider these examples as extreme. However, humanity manifests itself in diverse forms. Public administrators responsible for seeing that the constitutional rights of all citizens are honored, must be sensitive to every person. There are many ways in which we violate one another. Inhumane treatment is a matter of degree that can range from verbal putdowns to physical abuse; snide remarks to slanderous statements; sexual harassment to rape; and from physical torture to murder. These hurtful actions would not happen if we saw ourselves mirrored in the other person.

Certain important questions regarding the role of public administrators have been examined, discussed, and debated since the potential power of their positions was first recognized. Public administrators serve an important function as advisors to legislative bodies deliberating on public policy issues. They are crucial to the implementation of government programs, and form the first line of defense to an often critical citizenry.

Public administrators occupy authoritative positions and must decide where to draw the line. They are not elected officials responding to the public on the basis of a political platform. Further complicating their position is the crucial role they play in developing and interpreting the guidelines that accompany program legislation. Many scholars have commented that the guidelines can be more significant than the legislation itself.

The unity principle should be central to a philosophy of public administration. Acceptance of this truth will encourage public administrators to listen to the inner voice before making decisions on important issues, such as affirmative action, welfare, and health care. Individual administrators may differ in their views on controversial policies, but by enbracing the unity principle, they will not be inclined to judge the worth of individuals on the basis of their circumstances.

Substantial disservice is paid to people when they are judged better or worse than others. When public administrators confer special status on certain individuals, they undermine the neutrality essential to decision making. There is a temptation to do this because of our tendency to rely on facts to the exclusion of intuition and feeling. One person may seem more deserving than another simply because the facts support his or her case. The instruments and tools of decision making have replaced insight, preventing us from intuiting the deep connection we share with one another.

What happens every day in the office provides opportunities for personal and professional growth. Our daily work place is the laboratory where we sharpen our skills and either accept or reject the many instances in which we can function responsibly. We are part of everything we experience, whether or not an active participant. Shoddy work or the demeaning behavior carried out by one co-worker toward another affects us and reflects upon our own integrity. When we choose not to see these things or excuse them, we are not behaving in a responsible manner.

The only way public administration can accept the challenge of organizational renewal in the twenty-first century is if individual employees see clearly what is wrong and accept personal responsibility. This will happen when we gain the insight and wisdom to find the common thread that unites everyone and each situation we face. When we do this, we become less blaming, more accepting of individual differences, and less fearful of seeing ourselves through the eyes of others. Let us heed Jung's warning and avoid the trap of abdicating our responsibility for our own actions and the influence we may have on the actions of others (Jung 1978, 10:572).

> Since it is universally believed that man is merely what his consciousness knows of itself, he regards himself as harmless and so adds stupidity to iniquity. He does not deny that terrible things have happened and still go on happening, but it is always "the others" who do them.

Jung predicted that the gulf which exists between intellect and feeling that has caused much pain and is a blot on the history of the human race will disappear. The world will shrink into a more unified entity, resulting in changing perceptions (Jung 1978, 10:569–70). He believed that meaning cannot be found in western reasoning because it denies the hidden rationality that exists in everything and provides order and significance to life (Jung 1973, 8:922). Jung interpreted the words of Chuang Tzu, "you use your inner eye, your inner ear, to pierce to the heart of things, and have no need of intellectual knowledge" as an acknowledgment of the truths that exist in the unconscious mind, especially the intuitive sense that all things are united (923).

When we respect our own intellect and feeling, we become more open to the kind of knowing that comes from the inner voice. We are neither judgmental nor approving of the transgressions of others—we simply understand. Through this understanding we are able to connect with others and influence the course of events. This is genuine power and vitality.

NOTES

1. Zukav does not distinguish which group Bohm was addressing when he spoke these words. There is no citation in his notes to clarify this point.

2. Zukav is quoting from Max Planck, *The Philosophy of Physics* (New York: Norton, 1936, 83).

3. The reader is reminded of the discussion by Fox and Miller of the replacement

of the deterministic model of deconstruction of bureaucracy with the probabilistic model (see chapter 3). Fox and Miller argue that the success of probabilism is dependent upon sophisticated statistical methodologies. These methodologies, in turn, are dependent upon the theoretical underpinnings of quantum physics, which presents a universe whose contents are nothing more or less than probabilistic tendencies. This finding, which is in accord with ancient metaphysical teachings, is the foundation of probabilism.

REFERENCES

Bohm, David. 1983. *Wholeness and the Implicate Order*. New York: ARK Paperbacks.

Capra, Fritjof. 1991. *The Tao of Physics*. 3d ed. Boston: Shambala.

Einstein, Albert. 1991. *The World As I See It*. Translated by Alan Harris. Reprint, New York: Carol Publishing Group.

Jung, Carl G. 1973. "Synchronicity, An Acausal Connecting Principle." In *The Structure and Dynamics of the Psyche*. Vol. 8 of *Collected Works*. 2d ed. 1969. Princeton: Princeton University Press.

————. 1978. "The Undiscovered Self." In *Civilization in Transition*. Vol. 10 of *Collected Works*. 2d ed. 1970. Reprint, Princeton: Princeton University Press.

Krishnamurti, J., and David Bohm. 1986. *The Future of Humanity*. San Francisco: Harper and Row.

Merton, Thomas. 1969. *The Way of Chuang Tzu*. New York: New Directions.

Siu, R. G. H. 1991. *The Tao of Science*. Reprint, Cambridge: The MIT Press.

Weber, Renee. 1986. *Dialogues with Scientists and Sages: The Search for Unity*. New York: Routledge and Kegan Paul.

Zukav, Gary. 1989. *The Dancing Wu Li Masters*. Reprint, New York: Bantam Books.

PART 4

Commentary on Public Administration Tomorrow

CHAPTER 8

Journey's End

They thought it would be a disgrace to go forth in a group. Each entered the forest that *he* had chosen where there was no path and where it was darkest. (Campbell 1989, 73)

Now, dear reader, we have come to the end of our journey together. Each of us will continue along a path of our choosing. Like the knights of King Arthur's court who chose to seek the Holy Grail, some of us will enter the forest unaccompanied. The untraveled woods will yield many surprises, from sunny, open meadows to dark, secluded caves. The forest of the psyche is a strange place, and it awaits all who seek to unravel its secrets. Through its labyrinthian corridors and dark caves, the seeker of self-knowledge walks alone. None of us can dictate to another the path to choose, for there is no universal way of attaining self-knowledge.

We stood together at the divergence of two paths in the woods and decided to follow the one less worn. We left the path of reason, where we were safe and certain of what lay ahead in the bend of the road. Passing beyond rationalistic thinking and the ideas contained in the Cartesian Duality, we took a metaphorical trip to a different place on the philosophical landscape.

Looking toward the horizon, where the sun sets in the western sky, we watched the brilliant red glow soften to pink, then pale yellow, and finally the dusky grey of evening. The silence that replaced the light of day allowed us to listen to the stirrings of the voice within. Looking toward the horizon, where the sun rises in the eastern sky, we watched the night wake, to blush as a new day promised to light our path. Our journey led us to experience possibilities not honored in our western tradition. Some of us were unaware of the lost opportunities this lack has caused in our lives. Conditioned to open the gate where practical matters reside, we were oblivious to more contemplative, philosophical paths. Deprived of meaning, we ignored our need to realize the highest potential we are capable of attaining. Living in a structured society, we lost sight of our own passion.

As children of the twentieth century, we suffered the consequences of the shift away from mystery toward social/political reality. Some of us became overly rational. We failed to see ourselves as we truly are—united and free. We lost the "sense of transcendent energy that unites all of us, coordinates our cities, coordinates our lives" (Campbell 1989, 71). In an attempt to regain our center, we chose to travel together for a while, until we sufficiently restored our perspective, allowing us to choose our own way.

Along the road, we met many interesting people. Some were actual characters from the pages of history. For example, Confucius, Lao-tze, and Chuang Tzu were important contributors to Chinese culture. Vinoba Bhave and Krishnamurti bequeathed teachings rich in human value to the people of India. Our own western philosophers also met our acquaintance. We conversed with Rene Descartes, Frances Bacon, Immanuel Kant, and David Hume. They helped us understand the traditions that informed our consciousness and molded us into the people we are today.

Jergen Habermas and Jacques Derrida were postmodern thinkers we met in passing. Scientists like Albert Einstein, Niels Bohr, David Bohm, and Max Planck introduced us to worlds unknown. Werner Heisenberg confirmed the sense of uncertainty we always knew, but feared to face. Traveling further into the realms of mystery, we discovered Taoism through the writings and translations of Thomas Merton. The poetry of the eastern metaphysicians, the discoveries of modern physicists, the insights of human psychology, and the spiritual intuition of contemporary writers like Thomas Moore, rounded out our sojourn into new territory.

Although our journey focused on the ideas of the east, we were guided by western thinkers. Carl Jung helped us integrate eastern beliefs into our western mentality. Robert Frost placed us in the lap of nature and left us alone to discover its secrets. Aldous Huxley educated us to the common ground that exists among all beliefs and cultures. He gave us three gates from which to choose, and left us alone to ponder our decision, secure in the realization that the path to follow and the gate to open are personal decisions which allow no judgment and cast no aspersions. If we have learned anything from eastern philosophy, it is that the Tao follows its own course and is unaffected by attempts to control its natural progression.

Like most travelers at journey's end, we have reviewed our experience. Let us not forget the characters we met through parables. They serve us well as metaphors that will remain with us long after ideas are forgotten. The most significant character is Emily, for she is most like us. She was born and raised in the same culture and trained in its traditions. Emily revelled in the fields of allegory, swam in the deep lakes of silence, and walked through the quiet countryside, accompanied only by her thoughts. Her relationship to the natural world is a metaphor we can apply to our daily lives.

It is possible to discover a part of ourselves that we either forgot about or never knew. Our mind can open and we can learn new truths. We do not need to live on a New England farm to hear the inner voice. The experiences life provides are opportunities for us to delve within and find the wisdom that lives in the heart. Jung speaks of it as a jewel that is our birthright. Ancient Chinese philosophers traveled the inner road in search of their own jewel:

> The sages awaken through self-cultivation;
> Deep, Profound,
> Their practices require great effort. (Olson 1992, 41)

Emily's insight was also the result of great effort exerted over a lifetime of silent reflection. Her predilection toward introspection and philosophical probing is shared by few in contemporary western society. Emily is reminiscent of the nineteenth-century poet and essayist, Ralph Waldo Emerson, who symbolizes all that is fine and elevated in American thought. Influenced by Plato and the sacred books of the east, Emerson was a transcendentalist. The value he placed on intuition and matters of the spirit was not unusual among the men and women of his time and station. His ideas speak to us today, if we consider the practice of public administration more a calling than an occupation. Emily certainly did.

The following words taken from Emerson's essay "The Over-Soul" provide insight into his character and, by extension, to Emily's as well. Both enjoyed the security that comes from a sense of connection with others. Their capacity to live in a community was based upon a genuine respect for spirit as the unifying force that gives meaning to life (Emerson 1987, 164):

> I am certified of a common nature; and these other souls, these separated selves, draw me as nothing else can. They stir in me the new emotions we call passion; of love, hatred, fear, admiration, pity; thence come conversation, competition, persuasion, cities, war. Persons are supplementary to the primary teaching of the soul. . . . But the larger experience of man discovers the identical nature appearing through them all.

Emily accepted her emotions and intuitive feelings without judging them. Through careful evaluation of herself and her reaction to experiences, she saw others as her teachers. They taught her about herself and she, in turn, taught them about themselves. The incident in Skokie evoked a recognition in Emily of the underside of the "identical nature appearing through . . . all" (Emerson 1987, 164). Positive and negative experiences became lessons to be learned. With this attitude, Emily was able to accept each person as her teacher, cultivating spirit in herself and others. In this manner, her career as a public administrator became a vocation rather than a job.

Emily's journey led her to the realization that all of life is predicated upon a fundamental oneness, manifested in the world through the interaction of positive and negative forces. Working together in a kind of give-and-take relationship, these forces achieve an ultimate balance. Through silent reflection, Emily learned to appreciate the basic harmony that this dynamic relationship gives to the universe. Accepting the coexistence of positive and negative aspects of reality is at the forefront of ancient eastern teachings, as well as Jungian analytical thought.

SILENCE AND UNITY

> We live in succession, in division, in parts, in particles. Meantime within man is the soul of the whole; the wise silence; the universal beauty, to which every part and particle is equally related; the eternal One . . . the act of seeing and the thing seen, the seer and the spectacle, the subject and the object, are one. We see the world piece by piece, as the sun, the moon, the animal, the tree; but the whole, of which these are the shining parts, is the soul (Emerson 1987, 160).

Picture Emily sitting beside the pond at the edge of the west meadow. She is propped against the trunk of a large willow tree, reading from Emerson's essays. Imagination transports her from the humdrum life of the farm to a world of independence and freedom. Inspired by Emerson's ideas, Emily rests the book across her chest, setting her gaze on the cat tails lining the far side of the pond. She ponders Emerson's words.

Reflection puts us in touch with our thoughts, and we learn it is the finite that causes us difficulty and suffering. The infinite truth that lies within brings peace from worldly concerns. This discovery leads to the realization that life is "embosomed in beauty." Like passing clouds, all our experiences have a pleasing form. Even the tragic aspects of our lives contain an element of grace and beauty. Our inner voice teaches that all pain is confined to the experience of a particular person or situation. Upon reflection, we learn there is no imperfection in the whole, of which we are an essential part (Emerson 1987, 77).

Those who perceive beauty in every aspect of living, the sad as well as the joyous, have accepted a gift available to everyone. This gift awaits all who take the time to consider their surroundings; it includes everything that is part of daily life: people, objects, and ideas. When we appreciate small and seemingly unimportant aspects of our profession, it is easier to perceive public administration as a calling. Our thinking becomes elevated, and like Emily we are able to see significance and unity in the most mundane tasks.

Silence allows us to remove ourselves from preoccupation with the external world, since it it is not necessary for us to maintain a continuous presence. We are often more effective when we sit in quiet contemplation and allow our inner voice to guide us. Our genius as human creatures lies in our impulse to enter the depths of our being. In that place, we experience a connection with the universe which prepares us for a return to our responsibilities. Through this process, we become assimilated to the Tao (Rousselle 1985, 59).

When individuals fail to take the time to engage in silent consideration of their actions and the part they play in the drama of work, society pays the price. For instance, markets have suffered from violations of Security and Exchange Commission regulations, designed to protect the public from insider information which separates and isolates members of the financial community. Retail markets have suffered from unethical and unfair trading activities, price gouging, and monopolistic practices which alienate individuals from one another. Education has been compromised by disinterested administrators and unresponsive teachers who see their students as different from themselves. The reputation of government workers has been sullied by untruthful politicians and dishonest vendors who consider themselves to be privileged and above the law.

It is easy to get caught up in the fast-paced momentum of our ever-changing lives. Like a revolving top, our ambitions can spin out of control. Blind acceptance of outside pressure is a common occurrence when we take ourselves and our jobs too seriously. Professional codes of ethics are adopted to stem the tide of corruption that periodically sweeps over our insititutions. There is no substitute, however, for the fundamental honesty that finds its source within the individual.

As she inched her way along the path toward metaphysical truth, Emily grew in maturity and integrity. Her authenticity benefitted all who knew and worked with her. Secure in the belief that there is unity and harmony in the universe, she knew nothing could disturb her peace of mind without her participation. Emily assumed complete responsibility for all her actions as a public administrator.

The Tao of full maturity involves the total psyche, bringing unconscious truths to consciousness. Strengths and weaknesses are perceived simply as dual aspects of the integrated Self. With greater understanding for oneself, one becomes more tolerant of others. As the individual advances in maturity, he or she becomes less judgmental and more open to new ideas and perspectives. The world appears more connected, and a sense of unity replaces ego-driven isolation. The false veneer of a manufactured image starts to peel away, like varnish stripped from an old piece of furniture.

Authentic individuals like Emily have engaged in the process of individuation that Jung discussed, silently listening to the truths of the inner voice. The freedom and knowledge that ensue command a heavy price. Those who embark on this quest must eventually die to the old Self. They must abandon previous beliefs in a certain world and accept their inability to control it. Despair and fear are their temporary companions as they walk through the passage leading from the darkness of illusion to the light of truth. It is a transforming and paradoxical experience, in which an individual is set apart from and united with others at the same time.

The Golden Flower

Richard Wilhelm was a famous translator of Taoist texts who was a friend and collaborator of Carl Jung's. After fifteen years of studying the processes of the collective unconscious, Jung received a copy of *The Secret of the Golden Flower* (1962) from Wilhelm. The book was received with great hope, for it represented the first time Jung could compare his findings with other ideas. There was nothing in western medicine or psychology that was remotely related to his work. Finally, he was able to see connections between the phenomena he had discovered in his research and the ancient teachings of eastern metaphysics.

Jung perceived a restlessness in the west that he attributed to the repression of instinctual nature, characteristic of rationalism. His research convinced him that the fully realized human being has achieved integration through the unity of the positive and negative aspects of the Self. Denying the irrational side of one's nature does not obliterate it. In time, hidden unconscious desires will manifest themselves in destructive ways, causing pain and unhappiness in personal and professional life. Jung believed that truth does not speak to the head alone. He longed to restore to the western mind the peace that comes from listening to the heart in silent appreciation of its teaching.

Wilhelm's work with eastern metaphysics was a vehicle that Jung used to bring new ideas to European consciousness, which he thought was seriously unbalanced. He was impressed with Wilhelms's ability to set aside the rationalism of western culture with its "one-sided differentiation" (Wilhelm 1962, 147) and embrace the more comprehensive orientation of eastern culture with its emphasis on all aspects of unity. Eastern metaphysics emphasizes unity of mind and body, conscious and unconscious, heart and soul, positive and negative; and the fundamental unity of all living things. Jung memorialized Wilhelm as a messenger who transplanted to the west a "tender seedling, the Golden Flower, giving us a new intuition of life and meaning as a relief from the tension of arbitrary will and arrogance."

Cary Barnes, who translated *The Secret of the Golden Flower* from German into English, contrasted the tendency of western individuals to ignore or even mistrust inner life, with the tendency of eastern individuals to exclude outer reality. He argued that both the east and west have suffered the consequences of their preoccupation with one-sided thinking. The east has paid handsomely for ignoring the realities of the external world, suffering one catastrophe after another. The west, with its emphasis on the outer world, gets into trouble by denying the negative forces of the unconscious. This is evidenced by the continuing problems we have relating to one another, although we perceive ourselves as cultured and civilized. Barnes attributes this unfortunate tendency to an imbalance between science and spirit (Wilhelm 1962, 8): "We have to see that the spirit must lean on science as its guide in the world of reality, and that science must turn to the spirit for the meaning of life."

Spirit and Science United

The characters we met on our journey toward the Self exemplified what it means to regain a familiarity with our spiritual side. Upon reflection in the quiet of the night, Vinoba Bhave saw his own shadow as it evolved in the days activity. Upon awakening the next morning, he resolved to correct his self-serving mistake of the previous day. Ptah-hotep's advice to his son can restore our own peace, if we learn to value silence and kindliness more than empty words and self-serving behavior. Shankara, through silent contemplation, saw beyond the inconsistencies of a divided world.

Our journey provided us the opportunity to listen to a conversation between King Janaka and Yagnavalkya. We were invited, as the king asked the sage a penetrating question regarding the true meaning of life. The answer etched an indelible mark on us. We were told to trust our own inner voice as the source of meaning in our lives. Some of us may have identified with Narada, who experienced doubt in his attempt to reach the Self. His teacher, Sanatkumara, shared with him the importance of silence as the key to self-knowledge. Our acquaintance with Narada taught us that through quiet reflection we come to a realization that we do not stand apart. This understanding enables us to assume greater responsibility for ourselves and others.

Emily is the incarnation of the Golden Flower of the east. She is always with us and represents the epitome of what a western individual can achieve. Fully committed to the world that science has provided, Emily polishes the rough edges with spirit and intuitive truths. She shows us how to negotiate the tenuous path between the world of science and the world of the spirit. When circumstances require a reality check, Emily listens to the inner voice and trusts its message.

As she watched nature play itself out on the farm, Emily learned to appreciate its alternating forces. She learned from the changing seasons there is a time for everything. A delay in their normal progression created many hardships. The fields lay fallow when the rains of spring did not fall. They came with a vengeance the following autumn, turning the usually glorious meadows into pastures of thick black mud. Eventually, nature would restore the balance and the times of the year would work together once again. Emily likened herself to the seasons, and tried not to repress those parts of her personality that were less than perfect. She experienced her professional life as a composite whole, made up of positive and negative aspects that she could not always conrol.

Emily understood the principle of reality contained in the Tao. She knew that primal opposing forces come together in unified form and that separation among the ten thousand things is an inexplicable phenomenon. Emily knew the secret of the Golden Flower. Through silence and reflection, she replenished the rich soil of her heart, allowing the seed to grow into full awareness of the truths it harbors:

> The Golden Flower is the Elixir of Life (possessing) . . . a secret charm which, although it works very accurately, is yet so fluid that it needs extreme intelligence and clarity, and the most complete absorption and tranquility. People without this highest degree of intelligence and understanding do not find the way to apply the charm; people without this utmost capacity for absorption and tranquility cannot keep fast hold of it." (Wilhelm 1962, 23)

The intelligence required to learn the secret of the Golden Flower is not the power of reason, as westerners may assume. Rather, it is the capacity to sit in absolute silence and wait for the spontaneous manifestation of our innate nature. This experience has been called, variously, the appearance of "true energy (prana), seed, spirit, animus, and anima" (Wilhelm 1962, 23). The eastern masters tell us that when silence is total, the heavenly heart is visible and we can attain the spiritual intelligence required to live at the deepest levels of human life. When spirit and science are united, we attain knowledge that enables us to see more clearly into the true nature of our experiences. As a result, decisions are made on the basis of sound judgment and reasoned action.

SILENCE AND WU-WEI

> But real action is in silent moments. The epochs of our life are not in the visible facts of our choice of a calling, our marriage, our acquisition of an office, and the like, but in a silent thought by the wayside as we

walk; in a thought which revises our entire manner of life, and says, "This hast thou done, but it were better thus." (Emerson 1987, 93)

The intuitive voice is only heard through the silent reflections of consciousness, leading us toward spiritual intelligence. The knowledge we attain taps into the source of creativity buried within the unconscious mind. The long, lonely days on the farm taught Emily the value of simply letting go. Perched on a hill overlooking one of the meadows, she would watch the branches of the trees far below as they engaged in a kind of playful dance with one another. Swaying back and forth, they gave themselves completely to the movement of the wind. Their graceful motions needed no orchestration apart from the gentle breeze.

Emily learned to accept nature on its own terms, for whenever she tried to arrange something to her liking she was disappointed. On October afternoons, she would climb to the top of a hill, drawing board in hand. She was eager to capture on her canvas the rich crimson color of the leaves she had observed the day before. Crimson turned to mauve overnight, and Emily appreciated the panoply of colors that stretched before her in the valley below. Nature never seemed to cooperate with her wishes, and she welcomed whatever it was willing to share with her on any given day.

Like Chang, who came to Lao-tze in desperation, Emily had to learn not to grasp the Tao. Her teacher was nature itself. Through observation, she learned the truths that Lao-tze taught his distraught pupil. Emily and Chang had to learn to rest, know when to stop interfering, let go of the urge to control others, be independent, and know when to remove themselves from a situation. They were taught to accept their emotions and appreciate their feelings. Lao-tze advised Chang to be as expressive as a newborn infant, without paying the consequences. Nature taught Emily to respond to her own needs without hurting herself. Emily and Chang learned to relinquish control over what is uncontrollable, and accept the Tao as the gift it is.

As students of life, they eventually came to the realization that there is a balancing force at work in the universe. Chang understood yin and yang as the ordering principle that maintains harmony with the Tao. He learned from ancient Chinese teachings not to interfere with the chaos resulting from the interplay of opposing forces. As he grew in wisdom, Chang became inured to the vicissitudes of daily life. He finally attained the toleration that comes from quiet introspection. The words of his master became a part of his daily meditation, "who can (make) the muddy water (clear)? Let it be still, and it will gradually become clear. Who can secure the condition of rest? Let movement go on, and the condition of rest will gradually arise" (Müller 1927, 58).

Emily understood the vagaries of nature as the ordering principle that maintains harmony in the natural world. She learned from observing its patterns that nature is a willful mistress, who will not tolerate interference.

Her favors are bestowed on those who patiently accept her apparent inconsistencies. As she grew in wisdom, Emily accepted each situation she faced without judgment. With the insight that silence brings, she learned to appreciate the way events evolved independent of her direction.

Emily experienced many different situations as a public administrator in a large urban setting. Some were disturbing and, like the event in Skokie, called for reflection. Most often, these circumstances were made worse when her colleagues misjudged a situation and exerted unwarranted control. As she pondered their actions, she remembered Emerson's words (1987, 58):

> Nature hates monopolies and exceptions. The waves of the sea do not more speedily seek a level from their loftiest tossing, than the varieties of condition tend to equalize themselves. There is always some levelling circumstance that puts down the overbearing, the strong, the rich, the fortunate, substantially on the same ground with all others.

Emily conducted her professional life in accordance with her observations on the farm, the influence that Emerson's writings had on her, and her experiences as a public administrator. Through it all, she maintained a sense of responsibility for her involvement in situations. Her strength as a public administrator came from her capacity to sit in silent comtemplation. She believed that every thing contains the seed of its opposite, which will eventually be realized. Therefore, it is foolish to try to control all situations. When an artificial solution is imposed on an event that is following its own course, the situation worsens.

The best public administrators exercise good judgment and seem to instinctively know when to attempt to direct the course of events, and when to stand back and allow them to unfold naturally. This ability does not come easily, nor can it be taught. Neither reason, facts, nor intelligence are sufficient alone or in combination to produce good judgment. We need only consider the consequences of our mistakes. The war in Vietnam grates on our collective conscience. The disastrous decisions made about events in Waco and Ruby Ridge give us pause. In all these situations, facts and rational intelligence prevailed. We must go beyond reason if we are to solve the kinds of problems that can lead to war or the killing of our own citizens, however troubled they may be.

Our thoughts are very powerful tools of the mind because they motivate us to action. Through silence and reflection our thoughts can assess reality, enabling us to see clearly and make appropriate decisions. Men and women alike can strive for the qualities of Confucius' "ideal man" (Durant 1954, 671):

> In regard to the use of his eyes he is anxious to see clearly. . . . In regard to his countenance he is anxious that it should be benign. In

regard to his demeanor he is anxious that it should be respectful. In regard to his speech he is anxious that it should be sincere. In regard to his doing business he is anxious that it should be reverently careful. In regard to what he doubts about, he is anxious to question others. When he is angry he thinks of the difficulties his anger may involve him in. When he seeks gain to be got he thinks of righteousness.

As public administrators, we need to be "reverently careful" in conducting the public's business. Complex situations require us to carefully examine our own motivations before making a decision to act. It is easy for us to ignore the force of our own anger when faced with irrational people and potentially volatile situations. Having examined ourselves, we become more aware of any tendency we may have to rush in where angels fear to tread. Impulsive reaction is replaced with careful deliberation and consultation with others. Our general demeanor becomes more understated, and we are less inclined to take untoward action in a feeble attempt to make things right.

CHOOSING A GATE

Our decision to embark on this journey was made when we asked ourselves what it means to be a public servant. Upon reflection, we realized the answer was a deeply personal one, requiring introspection. We traveled together for awhile, intent on discovering our own path toward self-knowledge. Now we have arrived at the three gates of truth. Which gate we choose to enter depends upon many things. Each of us is responsible for delving as deeply as possible into ourselves so we may learn who we are and how we can contribute to the world while we are here. We will hear the inner voice, regardless of which gate we open. Those who choose one gate over another are neither superior to nor less than their colleagues. They are simply following the Tao that is natural to them.

Some may follow the direction of Carl Jung and attempt to unearth the hidden parts of the psyche. They will enter the philosophical gate, where metaphysical truth is found. Theirs is a long journey of intense inner work. The difficult path is strewn with pitfalls and dangers. Ultimately, it may lead to great spiritual revelation. Some will choose the contemplative gate, where human psychology and action intersect. They will observe themselves and others, and question conventional wisdom. Their self-examination will put them in touch with who they really are. Conviction and insight will be their reward. Some will open the gate where practice and morality intersect. Although more accepting of the status quo, they will also engage in a process of self-discovery. Their journey will make them more aware of who they are and their responsibility in the unfolding of events. And that, after all, is the real business of life.

REFERENCES

Campbell, Joseph. 1989. *An Open Life*. New York: Harper and Row.

Durant, Will. 1954. *Our Oriental Heritage*. Vol. 1 of *The Story of Civilization*. Reprint, New York: Simon and Schuster.

Emerson, Ralph Waldo. 1987. *The Essays of Ralph Waldo Emerson*. Cambridge: Harvard University Press.

Müller, Max, ed. 1927. *The Sacred Books of the East*. Vol. 39. London: Humphrey Milford, publisher to Oxford University Press.

Olson, Stuart Alve, trans. 1992. *The Jade Emperor's Mind Seal Classic*. St. Paul: Dragon Door Publications.

Rousselle, Erwin. 1985. "Spiritual Guidance in Contemporary Taoism." In *Spiritual Disciplines*. Edited by Joseph Campbell. Vol. 4. Princeton: Princeton University Press.

Wilhelm, Richard, trans. 1962. *The Secret of the Golden Flower*. Revised, New York: Harcourt Brace Jovanovich Publishers.

Selected Bibliography

Aiken, Henry D., ed. *Hume's Moral and Political Philosophy*. New York: Hafner Press, 1948.

Alexander, Franz. "Our Age of Unreason." In *Main Currents of Western Thought*. Edited by Franklin LeVan Baumer. New Haven: Yale University Press, 1978.

Aziz, Robert. *C. G. Jung's Psychology of Religion and Synchronicity*. Albany: State University of New York Press, 1990.

Bahm, Archie J. *The Heart of Confucius*. Berkeley: Asian Humanities Press, 1992.

Bataille, Georges. *Inner Experience*. Translated by Leslie Anne Boldt. Reprint, New York: State University of New York Press, 1988.

Baumer, Franklin LeVan, ed. *Main Currents of Western Thought*. New Haven: Yale University Press, 1978.

Bellah, Robert N., Richard Madsen, William M. Sullivan, Ann Swidler, and Steven M. Typton. *Habits of the Heart*. New York: Harper and Row Publishers, 1986.

Bennington, Geoffrey. "Mosaic Fragment: If Derrida were an Egyptian." In *Derrida: A Critical Reader*. Edited by David Wood. Cambridge: Blackwell, 1992.

Bernasconi, Robert. "No More Stories, Good or Bad: De Man's Criticisms of Derrida on Rousseau." In *Derrida: A Critical Reader*. Edited by David Wood. Cambridge: Blackwell, 1992.

Bohm, David. *Wholeness and the Implicate Order*. New York: ARK Paperbacks, 1983.

Bolen, Jean Shinoda. *The Tao of Psychology*. San Francisco: Harper San Francisco, 1982.

Bronson, Bertand H., George W. Meyer, Walter J. Bate, William C. DeVane, Lionel Trilling, Rubin H. Brower, Elizabeth Drew, Charles W. Dunn, C. S. Lewis, G. B. Harrison, Basil Willey, Douglas Bush, Herbert Davis, and Maynard Mack, eds. *Major British Writers*. Vol. 2. New York: Harcourt Brace and Company, 1954.

Burger, Peter. *The Decline of Modernism*. University Park: The Pennsylvania State University Press, 1992.

Butterfield, Herbert. *The Origins of Modern Science*. rev. ed. G. Bell and Sons Ltd., 1957. New York: The Free Press, 1965.

Cammerloher, M. C. "The Position of Art and Psychology in our Time." In *Spiritual Disciplines*. Edited by Joseph Campbell. Vol. 4. Princeton: Princeton University Press, 1985.

Campbell, Joseph. *The Power of Myth*. Edited by Betty Sue Flowers. New York: Doubleday, 1988.

———. *An Open Life*. New York: Harper and Row, 1989.

Capra, Fritjof. *The Tao of Physics*. 3d ed. Boston: Shambala, 1991.

Chan, Wing-Tsit, trans. and comp. *A Source Book in Chinese Philosophy*. Reprint, Princeton: Princeton University Press, 1973.

Chang, Stephen T. *The Great Tao*. 1985. Reprint, San Francisco: Tao Publishing, 1992.

Cooper, Terry. *The Responsible Administrator*. San Francisco: Jossey-Bass Publishers, 1990.

Cottingham, John, Robert Stoothoff, and Dugald Murdoch, trans. *Descartes, Selected Philisophical Writings*. 1988. Reprint, New York: Cambridge University Press, 1994.

Coward, Harold. *Jung and Eastern Thought*. New York: State University of New York Press, 1985.

Denhardt, Robert B. *Theories of Public Organization*. Monterey: Brooks/Cole Publishing Company, 1984.

———. *Public Administration, An Action Orientation*. New York: Wadsworth Publishing Company, 1995.

Descartes, René. "Introduction," "Discourse on the Method of Rightly Conducting the Reason and Seeking Truth in the Sciences," and "The Principles of Philosophy." In *A Discourse on Method*. 1912. Reprint, translated by John Veitch. Rutland, Vermont: Charles E. Tuttle Co., Inc., Everyman's Library, 1992.

DeTocqueville, Alexis. *Democracy in America*. Edited by Phillips Bradley. New York: Vintage Books, 1958.

Durant, Will. *Our Oriental Heritage*. Vol. 1, *The Age of Reason Begins*. Vol. 7, *The Age of Louis XIV*. Vol. 8, and *The Age of Voltaire*. Vol. 9 of *The Story of Civilization*. Reprint, New York: Simon and Schuster, 1954–1965.

Einstein, Albert. *The World As I See It*. Translated by Alan Harris. Reprint, New York: Carol Publishing Group, 1991.

Eliade, Mircea, ed. "Silence." Vol. 13 of *Encyclopedia of Religion*. New York: MacMillan Publishing Company, 1987.

Emerson, Ralph Waldo. *The Essays of Ralph Waldo Emerson*. Cambridge: Harvard University Press, 1987.

Fesler, James W., and Donald F. Kettl. *The Politics of the Administrative Process*. Chatham: Chatham House Publishers Inc., 1991.

Fox, Charles J., and Hugh T. Miller. *Postmodern Public Administration*. Thousand Oaks: Sage Publications, 1995.

Frost, Robert. *Complete Poems of Robert Frost*. 1949. Reprint, New York: Holt, Rinehart and Winston, 1964.

Gasche, Rodolphe. "Infrastructure and Systematicity." In *Deconstruction and Philosophy*. Edited by John Sallis. Chicago: The University of Chicago Press, 1988.

Golembiewski, Robert T. *Humanizing Public Organizations*. Mt. Airy, Maryland: Lomond Publications, 1985.

Goodsell, Charles T. "Emerging Issues in Public Administration." In *Public Administration, The State of the Discipline*. Edited by Naomi B. Lynn and Aaron Wildavsky: Chatham: Chatham House Publishers Inc., 1990.

———. *The Case for Bureaucracy*. 3d ed. New Jersey: Chatham House Publishers, Inc., 1994.

Goodsell, Charles T., and Nancy Murray, eds. *Public Administration Illuminated and Inspired by the Arts*. Westport, Connecticut: Praeger, 1995.

Green, Richard T., Lawrence F. Kellar, Gary L. Wamsley. 1993. "Reconstituting a Profession for American Public Administration." In *Public Administration Review* 53(6).

Gulick, Luther, and Lyndall Urwick. *Papers on the Science of Administration*. New York: Institute of Public Administration, 1937.

Hume, David. *Moral and Political Philosophy*. Edited by Henry D. Aiken. New York: Hafner Press, 1948.

Hummel, Ralph. *The Bureaucratic Experience*. 4th ed. New York: St. Martin's Press, 1994.

Huxley, Aldous. *The Perennial Philosophy*. 1945. Reprint, New York: Harper and Row Publishers, 1970.

Ingram, Helen. "Implementation: A Review and Suggested Framework." In *Public Administration: The State of the Discipline*. Edited by Naomi B. Lynn and Aaron Wildavsky. Chatham: Chatham House Publishers, Inc., 1990.

Jaffe, Aniela. *Was C. G. Jung a Mystic?* Einsedeln, Switzerland: Daimon Verlag, 1989.

Jung, Carl G. *Psychology and Religion*. New York: Yale University Press, 1938.

———. "Yoga and the West," "Transformation Symbolism in the Mass," and "A Psychological Approach to the Trinity." In *Psychology and Religion*. Vol. 11 of *Collected Works*. New York: Pantheon Books for Bollingen Foundation, 1958.

———. "Synchronicity, An Acausal Connecting Principle." In *The Structure and Dynamics of the Psyche*. Vol. 8 of *Collected Works*. 2d ed. 1969. Princeton: Princeton University Press, 1973.

———. "The Type Problem in Poetry." In *Psychological Types*. Vol. 6 of *Collected Works*. 1971. Reprint, Princeton: Princeton University Press, 1974.

———. "The Conjunction." In *Mysterium Coniunctiones*. Vol. 14 of *Collected Works*. Princeton: Princeton University Press, 1976.

———. "Symbols and the Interpretation of Dreams." In *The Symbolic Life: Miscellaneous Writings*. Vol. 18 of *Collected Works*. Princeton: Princeton University Press, 1976.

———. "Flying Saucers: A Modern Myth," "The Spiritual Problem of Modern Man," "The Undiscovered Self," and "What India Can Teach Us." In *Civilization in Transition*. Vol. 10 of *Collected Works*. 2d ed. 1970. Reprint, Princeton: Princeton University Press, 1978.

———. "Psychological Commentary on *The Tibetan Book of the Great Liberation*." In *Psychology and the East* and *Psychology and Religion*. Excerpts from Vols. 10, 11, 13, 18 of *Collected Works*. Princeton: Princeton University Press, 1978.

———. "Concerning Rebirth." In *The Archetypes and the Collective Unconscious*. Vol. 9, part 1 of *Collected Works*. 2d ed. 1968. Reprint, Princeton: Princeton-University Press, 1980.

Kant, Immanuel. "Analytic of Concepts: The Deduction of the Pure Concepts of the Understanding." In *The Critique of Pure Reason*. Edited and translated by Vasilis Politis. Reprint, Rutland, Vermont: Charles E. Tuttle, 1993.

Kolb, David. *The Critique of Pure Modernity*. Chicago: The University of Chicago Press, 1986.

Kornfield, Jack. *A Path With a Heart*. New York: Bantam Books, 1993.

Krishnamurti, J., and David Bohm. *The Future of Humanity*. San Francisco: Harper and Row, 1986.

Kuhn, Thomas S. *The Essential Tension*. Chicago: The University of Chicago Press, 1977.

Lao-tze. *Tao Teh King*. Translated by Paul Carus and D. T. Suzuki under the title *The Canon of Reason and Virtue*. La Salle: Open Court Publishing Company, 1991.

Lao-tzu. *Tao Te Ching*. Translated by R. B. Blakney under the title *The Way of Life*. New York: Mentor Books, 1983.

Leavey, John P., Jr. "Disinterrance: The Apotropocalyptics of Translation." In *Deconstruction and Philosophy*. Edited by John Sallis. Chicago: The University of Chicago Press, 1988.

Levine, Charles H., B. Guy Peters, and Frank J. Thompson. *Public Administration, Challenges, Choices, Consequences*. Glenview, Illinois: Scott Foresman/Little Brown Higher Education, 1990.

Luckmann, Thomas, ed. *Phenomonology and Sociology*. New York: Penguin Books, 1978.

Magill, Frank N., ed. "Francis Bacon: Novum Organum," "David Hume: A Treatise of Human Nature," and "Immanuel Kant: Critique of Pure Reason." In *Masterpieces of World Philosophy*. New York: HarperCollins Publishers, 1990.

Marini, Frank. "Leaders in the Field: Dwight Waldo." In *Public Administration Review* 53(5), 1993.

Mascaro, Juan, trans. Reprint, *The Bhagavad Gita*. New York: Penguin Books, 1980.

McCarthy, Thomas. *The Critical Theory of Jurgen Habermas*. 1981. Reprint, Cambridge: The MIT Press, 1991.

Merton, Thomas. *The Way of Chuang Tzu*. New York: New Directions, 1969.

Moore, Thomas. *Care of the Soul*. New York: HarperCollins Publishers, 1992.

Morgan, Gareth. *Images of Organization*. Newbury Park: Sage Publications, 1986.

Müller, Max F., ed. *The Sacred Books of the East*. Vol. 39. London: Humphrey Milford, publisher to Oxford University Press, 1927.

Murray, Nancy. "The Eastern Aesthetic in Administration." In *Public Administration Illuminated and Inspired by the Arts*. Edited by Charles T. Goodsell and Nancy Murray. New York: Praeger, 1995.

Olson, Stuart Alve, trans. *The Jade Emperor's Mind Seal Classic*. St. Paul: Dragon Door Publications, 1992.

Osborne, David, and Ted Gaebler. *Reinventing Government*. New York: Addison-Wesley, 1992.

Politis, Vasilis, ed. and trans. *Critique of Pure Reason*. 1934, 1991. Reprint, Rutland, Vermont: Charles E. Tuttle, 1993.

Prabhavananda, Swami and Frederick Manchester, trans. *The Upanishads*. Reprint, New York: New American Library, 1957.

Ramacharaka, Yogi, comp. *The Bhagavad Gita*. rev. ed. Chicago: The Yogi Publication Society, 1930.

Rohr, John A. *Ethics for Bureaucrats*. New York: Marcel Dekker, Inc., 1989.

Rorty, Richard. "Is Derrida a Transcendental Philosopher?" In *Derrida: A Critical Reader*. Edited by David Wood. Cambridge: Blackwell, 1992.

Rousselle, Erwin. "Spiritual Guidance in Contemporary Taoism." In *Spiritual Disciplines*. Edited by Joseph Campbell. Vol. 4. Princeton: Princeton University Press, 1985.

Schmidt, Mary R. "Grout: Alternative Kinds of Knowledge and Why They are Ignored." In *Public Administration Review* 53(6), 1993.

Scott, Richard. *Organizations: Rational, Natural, and Open Systems*. Englewood Cliffs: Prentice Hall, Inc., 1981.

Scott, William G., and David K. Hart. *Organizational America*. Boston: Houghton Mifflin, 1979.

Shafritz, Jay M., Albert C. Hyde, and David H. Rosenbloom. *Personnel Management in Government*. 3d ed. New York: Marcel Dekker, Inc., 1986.

Siu, R. G. H. *The Tao of Science*. Reprint, Cambridge: The MIT Press, 1991.

Stewart, Debra W., and Norman A. Sprinthall. *Ethical Frontiers in Public Management*. Edited by James S. Bowman. San Francisco: Jossey-Bass Publishers, 1991.

Storr, Anthony. *Solitude, A Return to Self*. New York: Ballantine Books, 1989.

Tillich, Paul. *The Courage to Be*. New Haven: Yale University Press, 1952.

Van Over, Raymond, ed. *Taoist Tales*. New York: New American Library, 1984.

Ventriss, Curtis. "Contemporary Issues in American Public Administration Education: The Search for an Educational Focus." In *Public Administration Review* 51(1), 1991.

Waley, Arthur, trans. *The Analects of Confucius*. New York: Vintage Books, 1938.

———. *The Way and its Power*. New York: Grove Weidenfeld, 1958.

Wamsley, Gary, Robert N. Bacher, Charles T. Goodsell, Philip S. Kronenberg, John H. Rohr, Camilla M. Stivers, Orion F. White, and James F. Wolf. *Refounding Public Administration*. Newbury Park: Sage Publications, 1990.

Weber, Max. *The Protestant Ethic and the Spirit of Capitalism*. Translated by Talcott Parsons. New York: Charles Scribner's Sons, 1958.

———. *The Theory of Social and Economic Organization*. Edited and translated by A. M. Henderson and Talcott Parsons. New York: Oxford University Press, 1947; The Free Press, 1964.

Weber, Renee. *Dialogues with Scientists and Sages: The Search for Unity*. New York: Routledge and Kegan Paul, 1986.

Wehr, Gerhard. *Jung, A Biography*. Translated by David M. Weeks. Boston: Shambala, 1988.

Welch, Holmes. *Taoism, the Parting of the Way*. rev. ed. Boston: Beacon Press, 1966.

Wilhelm, Richard, trans. *The Secret of the Golden Flower*. Revised, New York: Harcourt Brace Jovanovich Publishers, 1962.

Williams, Bernard. *Descartes, The Project of Pure Inquiry*. 1978. Reprint, New York: Penguin Books, 1990.

Zukav, Gary. *The Dancing Wu Li Masters*. Reprint, New York: Bantam Books, 1989.

Index

Action: action-oriented systems, 47;
based on inner direction, 14; constructivism, 71; end of, 44; ideal
course of, 36; and knowledge, 43;
morale and efficiency, 86; and problem-solving, 16; and psychology, 177;
and rules, 38; and silence, 174; standardized, 55–56; take-charge attitude,
7, 8; and thoughts, 176; when to
take, 85; when to wait, 63, 85; and
words, 28–29
Active imagination, 87, 90–92
Active listening, 98
Alexander, Franz, 57, 64
Analects (of Confucius), 121
Analytical psychology: aspects of reality,
170; concept of introspection and
wholeness, 9; Jungian, 5, 53; linkage
with eastern thought, 18, 79; and the
Tao, 86; and unity concept, 19
Aquinas, Thomas, 107
The Arabian Nights, 3
Archetypes, 30, 87, 91
Aristotle, 31, 69
Authority, 35–36, 40, 70

Bacon, Francis, 31–33, 35, 38–39, 168
Basel, 6
Bataille, Georges, 111
Bell's Theorem, 153
Bertalanffy, Ludwig von, 61
Bhagavad Gita, xiv, 100
Bohm, David, 108, 146, 168; conversa-
tion with Krishnamurti, 154–56; ex-
plicate order, 146; implicate order,
146–48; interconnectedness, 149
Bohr, Niels, 150–51, 168
Bollingen, 6
Buddhism, x, 9, 119

Campbell, Joseph, x, 29–30
Cartesian Duality, 14, 19, 145, 149, 159,
167. *See also* Descartes
Caruso, Enrico, 132
Categorical imperative, 108. *See also*
Kant
Challenges: toward a philosophy of administration, 4, 5, 47–48, 56, 123; toward organizational renewal, 4, 5, 48,
56, 61, 105, 162; toward technological
changes, 5, 48, 56, 105

Chicago, 82
Chih, 124
China, 6, 17, 121, 142
Chou Dynasty, 119
Chuang Tzu: and Chinese culture, 168; and hearing, 99; and interior life, 53, 162; parables of, 86, 126; and talking 97; and unity, 158; and wu-wei, 135–37, 141–42
Communitarianism, 54, 72 n.1
Comte, Augustus, 66
Confucianism, x, 142 n.1
Confucius, 142 n.3; and Lao-tze, 77, 126; myth and reason, 29; and the perennial philosophy, 129; and the Tao, 17, 120–29, 168
Conscious mind: and active imagination, 91; and causation, 160; experience of, 9; and Krishnamurti, 154; and meaning, 56; over-development of, 87; and spiritual intelligence, 175; split with unconscious mind, 19; synthesis with unconscious mind, 91; and truth, 87
Cost benefit analysis, 13
Coward, Harold, 8, 9
Creativity, 132–34
Culture: differences between east and west, 6, 11; and the east, 6, 58, 173; and the human brain, 157; influence of eighteenth-century humanism, 41; introspection and wholeness of the individual, 9; parallels between east and west, 86; and self, 54; and soul, 55; and the west, 5, 21, 40, 58, 66, 173; and World War II, 57

DeBroglie, Louis, 150
Decision Making: action vs non-action, 85, 134, 177; basis of, 14, 174; conflicting facts in, 16; consequences of, 85; and convention, 52; and creativity, 134; and discretion, 142; and ego, 103; and judgment, 54; Lebanon, 8; neutrality in, 130; objective and subjective, 160; on organizational structure and new technology, 48; patience and determination in, 84;

and perception, 136; and positive outcomes, 30; and psychology, 42; regarding self, 53; and responsibility, 80, 136; Ruby Ridge, 8; and silence, 18, 176; Waco, 8; on what cannot be measured, 71; what to classify, 69; which road to take, 64–65, 177; wishes and prejudices, 123; and wu-wei, 135–37, 142
Deconstruction, 69–71, 163 n.3
Democratic National Convention (1960), 21
Derrida, Jacques, 70
Descartes, Rene, x, xiv; absolute values of rationalism, 65; experience and deduction, 12; machine metaphor, 35; mathematical approach of, 12–13, 39; and objective world, 15; principle of certainty, 12; and public administration, 13; reality as duality, 14; subject/object split (Cartesian Duality), 14; and truth, 12–13
De Tocqueville, Alexis, 30, 63–64
Development: personal aspects, 4; technological, psychological, philosophical aspects, 4
Diderot, Denis, 44
Dirac, Paul, 150
Disjointed incrementalism, 13
Divine ground, 19. *See also* Huxley
Dragon, 77, 92, 129

Ego: and decision making, 103; demands of, 102; and judgment, ambition, success, 142
Einstein, Albert, 145, 147, 149, 168
Emerson, Ralph Waldo, 169–70, 176
Emotion, 44, 47, 79
Entropy, 61
Ethics, 62

Facts, 15, 16, 30, 35, 66, 161, 174, 176
Flash Gordon, 5
Frost, Robert, xii, 64, 106, 168

Gandhi, Mahatma, 21, 99–103
Golden rule, 123
Governance, 11, 21, 122, 125, 131

Han dynasty, 119
Hegel, George, 66
Heidegger, Martin, 66–68, 72
Heisenberg, Werner, 150–51, 168
Hinduism, x, 9
Holocaust, 160
Hostages, 8
Humanism, 123
Hume, David, x, 41–44, 46–47, 168
Humility, 20
Huxley, Aldous, x, xii, 9; and the age of noise, 95; hierarchy of gates, 10, 106, 129, 148, 177; and responsibility, 55; and silence, 97–98

Idealism, 54
Implementation, 13, 37, 71
India, 6, 95, 99, 101–2, 105–8
Individuation, 10, 87, 91–92, 172
Inner voice, ix, xii; awareness and understanding, 79–80; and career, 11; and collective belief system, 52; and the ego, 147; fear of insignificance, 48; and genuine intelligence, 158; guidance of, 171; and higher power, 133; and implicate order, 146; of individuals, ix, xii, 10; as inspiration, 60; intellect and feeling, 162; listening to, 17, 60, 63, 68, 90, 98, 123, 132, 134, 167, 172–73; lost to us, 53; and opportunities, 169; quiet introspection, 18; reason and truth, 30; and silence, 87; and Taoism, 120; and trust, 173; and truth, 52, 172; and the unconscious, 147; and unity, 161; whisper of, 80, 157; and the whole, 170; and wisdom, 149
Introspection: insight, 6, 7; solitude, 7; inner development, 8; wholeness, 9; inner voice, 18; and silence, 52

Japan, 6
Jaspers, Karl, 57–58, 64
Journey: and connection to others, 134; and fundamental oneness, 170; personal, 5, 177; professional, 4, 8, 177; and self awareness, 177; and spirtual

self, 173; subtleties of, 112; to the Tao, 117; within, 18, 111, 177
Jung, x, xi, xii, xiv, 168; active imagination, 87, 90–92, 94 n.1; alienation from self, 67; analytical psychology, 5, 86, 170; archetypes, 30, 87; concept of individuation, 10, 87, 172; eastern meditative techniques, 8, 90, 110; the Golden Flower, 172; the hero self, 111; intellect and feeling, 162; the jewel of the Self, 90; journey toward self, 18; on Lao-tze, 128; mass mindedness, 34, 52, 89; participation mystique, 52; power of myth, 29–30; psychic thunderstorm, 7; rationalism, 172; responsibility, 55, 162; search for philosophy, 64; state of contemporary society, 88; truth, 87, 162; the unconscious and the implicate order, 147; western culture, 5; wise old man, 53

Kant, Immanuel, x, xiv, 44, 46, 56, 69, 114 n.5, 124, 168; similarities with philosophy of Shankara, 106–11
Keats, John Maynard, 104
Kent State University, 21
King, Martin Luther, 21
Klein-Huingen, 6
Krishna, 100
Krishnamurti, Jiddu, 108, 168; conversation with David Bohm, 154–56; on intelligence, 157
Kuhn, Thomas, 32–33, 39

Lake Zurich, 6
Language, 14
Lao-tze, xiv; birth and background, 77; and the dragon, 129; on governance, 21; and his disciple, 137–41, 175; and Jung, 128; meeting with Confucius, 126; metaphysics of, 78; myth and reason, 29; and the perennial philosophy, 129; and reason, 118; on silence, 18; and the Tao, 117, 127–29, 168; Tao Teh King, 78; on unity, 20, 139; on wisdom, 18, 128

Laufen, 5
Lindblom, Charles, 13

Mahabarata, 100
Marini, Frank, 5
Merton, Thomas, x, 53, 86, 93, 99, 141, 158; and the teachings of Chuang-Tzu, 136–39
Metaphor: archer as, 123; candle as, 32; chain of command as, 36; dog as, 141; forest and woods as, 167; foundation of a building as, 71; Lao-tse as dragon, 129; limb of tree as, 54; machine as, 35, 36, 48, 57–62, 71; night as blushing, 168; parables, fields, lakes as, 169; public administrator as artisan, 59; vessel as, 38
Metaphysics: and absolutism, 67; of Aristotle, 69; eastern, 8, 55, 153, 172; and Huxley's gate, 10, 148, 177; of Lao-tze, 78; and positivism, 68; and practice of yoga, 88; and pragmatism, 46; and quantum physics, 145, 153; and the Tao, 117–18; and truth, 171, 177; and the unconscious, 147; and Upanishads, 109
Middle East, 6, 8
Ming Dynasty, 124
Myth, 29, 35, 92, 120, 134

Nature: and acceptance, 85–86; affinity with, 81; balance of, 174; and eighteenth-century mind, 40; and Jung, 5; laws of, 39; ordering principle of, 175; subjugation of, 89; and the Tao, 85, 175
Needs analysis, 10
Negentrophy, 61
Nehru, 101
New Age, 9
Newton, Isaac, x, 38–39, 149
New York, 6
Noumena, 107

Pantheism, 39
Pauli, Wolfgang, 150
Pendleton Act, 130
The Perennial Philosophy, 10, 19

Phenomena, 107
Philosophy: and administration, 5, 68, 80, 109, 131, 135, 161; Comte, Augustus, 66; deconstruction, 68–71; eastern, 7, 17, 153; goal of, 108; and governance, 131; Hegel, Georg, 66; Heidegger, Martin, 66–68, 72; and inner voice, 147; logical positivism, 46, 69; and meaning of life, 53, 55; merging of eastern and western traditions, 99; and metaphysical truth, 177; perennial, 10, 19, 57; and reality, 38, 57; of seventeenth century, 12–15, 19; and the 60's generation, 64; and the Tao, 117; unity concept, 19, 161
Picasso, 79
Planck, Max, 154, 168
Plato, 118, 169
Plutarch, 99
Policy, 11, 13, 14, 37–38, 71, 161
Politics/Administration dichotomy, 54, 131, 134
POSDCORB, 30
Postmodernism: and absolutist thinking, 51; and the world, 4
Principle of certainty, 12
Principles of logic: begging the question, 42; cause and effect, 41–45; deductive reasoning, 31–32, 40, 46; inductive reasoning, 32, 40, 46
Program evaluation, 13, 14
Psychology: and the human psyche, 41; and reason, 43

Quantum physics, 145; and common sense, 152; and light, 151; and metaphysics, 145; observer and observed, 151; and probability, 152, 159–60, 163 n.3

Rationalism: according to Weber, 60; and instinct, 172; and intelligence, 176; mathematics, 12; modern science, 11; and reason, 69; technical, 10, 18, 30, 34; western logic, 11
Reality: according to Descartes, 14; assessment of, 176; deeper levels of, 9;

existential grasp of, 86; explanation of, 42; and fundamental unity, 146; and individuation, 87; inner and outer, 7, 56; objective, 6; perception of, 43; and the play of opposites, 90; polarities of, 92; positive and negative aspects of, 170; and psychology, 90; science and spirit, 173–74; and shared ideas, 70; subatomic level of, 152; and ultimate human situations, 57; and the workplace, 62

Reason: and analysis, 10; and authority, 35; and causal pattern, 42; and change, 27–29; and the chosen path, 167; and dysfunctionalism, 8; and external world, 38; and facts, 30, 176; forces of, 37, 83; and the Golden Flower, 174; and Kant, 46, 69; and machine metaphor, 35; and misguidance, 89; and myth, 29–30; and nature, 38; and psychology, 43; and religion, 40; and the senses, 45; and the soul, 107; and the Tao, 117–18; value of, 41

Reform Movement: economy and efficiency, 4; technical education, 4

Responsibility: and behavior, 162; civic, 121; for decisions, 15; ethical and moral, 122–23; and inner striving, 55; of individual, 122–23; and motivation, 142; and multiple roles, 63; and neutrality, 60, 161; in open systems, 61; and personal accountability, 134, 147, 176, 177; and proactive stance, 62; and risk taking, 16; and the Tao, 171; and the unconscious, 63, 93; and unity, 147, 173; and wu-wei, 136

Rhine river, 6

Rousseau, Jean Jacques, 44

Ruby Ridge, 8, 176

Schopenhauer, 106

Schrödinger, Erwin, 150

Search for meaning, 8, 9, 53

Securities and Exchange Commission, 171

Self: accountability of, 147; and the Brahmin, 109; as concentration, 113; and cultural influence, 54; and the dragon, 92; as hero, 111; and individuation, 172; as insight, 113; integration of conscious and unconscious, aspects of, 87; the jewel of the, 90, 111; and jorney toward truth, 18; and Lao-tze, 79; as light, 110; lost self, 138; as mind, name, speech, will, 112; and others, 159; and the outer world, 129; personal decision, 53; and reductionism, 71; search for meaning, 8, 9; self-abnegation, 58; self-acceptance, 100; self-aggrandizement, 136, 158; self-centeredness, 98; self-cultivation, 122–23, 169; self-denial, 108; self-discipline, 55; self-discovery, 177; self-doubt, 173; self -effacement, 55, 86; self-esteem, 11; self-examination, 10, 177; self-expression, 96; self-forgetfulness, 57, 59; self-help, 6; selfhood, 56; self-importance, 86; self-integration, 149, 171–72; self-knowledge, 55, 57, 64, 66, 79, 92, 100, 111, 122, 125, 134, 167, 173, 177; self-mastery, 85; self-promotion, 103; self-reflection, 113; self-restraint, 107; self-transcendance, 107; self-understanding, 92, 171; and silence, 173; spiritual experience of, 87; and spiritual journey, 173; and the Tao, 117; and wisdom, 111

Shadow, 92–93, 128, 173

Shankara: similarities with Kant's philosophy, 106–11

Silence: degrees of, 97–98; and the Golden Flower, 174; and the inner voice, 87, 110; and insight, 85, 176; and Lao-tze, 18; looking within, 52; of the mind, 103–10, 156; of the mouth, 98–103; and problem solving, 18; and Self, 18, 173; and solitude, 96; and spiritual intelligence, 175; and stillness, 18; and the Tao, 86; and thought, 104–5, 176; and truth, 18, 102, 148; and understanding, 19; of the will, 110–13; and wisdom, 128; and wu-wei, 174–77

Spinoza, 38–39

Star Wars, 29
Switzerland, 5

Tang Dynasty, 119
Tao: and analytical psychology, 86; attainment of, 140; and the concept of Self, 117; of Confucius, 120–27; of Confucius and Lao-tze, 127–29, 142n.1; explanation of, 17; natural pattern of, 90, 168, 177; and nature, 85, 175; and public administration, 129–31; and reality, 117; and reason, 117–18; and responsibility, 171; and silence, 86; and truth, 171; and unity, 19, 86, 117; and virtue (*te*), 131; yin and yang, 175
Taoism, x; and Confuncianism, 142 n.1; and stories, 125–27; and the power of p'u, 20; development of, 119–20; the unnameable and the unknowable, 118
Tao Teh King, 18, 78
Texas, 8
Tillich, Paul, 67–68
Truth: absolute, 12; and beauty, 104; belief systems, 51; and change, 101; and conscious mind, 87; and Descartes, 12–13; faith and reason, 69; gates of, 177; and Heidegger, 67–68; of inner voice, 172; intuitive, 173; and Kant, 44; light of, 172; and mathematics, 69; metaphysical, 171, 177; in nature, 84; perceived universal truths, 52; profundity of, 9; pure reason and empiricism, 46; and reason, 30; as residing within, 53; and self-awareness, 113; and silence, 18, 102, 148; and subjective experience, 57; and Taoism, 118; and the Tao Teh King, 78–79; ultimate, 10, 153, 170; and the unconscious mind, 87, 128, 147; and unity, 18, 161; and wu-wei, 18

Unconscious mind: and archetypes (images), 91; and creativity, 175; and eastern practices, 90; and human psychology, 41; and the inner voice, 147; and intuitive sense, 162; meaning of life, 53; and myth, 29–30; participation mystique, 52; and psychic storm, 6, 9; and reflection, 56; and responsibility, 63; role of instincts, 9, 88; sense of connectedness, 19; significance of water, 6; split with conscious mind, 19; and truth, 30, 128; when idle, 133
Unity: and analytical psychology, 19; and connectedness, 54, 85; conscious and unconscious, 172; conversation between Krishnamurti and David Bohm, 154–56; heart and soul, mind and body, positive and negative, 172; and intuition, 19; and Lao-tze, 139; and philosophy of administration, 161; and quantum physics, 150–57; and responsibility, 147; spirit and science, 173–74; and the Tao, 86, 117–18; and virtue of humility, 20
Upanishads, 106–7, 109, 111

Vedanta, 107
Vedas, 99
Vietnam, 15, 176
Virtual reality, 5
Vocation, 11
Voltaire, 44

Waco, 8, 176
Waldo, Dwight, 5, 48
Weber, Max: and government officials, 59; ideal type, 35–36; rational-legal authority, 35; and rationalism, 60, 65–66; religious, economic, social values, 58; and search for philosophy, 64; sense of meaning, 55–56
Welch, Holmes, 20, 77–79
Wisdom: and acceptance, 89; conventional, 10, 177; conviction, 7; and imagination, 90; inner voice and, 149; inner wisdom, 55; and insight, 135, 141, 176; and meditation, 108; and power, 85; and a quiet mind, 113; and reason, 83; and self-understanding, 111; and silence, 128,

176; and the Tao, 17, 18, 125, 128;
and toleration, 175
Wordsworth, William, 104–5
Wu-wei: and balance, 136; and Chuang-
tzu, 136–41; and creativity, 132–34;
and decision-making, 135–37; and intrinsic knowing, 20; and introspection, 134–35; paradox of, 85; and
silence, 174–77; and the will, 136;
and yin and yang, 136

Yin and yang, 136
Yoga, 88, 90, 111

Zen, 9

About the Author

NANCY MURRAY is Associate Professor in the Department of Public Administration at Pace University. Among her earlier publications is the coedited *Public Administration Illuminated and Inspired by the Arts* (Praeger, 1995).

ISBN 0-275-95250-9

HARDCOVER BAR CODE